18.95

Morphology by Itself

Linguistic Inquiry Monographs
Samuel Jay Keyser, general editor

Morphology by Itself

Stems and Inflectional Classes

Mark Aronoff

The MIT Press
Cambridge, Massachusetts
London, England

This book was set in Times Roman by Asco Trade Typesetting Ltd., Hong Kong, and was printed and bound in the United States of America.

First printing.

Library of Congress Cataloging-in-Publication Data

Aronoff, Mark.
  Morphology by itself : stems and inflectional classes / Mark Aronoff.
      p.   cm. — (Linguistic inquiry monographs ; 22)
  Includes bibliographical references and index.
  ISBN 0-262-01136-0 (h.c.). — ISBN 0-262-51072-3 (pbk.).
  1. Grammar, Comparative and general—Inflection. I. Title. II. Series.
P251.A76   1993   93-20543
415—dc20   CIP

For France

Contents

Series Foreword

We are pleased to present this monograph as the twenty-second in the series *Linguistic Inquiry Monographs*. These monographs will present new and original research beyond the scope of the article, and we hope they will benefit our field by bringing to it perspectives that will stimulate further research and insight.

Originally published in limited edition, the *Linguistic Inquiry Monograph* series is now available on a much wider scale. This change is due to the great interest engendered by the series and the needs of a growing readership. The editors wish to thank the readers for their support and welcome suggestions about future directions the series might take.

Samuel Jay Keyser
for the Editorial Board

Preface

The title and subtitle of this work together are meant to warn the reader that in it I treat a narrow class of phenomena—stems and inflectional classes—from the perspective of a large claim: that certain delimited aspects of morphology can and should be viewed as an autonomous part of grammar. The reader in search of a general theoretical treatise on morphology should therefore look elsewhere, perhaps at Anderson 1992 or Beard, to appear, both of which are recent and written from a perspective similar to mine, or at Spencer 1991 or Carstairs-McCarthy 1992, which are the best current general surveys of the linguistic morphological theories that have appeared over the last twenty years.

On the other hand, although its subject is narrow, this work does not presuppose much more than a rudimentary knowledge of morphology and may indeed be easier for the uninitiated than for one steeped in traditional lore. The first chapter lays out the basic notions and terms that are used in the rest of the work and that most readers may not have been exposed to before. I have especially tried to clarify those notions that I draw from lexeme-based morphology. This work is not, however, an argument for lexeme-based morphology or against other types of theories, except insofar as two types of phenomena that I am interested in, stems and inflectional classes, may be more easily understood within a lexeme-based theory than in others. I use a lexeme-based framework because I am used to it and because it comfortably accommodates a number of interesting observations. If others find these observations enlightening and can easily understand them within a lexeme-based framework, then that may be the proper test of the general theory, but that is for the reader to judge and not for me. If, on the other hand, you find that what I have to say can be incorporated into some other general framework, so much the better.

I have tried hard in this work to avoid some of the questions that have preoccupied many morphologists for the last ten years or so, questions about morphosyntactic representations, the order of affixes, the nature of juncture, and the relation between morphological and phonological structure. This is not because I have no opinions on these matters, some of which I have discussed elsewhere, but because I believe that what I have to say about the nature of stems and inflectional classes stands on its own. For the same reason, I have tried to be as neutral as possible in syntactic theory. Some readers may feel that in framing my analysis in terms of item-and-process rather than item-and-analysis, I am endorsing a process-oriented or algebraic view of syntax of the sort adopted by some categorial theorists. This is not so. For if it is indeed true, as I assume, that morphological realization is separate from morphosyntax, then it is entirely possible that the two differ in this fairly fundamental regard. In accepting this possibility, I realize that I am denying the value of the uniformitarian argument that all the components or modules of a grammar should share some basic structural properties, but I must confess that I have never seen any value in this argument.

Morphologists, like specialists in any other academic field, form a community. More than most other linguistic communities, though, morphologists are open to discussion across a wide range of points of view. Maybe that is simply because there are so few of us that fashion and exclusion do not serve the same social purpose as in larger societies, like researchers in syntax or phonology. Nonetheless, it means that it is possible to acknowledge people who do not always agree (with each other or with me) on basic issues. I would like first to thank those whose writings have particularly helped to clarify my thinking in the years that I have been working on this monograph: Stephen Anderson, Robert Beard, Joan Bybee, Andrew Carstairs-McCarthy, Greville Corbett, Morris Halle, James Harris, Jack Hoeksema, Richard Janda, Rochelle Lieber, Alec Marantz, Peter Matthews, John McCarthy, Igor Mel'cuk, Yves-Charles Morin, Alan Prince, Richard Sproat, Laurence Stephens, Gregory Stump, Wolfgang Wurzel, and Arnold Zwicky. I have corresponded with some of these people about this work, and I thank them for this too, especially Robert Beard, Andrew Carstairs-McCarthy, and Richard Sproat, who provided sometimes very detailed comments on the whole manuscript. Other correspondents are too numerous to mention, but they know who they are. Here at Stony Brook, discussing this work in class has helped greatly, and I thank my students for this. Similarly, my colleagues Frank Anshen, Christina Bethin, Ellen Broselow, Dan Finer, Richard Larson, and Lori Repetti have helped me with many matters. Two colleagues deserve special thanks: S. N. Sridhar, whose joint work with me on Kannada sparked this whole enterprise, and Robert Hoberman, whose work on modern Aramaic turned me to Semitic again. Both have helped me think in new ways.

Earlier versions of parts of this work have appeared elsewhere. Chapter 2 was published in a somewhat different form in *Morphology Now* (SUNY Press, 1992), while part of chapter 4 appeared in *Yearbook of Morphology 1991* (Kluwer). I would also like to thank two organizations for material support: IBM provided equipment for this project early on, and Gyrodyne provided me with valuable time to think on a regular basis. Many of the basic ideas came out of a project funded by the National Science Foundation (BNS 8418914), and I began writing during a sabbatical leave granted by Stony Brook.

I also owe a great deal to two people at The MIT Press. Larry Cohen helped in many ways to ensure that this project would see the light of day. Alan Thwaits did a superb piece of old-fashioned editorial work: he read the manuscript and made it better. I thank them both.

Finally, let me thank my family for the love and joy that have sustained me and for not waking up too early, leaving the dawn hours to morphology.

Abbreviations

Throughout this book I frequently use the following abbreviations:

∅	null or zero element	inf.	infinitive
#	space	masc.	masculine
1	first person	N	noun
2	second person	n.a.	not applicable
3	third person	nom.	nominative
A	adjective/adverb	NP	noun phrase
abl.	ablative	num.	number
acc.	accusative	obj.	object
act.	active	part.	participle
adv.	adverb	perf.	perfect
C	consonant	pl.	plural
decl.	declension	PP	perfect participle
du.	dual	pres.	present
FP	future participle	sg.	singular
fem.	feminine	subj.	subjunctive
fut.	future	T	third-stem marker
gen.	gender	Th	theme vowel
imp.	imperative	V	verb
impf.	imperfect	V	vowel
ind.	indicative		

Morphology by Itself

Introduction

form ME *forme, fourme,* from OF, from L *forma,* perhaps modification of Gk *morphē*; perhaps akin to Gk *marmairein* to flash, sparkle—more at MORN

morn ME *morn, morwen,* dawn, morning, from OE *morgen*; akin to OHG *morgan* morning, ON *morginn,* Goth *maurgins* morning, L *merus* pure, unmixed, Gk *marmairein* to flash, sparkle, Skt *marīci* ray of light

Etymologies from *Webster's Third*

The term *morphology* is generally acknowledged to have been coined by Goethe early in the last century. As far back as I have been able to trace it, the linguistic sense of the term has always diverged somewhat from its etymologically expected sense, which is "the science of form" (*Oxford English Dictionary* [*OED*]) or its object. This expected sense is generally applicable in the biological and geological uses of *morphology,* all of which are about as old as the linguistic use. The standard linguistic use, by contrast, is peculiarly narrow. The *Shorter OED* defines it as "That branch of grammar which is concerned with word-formation and inflexion." In other words, linguistic morphology is restricted in its scope to the form of words and does not extend to larger domains of discourse.

Why is linguistic morphology confined so narrowly to words? Why are other formal aspects of language so conspicuously excluded from the domain of the science of linguistic form? One possible answer is that grammar in the nineteenth century did not go beyond words. So, for example, the *OED* provides the following 1869 quotation for the philological sense of *morphology* as an illustration of the narrow definition of the term: "By the morphology of a language we mean the general laws of its grammatical structure." From the conjunction of the narrow definition I gave above and the quotation, we can only infer that syntax was excluded from grammar, and hence from the form of language. This is certainly consistent with at least Chomsky's frequent assertion (1964, 1972) that nineteenth-century grammarians like Whitney and even de Saussure "expressed the view that processes of sentence formation do not belong to the system of language at all" (1972, 19). So the linguistic use of the term *morphology* may be so narrow because the nineteenth-century view of the nature of language was narrow in the same way.

But I prefer to explore instead a more narrowly linguistic or Kripkean explanation, in which words and their history are more central than ideas. I will begin with the term *formative*, which I first encountered in work of Chomsky's *Aspects* period (Chomsky 1964, 1965). In his earlier work (1957, 1962, 1975), Chomsky had used the neutral term *element*, and I had always assumed in my ignorance that *formative* was simply another symptom of the terminological ebullience of a period in which Chomsky coined such baroque technical terms as *subcategorization* and *Boolean conditions on analyzability*. The *OED*, though, reveals that the term *formative* has a long history in English, which I will review briefly.

First, the adjective *formative* precedes the noun, both historically and structurally. Structurally, *-ive* is an adjectival suffix. Of the more than 800 words ending in *-ive* listed in Walker 1936, only 25 are nouns, and most of them, quite curiously, are technical terms from linguistics, e.g. *infinitive*, *adjective*, *fricative*. Historically, the adjective *formative* is cited as early as 1490, while the noun is cited only from 1711. I emphasize the priority of the adjective because its sense is most relevant to my argument. Among the nonlinguistic senses of the adjective, the most relevant is "of or pertaining to formation or moulding."[1] This leads to the more narrowly linguistic sense of "serving to form words: said chiefly of flexional and derivative suffixes or prefixes." *OED* provides a citation from 1711 of the phrase *formative terminations*, but the phrase *formative letter* can be found much earlier, for example, in John Udall's 1593 translation of Pierre Martinez's 1567 Hebrew grammar in Latin.[2] From this sense we arrive at the noun *formative*, which the *OED* defines as "a formative element." Two nineteenth-century citations are given: "The element or formative, he seems to think, is employed to express the thing which modifies or connects itself with the idea suggested by the primitive" (1816). "In this language prefixed particles or augments are used as verbal formatives" (1865). The first quotation is revealing, but we must step back a little to appreciate it. Eighteenth- and nineteenth-century linguists were much concerned with uncovering the primitive origins of language. Roots were seen as "original primitive words" (*OED* citation, 1740), or as "general and abstract" material (de Saussure 1959, 186) from which words were moulded by means of formative elements. The formatives, from this point of view, are applied to primitive and amorphous roots, which are viewed as being beyond the scope of scientific study.[3] Formatives give form to abstract roots and produce the pronounceable forms, the stuff of language. Therefore, from a nineteenth-century linguistic perspective, morphology, the general science of form and forms, is the science of the forms of language and, more abstractly, of the formatives that give form to words. Syntax, by contrast, is concerned not with formation or forms or formatives but with comparatively insubstantial notions of order or arrangement, in keeping with the etymology of the term. Syntax is thus outside the scope of linguistic morphology, because of the abstract nature of the elements whose arrangement it deals with. On this account, syntax may still be a part of grammar (and most nineteenth-century grammars do deal with syntax, *pace* Chomsky), but it is not concerned with form in this more concrete sense of the word.[4] The formative nature of linguistic morphology is especially clear when we look at Semitic languages, where roots are mere collections of consonants from which all individual word-forms are quite dramatically given form by the laying on of templates and affixes. The ancient Greek and Roman grammarians were almost completely ignorant of morphology, as Robins notes: "As with the rest of western antiquity, Priscian's grammatical model is word and paradigm, and he expressly denies any linguistic significance to divisions, in what would now be called morphemic analysis, below the word" (1979, 56). It may thus well be that all Western linguistic morphology is directly rooted in the Semitic grammatical tradition, but that is an issue that takes us too far afield. My point in this introduction has been only to show that there is a clear historical connection between the seemingly narrow senses of the terms *morphology* and *formative* in linguistic discourse and their broader senses; this connection lies in an active interpretation of the term *formative* and a concurrently concrete interpretation of the term *form*. My goal in this work as a whole, then, is to show that this reconstructed "original" kind of linguistic morphology has a place in current theoretical linguistics.

Chapter 1
Preliminary Terms

Linguistics then works in the borderland where the elements of sound and thought combine; *their combination produces a form, not a substance.*

F. de Saussure

1.1 Introduction

The last two decades have witnessed a backlash against a concern with terminology and definitions. Whereas linguists for a century had reveled in the creation of new terms like *morpheme, phoneme,* and *subcategorization,* carefully distinguished and scrupulously defined, lately we find old and reasonably well-understood terms very often being used in novel ways, with or without definition. Consider, as a single example, the term *root.* The traditional technical sense of this term as denoting the ultimate elements from which words are derived, which goes back centuries, is fairly clear (though it may or may not be theoretically valid). Yet both Lieber (1981) and Selkirk (1982), to pick only two prominent examples, use the term *root* in ways that are totally unrelated to its normal technical sense. Lieber, who also uses the term in its orthodox sense (e.g., in referring to a Tagalog verb root, p. 29), introduces a formal definition of *root* only in her discussion of her novel notion of morpholexical rules. Here, she says the following:

If lexical classes are defined as partially ordered sets with morpholexical rules being the relations specifying the members of these sets, we immediately have a way of referring to the ROOT, or the more elementary item in a pair of lexical terminals: if a lexical class ϕ has an element a such that aRx for every x in ϕ, then a is the least element in ϕ (borrowing the set theoretic terminology). The least element in a partial ordering of lexical terminals will be called the ROOT. Therefore, in a partial ordering of nouns in German consisting of $\{(Mann, Männer),$ $(Geist, Geister), (Buch, Bücher), \dots\}$, the items *Mann, Geist,* and Buch are roots, since *Männer*, *Geister*, and *Bücher* are related to them by morpholexical rule (5b) [which umlauts the stem vowel and adds the suffix *-r*], and they themselves are not related to other items by this rule. Notice that given this definition, an affix morpheme as well as a stem morpheme can be a ROOT; that is, items like *-heit* and *-schaft* are the least elements in their ordered pairs, just as *Staat* is in its pair. Roots are thus a subset of stems and affixes.... This use of morphological terminology is admittedly non-standard with respect to earlier works on morphology, both traditional and generative. (Lieber 1981, 43)

Selkirk uses the term *root* for phonological purposes, to distinguish between what Siegel had earlier called class I and class II affixes, which were distinguished even earlier by Chomsky and Halle (1968) in terms of boundaries (class I = formative boundary (+); class II = word boundary (#)), or their effects on stress (nonneutral versus neutral). Though she provides no formal definition, Selkirk says,

I will be defending the claims (i) that there are two (recursive) category levels or types that play a role in English word structure—Word, along with a "lower" category type, Root—and (ii) that Class I affixes attach to (i.e. subcategorize for) categories of type Root (and with them form roots), while Class II affixes attach to categories of type Word (and with them form words). (1982, 77–78).

Selkirk does not attempt to relate this use to any other, but it is clearly nonstandard.[1]

Both of these extended uses of the term *root* seem to be grounded in some aspect of some sense of the word *root*. Lieber's, for example, is reminiscent of the term *root node* from tree theory, where the root node, as the origin, enjoys some privilege of place. But I do not think that it would be worth our while to explore the question in detail, for, whatever the answer, these senses are only remotely related to the usual linguistic sense of the word *root*.

"So what?" one may say. Are not authors free, like Humpty Dumpty, to use a word in whatever way they wish to use it, so long as they are clear about what they mean? Well, yes and no. English is a language thankfully without police, but if the purpose of academic discourse is to clarify our understanding through that discourse, then the multiplication of private senses only gets in the way.

Speculation as to why such proliferation of senses should have happened is worth no more than a note.[2] The results, though, have been disheartening. Not only do we find authors arguing vehemently over seeming issues that arise solely out of the protagonists' having adopted the same terms for very different concepts (as for example, in Jensen and Stong-Jensen's [1984] reply to Anderson [1982], which hinges largely on different assumptions about what the lexicon is), but we also find respectable scholars falling into the simple logical fallacy of equating two concepts simply because they have the same name. Consider the following example from my own work: In Aronoff 1976 (henceforth *WFGG*) I used the term *word* in several senses and specifically noted in the preface that I would not use the term *lexeme*. This refusal led to a number of problems. For instance, one of the major points of *WFGG* was that morphology was what I termed *word-based*, by which I meant *lexeme-based*. I especially did not mean that the base or stem for a word-formation rule had to be a complete word or free form, only that the base should be a lexeme and the stem some form of a lexeme. Furthermore, I did not discuss exactly what form of a lexeme could constitute the stem for a word-formation rule. Nonetheless, others naturally misunderstood my claim as being about the forms of stems and pointed out that there are many languages in which the actual form to which a morphological operation applies is often not a free form, which would thus falsify my apparent claim that a stem had to be an otherwise free form (word). This was understandable, but even more to the point was the fact that this particular homonymy confused me too. Thus my treatment of what I called *adjustment rules* stemmed from the observation that "we often find cases of regularly derived words, semantically transparent, formed with affixes which we know to be alive and regular in their operation, which on the surface do not appear to have been derived from words" (p. 88). The examples I gave, all from English, were like *nominee*, whose meaning seems to dictate that the base of the derived word is *nominate*, although the actual stem that appears on the surface, *nomin*, is not an occurring free form. Given the distinction between a lexeme and a free form, though, it is entirely possible, within a lexeme-based framework, to accept that *nominee* is derived from the lexeme NOMINATE (I follow Matthews's convention of putting the names of lexemes in small capitals throughout this book), but from the bound stem *nomin-* of that lexeme rather than from the free form *nominate* via truncation. The mere fact that a stem does not appear on the surface as a free form therefore does not mean that truncation must be invoked within a lexeme-based framework, not unless one also claims that a lexeme and a free form are one and the same. Clearly what led me to truncation was my own confusion of lexemes with free forms.[3]

This time I am determined to do better. I cannot guarantee that I will never confuse any notions by means of terminology, and while I am enough of a realist not to believe that ideas can be understood only within a theory, I am equally not so naive as to believe that we can begin an investigation with all our terms predefined, as if we knew from the outset what lay in an unknown country. Nonetheless, it is useful to have some idea of what we are looking for. So the terms, notions, and distinctions I am about to discuss are tentative, but I have tried to be clear, and I hope that the reader will find the exercise useful.[4]

1.2   Separationist Morphology and Lexemes

Robert Beard (1981, 1987, to appear) has developed an approach to morphology in which there is no direct connection between the side of morphology that deals with sound and the sides that deal with syntax and semantics. He calls this idea, whose first intimations can be found in the work of Bazell (1949, 1952), the *separation hypothesis*. I will call any morphological theory that incorporates this hypothesis *separationist*. As Beard points out, separationist morphology is more compatible with lexeme-based theories than with morpheme-based theories for the simple reason that the concept of the lexeme is essentially separationist (it treats sound and meaning as separate systems), while the concept of the morpheme is based on the isomorphism of sound and meaning beyond the morpheme. Beard (to appear) discusses this point at some length, but I will review only the essentials of it here.

The basic goal of most morpheme-based theories is to reduce language to simplex signs, each one of which is an arbitrary union of sound and meaning. In a language that is ideal from this point of view, arbitrariness will reside entirely at the level of the simplex sign: each simplex sign will consist of a one-to-one match between a stretch of sound and a meaning, and in the perfect language, at least, these matchings should be biunique: each distinct arbitrary form should have a single meaning, and each distinct meaning a single form. This aesthetic of the perfect or ideal language can be traced directly at least as far back as seventeenth-century philosophers of language and the universal language movement (Salmon 1988), though it also has earlier connections to the mystery of Adamic naming. It influenced the development of standard languages through the academies, and again emerged, strongly, in the eighteenth century in the French school of the synonymists. In the nineteenth century we see it at work in a different guise, coupled with Adamic naming again: the search for the original roots of the *Ur*-language. With the advent of synchronic linguistics in the work of de Saussure and especially of Baudouin de Courtenay, the ideal takes on a different, psychological form: deep down inside, every utterance should be reducible to some string of simplex invariant signs, which Baudouin called *morphemes*; morphology and syntax both proceed from this same string of morphemes. This reductionist doctrine that the essence of language lies in the psychological invariance of morphemes has its fullest development in Roman Jakobson's structuralism and early generative phonology, and it is in the latter that morpheme-based linguistics reached its apogee, in such phonological *tours de force* as Foley 1965 and Schane 1969, which are marked by a fierce drive toward morphological invariance at all cost.

By contrast, the notion of the lexeme, as developed by Matthews, though it has its roots in structuralist linguistics, is entirely independent of morphological invariance: some (probably most) lexemes have a unique form associated with them; others do not. But lexeme-based morphology starts from two decidedly unstructuralist assumptions: that the morpheme is not the basic unit of language and that morphology and syntax are not one and the same. Morphology is not a matter of concatenation of morphemes in a lexeme-based morphology but rather the complex process by which abstract morphosyntactic representations are realized morphophonologically. It follows that the search for invariance is only a methodological or aesthetic desideratum (albeit an important one) within such a framework and not of particular theoretical significance. Indeed, one can argue, as Anderson (1992) has quite convincingly, that the traditional morpheme is simply an embarrassment in a lexeme-based theory of morphology.[5]

As I noted above, the lexeme is a theoretical construct that corresponds roughly to one of the common senses of the term *word*. Matthews (1991) provides a careful and by now classic analysis of three quite distinct senses in which the term *word* is commonly used in linguistics, which I will distinguish by the terms *sound form of a word*, *grammatical word*, and *lexeme*. The sound form of a word is simply a stretch of sound, with no regard for its meaning. The three lexemes that we spell PARE, PAIR, and PEAR share the one sound form [per]. The notion of a homophone is rooted in the sound form of a word. Related to the sound form of a word is the *prosodic word*, a unit on the prosodic hierarchy that contains the sound form of a word and all its phonological dependents. (See Nespor and Vogel 1986 and Goldsmith 1990 for further details.) The prosodic word is the closest modern analog to the phonological side of Bloomfield's definition of *word* as a minimum free form. In the case of a lexeme, in contrast with a phonological or prosodic word, what matters is not being a sound form but having a sound form. A lexeme is a sign, and therefore has meaning and syntax as well as form. But not all linguistic signs are lexemes, for I restrict the class of lexemes to what traditional grammars call *vocabulary words*, and what Chomsky (1965) calls the *major lexical categories*: noun (henceforth N), verb (henceforth V), and adjective/adverb (henceforth A).[6] As a vocabulary word, a lexeme stands outside any syntactic context beyond that for which it is lexically specified or subcategorized. A lexeme is therefore inherently unspecified for those contextually variable syntactic, semantic, and pragmatically determined categories that are encoded by inflection, although it contains within itself sufficient information for realizing these categories morphophonologically.

A lexeme is abstract in at least three ways. First, in contrast with the sound form of a word or prosodic word, a lexeme is not a form, but rather a sign or a set of signs: form, syntax, and meaning bound together (Mel'čuk 1982). It is natural, in our material world, to think of a lexeme as a form, or at least to rely more on form than on meaning. That is because of the tangible imbalance between the (relatively) concrete form of a word and the abstract nature of syntax and meaning. It is easier to grasp a form, to be sure of its reality, and to study it, than it is to grasp a meaning.[7] Consider the simple fact that even linguists normally use a sound form of an expression when we want to mention its meaning and that so-called abstract entities, like traces, Pro, or the performative and causative verbs of generative semantics, are so difficult to control in large part because they have no detectable form. But a lexeme is not just a form, although a major strategy of American linguistics since Boas has been to trust form over meaning.[8]

In my view (Aronoff 1983), and here I depart from some, the lexeme is also abstract in that it is not necessary to assume for any given lexeme that it be lexical (in the sense of this term that is more or less equivalent in meaning to *arbitrary*) or listed in a lexicon. I will discuss this sense of *lexical* below in section 4. All vocabulary words that are members of a major lexical category, regardless of whether they are actual or potential, are lexemes. The set of potential (regularly derived and compounded) lexemes for any given language is therefore infinite. That at least some lexemes exist only potentially is the second abstract property of lexemes. Being a lexeme and being in a (Bloomfieldian) lexicon are thus separate matters.[9]

Not only is being in a lexicon or dictionary not a necessary condition for being a lexeme, it is not a sufficient condition either, so that idiomatic phrases, for example, although one would list them in an ideal dictionary, are not lexemes, because they are not words. Here I agree with Matthews (1974, 35), but not with Lyons (1977), who explicitly includes idioms among lexemes and uses the term *word-lexeme* for Matthews's lexeme. The reader should also note that some authors do not restrict the scope of the term *lexeme* to major lexical categories (Sadock 1988).

One aspect of the dictionary metaphor that does prove useful is the notion that a lexeme has status as a vocabulary item outside of any syntactic context, in the way that a dictionary entry "exists" outside context, even though in actual use it will occur only in the syntactic and pragmatic context of an utterance. This third and final major abstract property of lexemes is especially important in inflective languages like Latin. So, for example, a Latin noun must always have a particular case and number when used in a sentence, both in its meaning and in its form. But the lexeme ("in the lexicon" as some linguists say, remembering all along that not all lexemes are in the lexicon) has no case and no number. Similarly for verbs, the lexemes for which exist in Latin without the tense, aspect, mood, voice, person, and number that must all be specified in any actual use.[10] A lexeme, at least in its extrasyntactic state, is uninflected, both abstractly and concretely. It neither bears the particular morphosyntactic features realized by inflectional morphology nor carries the phonological markers (affixes and such) by means of which these features may be recognized.

To recapitulate, a lexeme is a (potential or actual) member of a major lexical category, having both form and meaning but being neither, and existing outside of any particular syntactic context. In actual use, though, any instance of a lexeme appears in a sentence, a grammatical and pragmatic context. It is here that the notion of a grammatical word comes into play: a *grammatical word* is a lexeme in a particular syntactic context, where it will be provided with morphosyntactic features (like case and number) and with the morphophonological realization of these morphosyntactic features as bound forms. Grammatical words are the members of the paradigm of a particular lexeme.

1.3   Other Basic Morphological Terms

I will now clarify my use of the central morphological terms *morphology*, *morphosyntax*, *lexeme formation*, *inflection*, *derivation*, and *compounding*. All these terms and the senses in which I use them are reasonably standard, but in discussing them together, I hope to provide some understanding of how these senses fit into a coherent picture within a lexeme-based theory of morphology and its neighbors.[11]

I will begin by trying to untangle the relationship between morphology and syntax. Consider first Bloomfield's definition of morphology from the opening sentences of his classic chapter on morphology: "By the morphology of a language we mean the constructions in which bound forms appear among the constituents. By definition, the resultant forms are either bound forms or words, but never phrases. Accordingly, we may say that morphology includes the constructions of words and parts of words, while syntax includes the construction of phrases" (1933, 207). Earlier in the book, Bloomfield had defined a word as a *minimum free form*, "a free form which does not consist entirely of (two or more) lesser free forms" (1933, 178). Together these definitions of *word* and *morphology* provide a quite traditional vision of morphology and syntax in terms of phonologically defined words: two halves of a single domain divided at the phonological word or minimum free form. On this traditional view, morphology leaves off at the level of phonologically defined words, and then syntax takes over, putting these minimum free forms together into phrases and beyond. Syntax trades in minimum free forms (phonologically defined words), and morphology deals in their parts.

But in the beginning of his chapter on syntax, which he devotes to grammatical constructions, Bloomfield cautions that "grammatical *constructions* ... are dealt with partly under the heading of morphology" (1933, 184). Thus syntax, if we conceive of it as trading in grammatical constructions and categories in the modern fashion that Bloomfield explicitly advocates, is not so neatly divided off from morphology, as Bloomfield goes on to show; the two are not halves of a whole. Instead, they are two very different things: morphology deals with (bound) forms, as Bloomfield claims, while syntax deals with grammar (in the very narrow sense of that term that distinguishes syntactic/grammatical constructions from semantics, phonology, and other components of the grammar), as Bloomfield also claims. The problem is that the very traditional picture, which I first ascribed to Bloomfield, that depicts syntax and morphology as forming two parts of a single domain is based on a phonological or prosodic distinction between words and larger units, which, while it may be useful for morphology, is simply not relevant to the modern conception of syntax.

On the view of syntax that most modern linguists share, it is entirely possible for a grammatical construction to be simultaneously morphological and syntactic. It is syntactic by definition (because it is a grammatical construction) and morphological if it contains bound forms. There is no paradox, because modern morphology and syntax are not two halves of a single domain, but rather two different dimensions of the language space. The major concern of morphology (so far as it relates to syntax) is the mediation between grammatical categories and phonological substance. Morphology deals with forms. Syntax deals with grammatical constructions and categories.

The core of morphology, in my modernized version of Bloomfield's view, is the arbitrary relation between the signified and signifier of bound forms, what I have called elsewhere *phonological operations*, what Zwicky (1986) calls *morphological realization*, and what Beard (to appear) calls the *morphological spelling component*. This sense of the term, though narrow, is, as I argued in the introduction, actually closer to the original sense. Morphology at its core deals with formatives, the dependent elements that give shape to words. Because it is the clearest, I will use Zwicky's term *morphological realization* to refer specifically to this core of morphology.

One might wish to extend the scope of this sense of *morphology* so that morphology encompasses all translation into phonological substance, including that of lexemic stems and free forms. On this latter account, the fact that we say [pul] in English or [pisin] in French are facts about morphology. This extension is in fact close in spirit to what led Baudouin de Courtenay to coin the term *morpheme*. It is also close to Kiparsky's (1982) view, in which all forms are rules. However, because it may be useful to distinguish both between lexemes and morphosyntactic properties syntactically and between free and bound realization morphologically,[12] I will stick to the narrower definition, which restricts morphology to the realization of morphosyntactic properties through bound forms and which (more important for me) puts morphology and syntax on two different planes.[13]

From this point of view, the traditional definition of *morphosyntax* as the aspect of syntax that is relevant to morphology is perfectly reasonable. I will therefore adopt it, but I will have very little to say in this work about morphosyntax. Interested readers should consult Anderson 1992 for a treatment of the subject that is more concerned than most with the implications of morphosyntactic structure for morphological realization.

This brings us to *word formation*, or what I prefer to call *lexeme formation*, for it is here that the notion of a dividing line along a single dimension becomes useful, not a dividing line between syntax and morphology but rather between syntax and lexeme formation, and not at the phonologically defined level of the minimum free form but rather at the syntactically defined level of the minimal projection of X-bar syntax: X^0 or X-min.

Lexeme formation deals with the inner linguistic structure of what Chomsky (1965; henceforth *Aspects*) calls *lexical formatives*, the basic uninflected members of the major lexical categories (noun, verb, and adjective) on which the syntax operates. Chomsky opposes lexical formatives to *grammatical formatives*.[14] Lexical formatives are also called *minimal projections* (in *X*-bar theory) or *syntactic atoms* (in DiSciullo and Williams 1987) or *lexemes* (Matthews 1991), the term I use here. Lexeme formation (at least its syntactic side) thus stands in polar opposition to one traditional delineation of the scope of syntax: it deals with the internal (syntactic) structure of minimal projections, while syntax deals with their external syntax. Together, syntax and the syntactic side of lexeme formation, which Beard (to appear) calls *L-derivation*, divide up a single linguistic dimension, which is unfortunately sometimes also called syntax (as opposed to semantics). Because the term *syntax* is ambiguous, having scope in the broad sense over the entire domain (the syntax of lexeme formation together with supralexical syntax) and in the narrower sense over only supralexical syntax, it might be useful to coin a new term to distinguish the wider and narrower senses of the term. In this work, at least, I will use *syntax* and the related adjective *syntactic* narrowly, to refer only to supralexical syntax. I have no good term to suggest for the wider sense, which one might call *wide syntax* when necessary.[15]

I do not use the more common term *word formation*, because, unlike *lexeme formation*, it is confusing. That is because the term *word* is ambiguous among quite separate and independently important concepts, as I have already noted. A (phonological) word and a lexeme are not always coextensive. There are lexemes (minimal projections) that contain more than one phonological word: compounds, which, in Germanic languages like English, may be many words long, or phrasally based lexemes, like *stick in the mud*.[16] Conversely, there are single phonological words that do not belong to major lexical categories and are therefore not lexemes by the narrow definition, which distinguishes between major and minor categories.[17] Finally, there are single words that are syntactically complex, and thus constitute more than lexemes, because they contain material from the syntactic domain beyond the minimal projection, like inflections and clitics.[18]

Another problem with the term *word formation*, and especially the term *word-formation rule*, is that for some authors (e.g., in Anderson 1992), it is synonymous with *morphology*. For others (e.g., me in *WFGG*), the term encompasses both the internal syntax and the internal morphology of minimal projections. I will therefore use the term *lexeme formation* exclusively in this work.[19] Within a separationist framework, however, it is important to distinguish the internal syntax of minimal projections from their morphology. I will therefore restrict its use as far as possible to lexeme-internal syntax, (essentially following Beard, to appear) as opposed to morphology. This restriction allows me to treat conversion or zero-derivation as lexeme formation that has no morphological realization, which seems correct (Beard 1981, Pinker 1991, Williams 1981).[20]

Having thus drawn a dividing line between lexeme formation and syntax along a single dimension separate from morphology, we may now better understand what the lexicalist hypothesis means for the narrow construal of morphology within a separationist framework: nothing. The lexicalist hypothesis, at least in its more common weak version (Anderson 1992; *WFGG*; Aronoff, to appear; Chomsky 1970), is a hypothesis about syntax and not about morphology. It consists simply of drawing a dividing line along the syntactic dimension between lexeme formation and supralexical syntax. To draw this line is to claim only that syntax operates differently in the two domains, above and below it. For the line to exist, it is not necessary, as some claim (e.g., Lieber 1992) that entirely different mechanisms are at work in the two domains. The very same mechanisms may be at work, but if they work at all differently, then the weak lexicalist hypothesis is true. If they do not, then it is false. In either case, the lexicalist hypothesis tells us nothing about morphology in the narrow sense of morphological realization, which is entirely orthogonal to the issue. It is thus perfectly reasonable to put aside the question of the lexicalist hypothesis in a work on morphology, except in one instance: the distinction between inflection and derivation.

Within a separationist lexicalist framework, *inflectional morphology* as traditionally conceived deals with the bound realization of syntactic categories and elements that lie above the minimal projection (the morphology of syntax), while *derivational morphology* deals with the bound realization of categories and elements that are entirely internal to minimal projections, (which is to say the morphology of lexeme formation). This is more or less the position of Anderson (1982, 1992).[21] Whether inflection and derivation are morphologically distinct is therefore a separate and most likely subsidiary issue. In fact, the morphology of inflection and derivation seem to be very similar to a great extent in most languages that have been investigated in any depth. Nonetheless, there are sometimes intriguing empirical differences. For example, in English, the two non-syllabic productive suffixes -/s, z, əz/ and -/t, d, əd/ are inflectional, and all prefixes are derivational. Also, productive inflection in English always involves stress-neutral suffixes, while productive derivation is divided between stress-neutral and stress-changing affixes. In Kannada and other

Dravidian languages, all inflection is suffixal and the few prefixes that can be isolated are derivational and relatively new (Aronoff and Sridhar 1988). In other words, it is certainly possible to find phonological distinctions between inflectional and derivational morphology, though their theoretical import is not yet clear.

We can now also distinguish derivation from compounding. Compounding is lexeme formation, but it is not morphological, at least in the sense of the term that I have adopted here: it does not necessarily involve bound morphological realization. Instead, compounding is a type of lexeme formation that operates primarily at the level of syntactic categories, without reference to the morphological content of the construction. Thus the prototypical English compound is one in which a noun is adjoined to a noun to form a noun:

(1) $[[\ ]_N[\ ]_N]_N$

There is no mention of the form of either noun. The same is true for other compound constructions.[22] Compounding is thus lexeme-internal syntax, as pointed out by Anderson (1992).

This point may be clearer when put from another perspective. Remember that a word-formation rule as explicated in *WFGG* (which I would now term a lexeme-formation rule) is a multidimensional function with syntactic, semantic, and phonological parts to it. The syntactic part stipulates a base (in terms of its syntactic category) and an output (also in terms of its syntactic category); the semantic part of the rule may provide more detailed semantic specification for the base and the output beyond their simple categories (in a theory that distinguishes semantic from syntactic properties); the phonological part consists of a realization rule in which are stipulated a stem and a morphological operation. Within such a framework, compounding is a lexeme-formation rule with no phonological subpart beyond concatenation.[23]

To sum up, lexeme formation (including compounding) deals with the internal syntax of lexemes. Derivation and inflection are both restricted to morphology in the narrow sense of morphological realization, but they differ from one another on the basis of what they realize: lexeme-internal versus lexeme-external syntactic elements.

1.4 *Lexical, Lexemic,* and the Lexicon

The term *lexical* was to linguistics in the 1980s what the word *natural* was to the 1970s, a feel-good buzzword that attached itself to a number of unfortunate theories with no necessary connection to each other or to anything else. I will not deal with all of these theories but rather only try to untangle the two senses of the term that seem to be most important, showing that one of these senses is rooted in the notion of the lexeme. Additionally, by disentangling these two senses of *lexical*, we can also clarify the term *lexicon*.

In its most unadorned sense, *lexical* means 'having to do with words'. Etymologically, it is derived by means of the Latinate adjectival suffix *-al* from the borrowed Greek noun *lexicon*. The latter is originally a neuter adjective, and its nominal sense is derived by clipping from the phrase *lexicon biblion* 'wordbook'. The adjective stem *lexic-*is based on the noun *lexis* 'what is said, word', which derives finally from the verb *leg-*to 'say, speak'. *Lexical* itself is not an old word, although its Greek progenitors are all venerable. The first citation in the *OED* is 1836, and it is not listed in any dictionary of medieval Latin.

In its two most important technical linguistic uses, *lexical* has a narrower sense than just 'having to do with words' and is contrasted with *grammatical*. I will devote the rest of this section to these two senses and ignore any other noncontrastive senses. Etymologically, *grammatical* is quite parallel to *lexical*. It is based on the Greek noun *grammatike*, which is originally a feminine adjective. Its nominal sense is derived by clipping from the phrase *grammatike texne*, which had a number of distinct senses, one of them being more or less equivalent to *grammar*. The adjective stem *grammatik-* is derived from the noun *grammata* 'letters', which itself is derived from *graph-* 'write'. The two words *lexical* and *grammatical* are thus perfectly parallel in their etymological history, each being an adjective derived from a noun derived from an adjective derived from a noun derived from a verb.

Traditional grammarians divided a language into two major parts: grammar and lexicon. The latter contains the basic elements, the words, while the former contains the rules for combining these basic bits. If words and grammar are conceived of as being maximally distinct, so that all the rules of the language are concentrated in the grammar, then we arrive at the kind of theory that has dominated theoretical discourse since at least the seventeenth century, in which the words, by contrast with the grammar, are treated as the seat of everything irregular.

Early theorists went so far as to equate grammar with logic, and they constructed purely logical artificial languages in which "real characters" substituted for untrustworthy words. These same theorists were only strengthened in their dichotomous conclusions by the simultaneous recognition that words were arbitrary signs. Words and the adjective *lexical* thus came to be associated with arbitrariness and idiosyncrasy in contrast with grammar and *grammatical*.

The equation of *lexical* with *idiosyncratic* was strengthened in the twentieth century, under the theoretical influence of Leonard Bloomfield. Sometime before 1881, Baudouin de Courtenay coined the term *morpheme* to refer to minimal meaningful forms.[24] Bloomfield adopted the term but gave it a characteristically formal definition free of mentalistic baggage. In his postulates, he defined a morpheme as "a recurrent (meaningful) form which cannot in turn be analyzed into smaller recurrent (meaningful) forms" (1970 [1926], 130). For Bloomfield, as for Baudouin de Courtenay, the basic elements of language were not words but morphemes. This theoretical innovation resulted in another terminological change, for which Bloomfield alone seems to have been responsible: the lexicon, the list of basic elements in a language, was now defined as a list of morphemes rather than as a list of words: "The total stock of morphemes in a language is its *lexicon*" (Bloomfield 1933, 162). Furthermore, since "every morpheme is an irregularity," the lexicon is "a list of basic irregularities" (Bloomfield 1933, 274). This definition makes the word *lexical* synonymous with *idiosyncratic* and leaches it of any real connection with words.[25]

Bloomfield's new senses of *lexicon* and *lexical* prevailed for the next forty years. Together with the emphasis on the phoneme and the subsequent influence of information theory, these definitions led, in phonology, to the sparse lexical phonological representations of the 1960s and 1980s, from which all predictable nonarbitrary redundancy is excluded. In syntax and semantics too, lexical properties became those that were not predictable but were rather part of what must be memorized about individual lexical items. As Chomsky puts it, "In general, all properties of a formative that are essentially idiosyncratic will be specified in a lexicon" (Chomsky 1965, 87). I call this sense of *lexical*, which I have traced to Bloomfield, *idiosyncratic-lexical*.

The other important sense of *lexical* also finds its roots in the traditional distinction between *lexical* and *grammatical*, but on the substantive side, in the contrast between lexical (content) elements, sometimes called *full words*, and grammatical elements, sometimes called *function words*, what Bloomfield calls *formatives*.[26] This sense is explicated most clearly by Sapir in his *Language* (1921), although it should be noted that Sapir himself does not use the term *lexical* but rather a variety of other terms, especially *radical*. In Sapir's work, as in traditional grammar, the lexical/

grammatical dichotomy is grounded in semantics. Lexical (radical) concepts are semantically concrete, while grammatical concepts are archetypically abstract and relational. Sapir divides radical concepts into three types—objects, actions, and qualities—which correspond respectively to the three open or lexical classes: nouns, verbs, and adjectives. Sapir devotes the longest chapter of *Language* to an attempt to develop a classification system that will distinguish the concrete concepts of radical elements from the relational concepts of grammatical elements. He is careful to point out in the end of that chapter that no sharp dichotomy can be made. Nonetheless, the lexical/grammatical dichotomy still stands as a way of expressing the distinction between the three open lexical classes and all other (closed) classes of forms, which are grammatical. This second sense of the term *lexical*, which is based on the identification of lexical categories, is clearly related to the notion of a lexeme: the members of the open (major) lexical classes are lexemes. We may therefore substitute for the term *lexical* in this second sense the term *lexemic*, which can be defined informally as 'having to do with lexemes'.

Compared with Bloomfield's 'idiosyncratic' sense of *lexical*, this lexemic sense of the term enjoyed little popularity until very recently, largely because of its overt connection with traditional semantic definitions of parts of speech, which were a favorite target of structuralist ire. However, this sense has come to the fore in syntactic research in the last twenty-five years.

Let us therefore turn to the use of the term *lexical* in syntax, whose *locus classicus* is in *Aspects*. There Chomsky uses the term in both the senses under discussion. Thus, early in the book (1965, 65), he distinguishes between lexical and grammatical formatives or items and suggests that the lexical categories are at least N, V, and A.[27] Chomsky searches, as Sapir did, for some independent characterization of the lexical/grammatical distinction. His answer is very different from Sapir's. In the case of lexical categories, Chomsky suggests, phonetic-distinctive feature theory provides a language-independent representation, while the substantive representation of grammatical formatives is provided by Universal Grammar.[28] It is thus clear that, although his criteria are novel, Chomsky is pursuing a lexemic definition of the term *lexical*. In accord with this definition, Chomsky then defines the lexicon as "an unordered list of all lexical formatives" (1965, 84).

On the other hand, Chomsky also says, following the Bloomfieldian tradition, that "In general, all properties of a formative that are essentially idiosyncratic will be specified in the lexicon" (1965, 87), with an accompanying footnote recalling Bloomfield's characterization of the lexicon as a list of basic irregularities and noting a remark of Sweet's according to which "grammar deals with the general facts of language, lexicology with the special facts." Chomsky's definition here is thus explicitly within the Bloomfieldian idiosyncratic lexical tradition (both in nature and in attribution), according to which even grammatical formatives must be listed in the lexicon. A definition of *lexical* combining both senses is given in *The Sound Pattern of English*: "formatives which are provided by the lexicon, i.e. the lexical formatives as well as certain grammatical formatives which happen to appear in lexical entries. There may be other grammatical formatives introduced directly by the syntactic rules themselves" (Chomsky and Halle 1968, 9).

The syntactic theory of *Aspects*, however, is based only on the lexemic sense of *lexical*. Grammatical formatives are introduced by the categorial component. This component generates strings consisting of various occurrences of the variable Δ, which marks the position of lexical categories, and grammatical formatives. Lexical formatives (lexemes) are then introduced into these strings by the substitution transformations, which substitute complex symbols for occurrences of Δ. Nonetheless, because both senses of *lexical* are used in *Aspects* without explicit differentiation, it seems that the confusion in the subsequent literature begins at the source.

Aspects is followed by Chomsky 1970 (henceforth "Remarks"), which most of us regard as the cornerstone of lexical grammar. Bresnan, for example, says, "The existence of a class of lexical rules of word formation was postulated by Chomsky (1970)" (1978, 5). In fact, the lexical theory of "Remarks" is essentially identical to that of the last chapter of *Aspects*. In this account, there are no word-formation rules of the sort that Bresnan attributes to Chomsky. Instead, Chomsky uses lexical entries that are unspecified for lexical category to allow derivationally related lexemes to share subcategorization frames. This permits Chomsky to express common properties of these related lexemes without word/lexeme formation rules. Thus the theory of "Remarks" that Bresnan alludes to is lexical in the idiosyncratic sense of the term and not in the lexemic sense, as Bresnan implicitly claims. The fact that the theory is recalled as being lexical in the lexemic sense must be due to confusion between the two senses, which is one legacy of *Aspects*.

Aspects leaves us, nonetheless, with an interesting question: are the two senses of *lexical* conceptually related in some way? In particular, are members of major lexical categories necessarily listed in the lexicon? Many authors assume that they are. Thus Anderson (1988) says that stems, or words minus productive inflectional affixes, function as the base of word-formation rules and are "the lexical items that are entered in the dictionary of a language" (p. 28), and that productive inflection applies to these lexical items. Given this much, it would appear that Anderson is using *lexical* here in its lexemic sense. Later on in the same article, though, Anderson makes the following argument. He first notes that idiosyncratic realizations of inflectionally relevant properties must be present in lexical representations. He then concludes that "nonregular (hence lexical [inflectional]) morphology may appear in derivational forms or compounds because it is in the lexicon" (1988, 40). But this conclusion, which Anderson calls a theorem, follows only if the two senses of *lexical* define the same object. If they do not, then there is no logical reason to assume that idiosyncratic inflected forms will interact with unlisted uninflected stems. They may interact, but this does not follow from any theory. Perlmutter (1988) makes exactly the same argument in a closely related paper in the same volume.

The reader might object here that there is a good deal of evidence showing that irregularly inflected forms do appear in compounds and derivatives. But the reader should also realize that this observation, if it is true, does not follow from any current theory of morphology. If it is true that the two senses of *lexical* are extensionally equivalent, then we do not have any idea why this should be. Thus what Anderson characterizes as a "rather precise claim [that] follows as a theorem from the proposed organization of the grammar" (1988, 42) is in fact an important empirical question yet to be answered and not a logical one.

We have indeed been fooled by our own terminology. Using the same term for two quite different notions has led us astray. But the solution to this problem is not simply terminological, for if one important theoretical point has emerged from this lengthy etymological excursus, it is that one sense of the term is rooted in the notion of the lexeme. Within a lexeme-based theory of morphology, we don't need any new terms. All we have to do is to restrict our use of the term *lexical* to its 'idiosyncratic' sense, which is indeed the better entrenched of the two in the rcent literature. We do not need a new term for the other sense, since we already have *lexemic*. Furthermore, and most important, the two concepts each find a natural home in a lexeme-based morphology and syntax.

But what about the lexicon? The two senses of *lexical* have led, over the last twenty years, to two quite distinct notions of a lexicon. On the idiosyncratic sense, the lexicon is a list of arbitrary pairings of form and meaning, regardless of the category they belong to. This view has been best articulated by DiSciullo and Williams (1987). On the lexemic sense, we might call the set of all lexemes the lexicon, regardless of whether they are all arbitrary (and some are clearly not). These two senses of *lexicon* are sometimes given different names, respectively, the *permanent lexicon* (Lieber 1981) versus the *conditional lexicon* (Allen 1978). But even this nomenclature is deceptive, for it is clear that we are not dealing with two types of lexicons, one permanent and one conditional, but with two largely unrelated theoretical entities: an arbitrary list of signs that a speaker happens to hold in memory as opposed to a well-defined infinite set. In fact, since the extensional notion of a potential lexicon plays no significant role that I know of in any theory of morphology, while the Bloomfieldian theory is crucial to a proper understanding of blocking and productivity, it seems best to simply dispense with both the notion of the potential lexicon and the name. The term *lexicon* should therefore be understood, in this work at least, as referring only to the permanent lexicon: the list of all idiosyncratic signs, regardless of their category or complexity. The endless list of all lexemes, by contrast, will remain nameless.

1.5   The Morphomic Level

Morphosyntactic elements are frequently morphophonologically diverse, contrary to our best expectations. For example, although linguists often think of the English Plural in nouns as consisting of an underlying /z/, there are many nouns with other plurals, some of them even partially regular (as with the lack of an overt marker for nouns denoting game animals and quantitative nouns). (Quirk, Greenbaum, Leech, and Svartvik [1985] devote eight pages to irregular English plurals and one to regulars.) This diversity of plural forms forces us to recognize that Plural does not have a unique morphological form but rather varies according to the noun whose plural marker we are specifying: /z/ is not its signifier but rather its default realization. The same is true for English Past Tense, but to a much greater degree, there being some 250 irregular verbs, which Quirk et al. (1985) analyze as falling into seven different classes and many subclasses, based on their past-tense and perfect-participle forms. Indeed, the base-dependent morphological realization of these categories is one of the simplest arguments for an abstract morphosyntactic level and against the traditional morpheme sign with a unitary underlying sound form (Matthews 1972).

   In traditional morphology there are many instances where phonologically quite diverse forms occupy a single morphosyntactic cell in the general morphological paradigm, their distribution being determined by base lexemes or inflectional classes of lexemes.[29] Indeed, it is unusual, except in an ideal regular agglutinative language, to have very many cells in a paradigm that have completely constant realizations.[30] Though the distribution of plural markers and such may seem complicated, from a simple mathematical point of view, it is not. Such distributions may be described mathematically as functions. Consider the English Past Tense. For each verb lexeme, which we may call the elements in the domain of the plural, there is a single past-tense form, which we may call the range of the plural. The morphophonology of the Past Tense is therefore a function from verb lexemes to past-tense forms. These functions are sometimes discontinuous (not all past-tense forms can be described by the same equation), but the mapping is always one-to-one: a given speaker in a steady state does not have more than one past-tense form for a given verb.[31]

But this characterization raises another question, which is how to characterize the relation of these functions to their morphosyntax. For something like Plural, we may perhaps assume that there is a single syntactic element, Plural, with a well-behaved semantics, that is mapped directly onto the single morphophonological function F_{plural}. Similarly, perhaps, for F_{past}. But this is not always true. Some morphophonological functions may not have single morphosyntactic values. Consider the member of the English verb paradigm that Chomsky (1957) singles out with the abstract suffix marker -en, often called the *past* or *passive participle*. I will call it the *perfect participle*. Every nonmodal English verb has such a form. Although Chomsky syntactically treats -en as a suffix, which allows him to include it in his classic affix-hopping account of verb morphology, it is quite complex morphophonologically and is certainly not always a realized as a suffix. For most verbs, which is to say in the default case, the perfect participle is formed by adding to the verb stem a suffix, which I call D, which is also the default marker of the past-tense form. This suffix, as is well known, has three allomorphs, *d, t, əd*, whose distribution is completely predictable from the phonological value of the last segment of the verb stem.[32] But even abstract D is only the *default* realization of the perfect participle. With lexically marked verbs, the perfect participle may be formed instead by a variety of means: with the suffix -n (e.g., *gotten*), with the suffix + *t* (as in *left*), by ablaut of one sort or another (e.g., *sung*), or by a combination of two or more of these (e.g., *broken* with ablaut and -n, *thought* with ablaut and + *t*, or colloquial *boughten* with all three).[33] Since ablaut is not a suffix, we cannot call the perfect-participle formative a suffix, let alone assume that it has any constant underlying sound form (as calling it -*en* leads us to presume). We must therefore conclude that the perfect participle is a kind of abstract category realized in the context of a given verb through the operation of one or more of a set of realization rules of suffixation or ablaut, the default realization being D.[34] Perfect Participle is therefore a discontinuous morphophonological function similar to Past Tense or Plural: for every verb lexeme, there is a single perfect participle, although not all perfect participles are derived by the same rule. Let us call this morphophonological function from verb stems to perfect participles F_{en}. What morphosyntactic value is mapped onto F_{en}?

The English Perfect Participle has two major uses syntactically: to form the passive verb and to form the perfect verb (always in company with the verb HAVE). Within recent Chomskyan syntax, the most widely accepted treatment of the passive is in terms of thematic role or case absorption. Jaeggli (1986) and Roberts (1987) treat the passive morphology as absorbing the thematic role and the case, while Baker, Johnson, and Roberts (1989) analyze passive syntax as resulting universally from an abstract subject pronoun of sorts in Infl. Presumably this abstract pronoun or some structure containing it is realized through the morphological function that I have labeled F_{en}. What about the perfect construction? The most recent detailed analysis of its semantics (Klein 1992) makes no connection to the passive. Nor is there any currently popular analysis of its syntax that attempts to accommodate the perfect to recent accounts of the passive (which pretend to universality). As far as I know, the two may be totally independent of one another syntactically, although there are good historical reasons for the synchronic fact that both participles are identical (Benveniste 1966). From a universal perspective, it would be odd for passive and perfect constructions to be identical at some deep syntactic level, since the two only rarely coincide morphologically. Let us assume then, for the sake of argument, that passive and perfect are not closely related syntactically.[35] Nonetheless, the two must be identical on some level, since there are no English verbs for which they are morphologically distinct. The complete morphological covariance of the two is striking, since innovation in the F_{en} participle is rampant among children. Furthermore, though there have been many changes in individual F_{en} participles over the centuries, with certain verbs showing variants today (e.g. *kneeled*/ *knelt*), the two participles remain firmly linked throughout the innovation for any given verb: no speaker has an innovative passive participle and a conservative perfect participle; if a speaker varies, then both participles vary. I therefore assume that passive and perfect are paired by means of the morphologically abstract entity F_{en}, regardless of any possible syntactic and semantic differences between the two. In other words, there is a mapping to the function F_{en} from either Passive or Perfect. The subsequent phonological realizations of F_{en} must ignore any distinction between Passive and Perfect as syntactic entities, for otherwise we would not be able to account for the complete morphological coincidence of the two constructions.[36]

What is F_{en}? Formally, we may say that both Passive and Perfect are syntactic elements mapped onto the morphological function F_{en}. This function occupies a cell in the morphological paradigm of English that is neither syntactic nor phonological. Because the function itself is mapped from either Passive or Perfect and because the domain of the function (the class of verb lexemes) is morphological or lexemic, and not syntactic, its effect is to erase any possible distinction between the two syntactic elements in their realizations on the verb itself (though the difference in the auxiliary will distinguish the two constructions). F_{en} is neither morphosyntactic nor morphophonological but rather purely morphological— morphology by itself. Let us call the level of such purely morphological functions *morphomic* and the functions themselves *morphomes*. What is novel about this level, and what warrants giving it a special name, is that it embodies an empirical claim: the mapping from morphosyntax to phonological realization is not direct but rather passes through an intermediate level.[37] Note that not all mappings from syntax to morphology are necessarily so indirect. It is possible to have a singleton morphosyntactic set mapped onto a singleton morphomic set, which itself is mapped onto a singleton morphophonological set, although such direct mappings are less common than one would like to believe. It is also possible to have cases intermediate in complexity between the two extremes. All of these mappings technically involve morphomes, but it is morphomes like F_{en} that truly earn their name.

Once we recognize the possibility of these neutralizing morphomes, examples spring to mind quite easily. The clearest often inhabit traditional grammars under the name *participle*. Consider Hebrew participles. Aside from their expected use as "adjectival verbs" (in Biblical Hebrew relative structures for example), they function as agentive nouns and, in Mishnaic and later stages of the language, as the present tense. As present tense verbs, participles show no nominal syntax whatsoever, only nominal morphology, which entails that they agree with their subjects in number and gender always, but never in person, while other verb tenses agree in number, gender, and person but do not show gender agreement in the first person.[38] The actual forms of the agreement affixes to the present-tense participle are also identical to nominal agreement affixes. Apart from their agreement morphology, though, present-tense forms show syntactic patterns exactly like all other verbs. For example, definite direct objects of verbs are preceded by the particle *'et* (which shows morphological and syntactic patterns like a preposition). This particle is found after present-tense verbs. The direct object of nouns, by contrast, never shows the *'et* particle but appears instead together with its governor in a genitivelike construction called the *construct*. The construct differs from the English genitive in that the head noun occurs in a construct form. This construct form is very clearly demarcated with plurals of nominals. The default (masculine) nominal plural suffix is *-im*. Nouns in the construct always show *e* instead. So the nonconstruct plural of *sus* 'horse' is *susim*, but its construct is *suse*, as in the following example:

(2) sus-e   far'o
    horse-pl   Pharaoh

The nouns in a construct phrase form a single word phonologically, as shown by the spirantization of the initial /p/ in *far'o* (underlyingly *par'o*) in the Masoretic text. The construct can be used as a diagnostic for syntactically distinguishing those participles that are nouns from those that are verbs: when participles are agentive nouns with objects, they will appear in the construct form; when they are present-tense verbs with objects, they will not appear in the construct; also, when their objects are definite, they will be followed by the direct-object particle *'et*.[39] These differences are illustrated in the following examples:

(3) Hem šomr-im   co'n.
    they watch.part-pl sheep
    'They watch sheep.'

(4) Hem šomr-im   'et ha-co'n
    they watch.part-pl obj the-sheep
    'They watch the sheep.'

(5) Hem šomr-e   co'n.
    they watch.part-const.pl sheep
    'They are watchers of sheep.'

(6) Hem šomr-e   ha-co'n.
    they watch.part-const.pl the-sheep
    'They are (the) watchers of the sheep.'

Both (3) and (4) contain present-tense participles; (4) shows the object marker before a definite object of a verb. This marker is missing in (6), because the participle in (6) is not a verb. Both (5) and (6) betray their nominal syntactic nature in the construct form of the participle. With some nouns, especially certain types of masculine singulars, including participles, there is no special construct form (Gesenius and Kautzsch 1910, sec. 93). In such instances, it is impossible to distinguish between an agentive noun and a present-tense verb with an indefinite object. The following example is therefore ambiguous:

(7) Hu šomer   co'n.
    he watch.part sheep
    'He watches/is a watcher of sheep.'

Nonetheless, despite the absolute morphological homophony, the syntactic distinction between the present-tense verbs and the agentive nouns is clearcut. As Berman puts it, "Two syntactically distinct items—verb and noun respectively—coalesce into one single form on the surface. But these two items are either very clearly verbal, in that they take the same complements and modifiers as any finite verb, or strictly nominal, in which case they pattern syntactically like any other 'basic' or non-derived noun in the language" (1978, 397). Furthermore, although all verbs have a present tense, not all verbs have an agentive noun. On the basis of certain diagnostics, Berman notes that the participle of the verb *ntn* 'give', *noten* 'giving', is not used in Israeli Hebrew as an agentive in the sense 'giver', although the corresponding form *torem* 'contributor' is perfectly acceptable as an agentive. There are many other similar pairs. Also, agentives may be semantically noncompositional. So, to again cite Berman, the verb lexemes whose participles are *cofe* and *maškif* both have the sense 'watch, observe', but the first, as an agentive noun, means '(boy) scout', while the second means '(UN) observer' (1978, 398). Some agentives also occur in only one gender. There are thus ample syntactic grounds for claiming with Berman that participial agentive nouns are the result of derivation, while the present tense is an inflected form of the verb. The two are unrelated syntactically.

Morphologically, however, these agentives and present-tense forms are identical in form. As I will show in chapter 5, the form of the participle of a Hebrew verb is not constant but is rather a function of its inflectional class. There are five (seven on some analyses) inflectional classes in Hebrew, and each has its own participle. The forms of the participial agentive and of the present tense will therefore depend on the inflectional class of the verb lexeme, but they will always be identical for a given lexeme. The situation is thus exactly analogous to that of the English passive and perfect participles. Both agentive and present tense are realized by a single morphological function F_{part}. Similar data from Chukchee and Koryak, with a very similar analysis, can be found in Beard 1990.

The morphome is purely morphological in the narrow sense that it lies between morphosyntax and morphophonology. Other mappings can also be fruitfully analyzed as morphological in this same narrow sense. In chapter 3, I will discuss a number of cases of systematic homonymy, which, while less complete than what I have described here, nonetheless also involve an intermediate purely morphological level. Another example is the inheritance of irregular morphology from a root or morphological head, even in the absence of compositionality. Thus all English verbs of the form *stand*, regardless of their sense, and all verbs whose root is *stand* have *stood* as their past tense and perfect participle (Aronoff 1976). The same is true of other irregular verbs, and irregular noun plurals like *child/ children* are parallel. This general phenomenon is discussed at length by Hoeksema (1985). In each case, the set of irregular forms is obviously not a single lexeme (WITHSTAND and UNDERSTAND are not semantically related), so their unity must be expressed at a purely morphological level.

The linguistic literature is replete with examples of morphological mappings that go awry because of a failure to recognize that certain phenomena are purely morphological. One of the most interesting such examples can be found in Chomsky's (1975) analysis of the /-z, -s, -əz/ suffix that is the default marker for plurals in nouns and also for the third-person singular present in verbs. Chomsky unites these diverse syntactic elements into a single morpheme. In his expansion of the auxiliary node, the first member (which is tense in later treatments) is a disjunction. One of its members is *-ed* (past in later treatments), and the other member is C, which Chomsky characterizes as "an element of P (i.e. a 'lowest level' element of the level P [phrase structure]) which carries the long component of number" (1975, 232). Chomsky analyzes C into morphemes as follows:

C will in turn be analyzed by a mapping ... whose content will be roughly as follows, where, for noun phrases, S is taken as the plural morpheme, and $\emptyset$ as the singular morpheme (thus each NP becomes either $NP\widehat{\ }S$ or $NP\widehat{\ }\emptyset$):

C goes into S in the environment $NP\widehat{\ }\emptyset$____, and into $\emptyset$ in the environment $NP\widehat{\ }S$____.

Thus the long component of number has the peculiar feature that the verb is "singular" when the subject is "plural," and *vice versa*. That the same morpheme is affixed to both the noun and the verb is evident from the fact that this is a long component, and from the fact that the same morphophonemic statements must be made about both elements (e.g., both are voiced after voiced consonants, etc.). (1975, 233–234)

Two footnotes to this passage are especially revealing. In the first, Chomsky points out that " 'I' and 'you' are 'plural' from the point of view of this rule of 'disagreement in number.' " In the second he notes that the voicing alternation between /-z/ and /-s/ cannot be phonemic, because we find pairs like *peers/peirce*.

As is well known by now, this *S* element not only occurs as a plural marker on nouns and as a third-person singular marker on verbs; it is also the possessive marker and the reduced form of the auxiliary verbs *has*, *is*, and even *does* in colloquial registers. To extend Chomsky's analysis to these other cases (e.g., to rewrite HAVE or BE as the plural morpheme when cliticized) would either quickly lead us to grief or force us to abandon the content of the notions 'plural morpheme' or 'number'. If, however, we recognize the identity of these elements at a purely morphological level, independent of their syntax and semantics, then we are at least on our way to understanding the problem. I should note in closing this discussion that Chomsky uses essentially the same analysis of the identity of the two sets of suffixes in his best-known discussion of English verb morphology, Chomsky 1957. He notes in a footnote, however, that "identification of the nominal and verbal number affix is of questionable validity" and omits the first and second persons from the purview of the analysis (Chomsky 1957, 29).

I now turn to a more complex, purely morphological phenomenon in which a number of syntactically distinct elements in Latin, rather than simply being identical in form, are instead all built on the same stem, a stem, moreover, that is not constant in form but can instead be identified only as a cell in the morphological paradigm of the verb.

Chapter 2
Stems in Latin Verbal Morphology

What are the formal patterns of the language? And what types of concepts make up the content of these formal patterns? The two points of view are quite distinct.
E. Sapir

In this chapter I will examine the role of morphological stems, defined purely in terms of functions from sound forms of lexemes to sound forms of lexemes or grammatical words. I will adopt the traditional definition of a stem as the part of a complete word form that remains when an affix is removed.[1] And I will explore the consequences of treating stems as sound forms from the general perspective of such lexeme-based theories of morphology as those of Anderson 1992; *WFGG*; Beard, to appear; Hoeksema 1985; Matthews 1972; and Zwicky 1989.

2.1 Priscianic Formation of Latin Future, Active Participles

I will begin with Matthews 1972, since that is where lexeme-based morphology originates. Matthews devotes a great deal of attention to what he calls *Priscianic* or *parasitic formation*, in which one member of a paradigm seems to be formed not on the lexical root of the paradigm[2] but instead on the stem of another member of the paradigm.[3] The best-known case of a putative Priscianic formation, and the one to which Matthews devotes most of his attention, is the Latin future, active participle. This participle is invariably marked by the suffix -*ūr*-, and since it is an adjective morphologically, it agrees in gender, number, and case with its modified head noun or subject,[4] as in the following examples:[5]

(1) a. Cum hōc   equit-e   pugn-ā-t-ūr-ī   es-tis.
      with this.abl.sg cavalry-abl.sg fight-Th-T-FP-nom.pl be-2pl.pres.ind.act
      'You are about to fight with this cavalry' Livy

b. qu-ōs   Cn. Pompēius fac-t-ūr-us   est
which-acc.pl Pompey   do-T-FP-nom.sg is
'which Pompey is to do' Cicero

Two things are noteworthy about the future active participle. First, it is formed not directly on the verb root but instead on the stem of the perfect (passive) participle, as shown in table 2.1.[6]

The perfect-participle marker is usually the suffix -*t*, attached directly to the verb theme (the root followed by the theme vowel), as in *am-ā-t-* 'love PP', *aud-ī-t-* 'hear PP', or attached directly to the verb root, as in *duc-t-* 'lead PP'.[7] Often, however, there is some irregularity, either in the perfect-participle suffix, which may be *s* instead of *t*, or in the form of the verb to which the perfect-participle suffix is attached.[8] In these cases, the perfect participle must be listed. The perfect participle, like the future participle, is an adjective morphologically and therefore always carries a marker for the gender, number, and case of its head noun or subject in the form of a suffix following the perfect participle suffix.

Generally, if the perfect participle is irregular, the future-participle stem is identical to it, as shown in table 2.2. There are only a handful of exceptions to this statement.[9] This covariance has led grammarians to an analysis whereby the future participle is formed by suffixing -*ūr* to the stem of the perfect participle.[10] However, this analysis has an unfortunate side effect, which is the second interesting property of the future participle: the perfect participle is usually passive, but the future participle is always

Table 2.1
Perfect and future participles

Present active infinitive	Perfect participle	Future participle	Gloss
laudā-re	laudāt-	laudāt-ūr-	'praise'
monē-re	monit-	monit-ūr-	'warn'
duce-re	duct-	duct-ūr-	'lead'
audī-re	audīt-	audīt-ūr-	'hear'
cape-re	capt-	capt-ūr-	'take'
vehe-re	vect-	vect-ūr-	'carry'
haerē-re	haes-	haes-ūr-	'stick'
preme-re	press-	press-ūr-	'press'
fer-re	lat-	lat-ūr-	'bear'
loqu-ī	locut-	locut-ūr-	'speak'
experī-rī	expert-	expert-ūr-	'try'

active.[11] Indeed, although there exists a future *passive* participle (the *gerundive*), it is formed on the present stem of the verb and not on any future or passive stem.

If we derive the future participle from the perfect participle, then what do we do with the passive meaning and syntax of the perfect participle? Matthews says that the future participle is based on the perfect participle solely in terms of its sound form and not in terms of its meaning. The future participle is in this way parasitic on the perfect participle. Hence his term *parasitic* for a formation of this sort, where one item is built on another solely in terms of their sound forms and not in terms of their meaning or syntax. Mel'čuk (1991) discusses this discrepancy between semantic and formal effects very clearly. According to him, on the assumption that the -*t*- suffix marks the perfect participle, the suffix of the future participle is an additive sign that contains an additive signifier (-*ūr*-) but a replacive signified: it replaces the original meaning of the -*t*- with its own future active meaning.

2.2   Stems in Lexeme-Based Morphology

I would like to provide an analysis of the Latin future participle within a lexeme-based or word-based framework. To some, it might seem odd to attempt any analysis of Latin morphology from a word-based point of view, since Latin is a paradigm example of a language with what Bloomfield calls *stem-inflection*, which he contrasts with *word-inflection* (1933, 225). More generally, Bloomfield contrasts a language like English, which "may be said to have *word-inflection, word-derivation*, and *word-composition*" (p. 225) with German, which, he says on the same page, "is an example of *stem-inflection, stem-derivation*, and *stem-composition*." Even more generally, one may extend Bloomfield's terminology

Table 2.2
Perfect and future participles of irregular verbs

Present active infinitive	Perfect participle	Future participle	Gloss
fer-re	lāt-	lātūr-	'bear'
siste-re	stat-	statūr-	'place'
esse	—	futūr-	'be'
posse	—	—	'be able'
velle	—	—	'wish'

and speak of *word-based* versus *stem-based* morphology, so that a language in which realization rules are usually defined on stems that occur as free phonological words will have word-based morphology and those whose realization rules are usually defined on stems that do not occur as free words will have stem-based morphology (Wurzel 1989). If we speak in this way (and I do not think that we should), then Latin morphology is obviously stem-based, while English is word-based. In such a terminological world, a word-based theory of morphology or word formation, such as that of *WFGG*, would be inapplicable to Latin or to any other highly inflective language. But this conclusion follows from the misinterpretation of the use of the term *word* in *WFGG* that I discussed in chapter 1. The theory of word-based morphology or word formation is a theory of lexeme-based morphology or lexeme formation, and the word-based hypothesis is a claim about the semantics and syntax of word formation and morphology as much as, or perhaps more than, a claim about affixation. Thus, although English may differ from Latin in whether an affix attaches to a morphologically free or bound form, this difference is orthogonal to the question of whether morphology and lexeme formation are based on the word (or lexeme).[12]

Having laid this misunderstanding to rest (for the duration of this chapter at least), we may now return to the Latin data. My claim is that there is no need for a parasitic formation but that instead both participles are formed on the same stem and that this stem is semantically neither active nor passive. In fact, when the nature of stems is properly understood, the semantic question becomes irrelevant, because, being purely a sound form, this Latin stem has no semantic value at all. The factual evidence for my claim is largely negative: there is no reason to believe that the future participle is derived in any way from the perfect participle. In fact, there are a number of morphological operations, both inflectional and derivational, that are based on this same stem, with little evidence that any one of them is basic to another. The question then arises of how one can accommodate a stem with no semantic value in a theory of morphology. As I will demonstrate, in a lexeme-based separationist theory, where meaning or syntax and sound are distinct, the notion of a stem divorced from meaning is entirely natural.[13]

2.2.1 Form versus meaning

To begin with the future participle and perfect participle, what evidence is there for deriving one from the other? Certainly there is no semantic evidence. Morphologically, though, since the perfect participle is marked only by the *t* and the future participle by *-t-ūr-*, it seems reasonable to claim that the perfect participle is basic. There are, however, several arguments against this simple solution. Most obviously, there are verbs that lack a perfect participle (being intransitive) but nevertheless have a future participle. Some examples are given in (2).

(2) a. caleō, calitūr-, 'burn, be hot',
     b. doleō, dolitūr-, 'suffer pain'
     c. iaceō, iactūr-, 'lie'
     d. recidō, recāsūr-, 'fall back'
     e. ēsuriō, ēsuritūr-, 'be hungry'

Kuhner and Holzweissig (1912) say that these future participles are constructed by analogy to other verbs that have a perfect participle, but their claim is unprovable. There are also cases like *discō, discitūrus* where Kuhner and Holzweissig can find no analogous forms. In the absence of a perfect participle, it is difficult to see how these future participles can be derived, unless this stem, which I will call the *third stem*, has some independent status.[14]

2.2.2 The supine

The second commonly remarked obstacle to deriving future participles from perfect participles (the semantic problem being the first) is the form called, in traditional Latin grammar, the *supine* noun, which is identical to the perfect participle in being marked by the third stem alone.[15] The supine is traditionally characterized syntactically as a kind of infinitive (albeit one that permits case markers) with a very limited distribution. It occurs in two case forms, the accusative and the ablative singular. In the accusative, it is used mainly as the verb of a purpose clause after verbs of motion, as in the following examples:

(3) a. Ab-i-it   pisc-ā-t-um.
         away-go-3sg.perf.ind.act fish-Th-T-acc.sg
         'He/she has gone fishing.' Plautus
     b. Ses-s-um   it   praetor.
         sit-T-acc.sg go.3sg.pres.ind.act praetor
         'The praetor is going to sit down.' Cicero

In the ablative, the supine occurs after adjectives as a kind of specifier. In this use, it is almost always bare, as in (4):

(4) Sī hoc   fās   est dic-t-ū.
     if this.acc.sg allowed is say-T-abl.sg
     'If it is permissible to say this.' Cicero

From its two forms -*um* and -*ū*, we may conclude that the supine is morphologically a fourth-declension masculine noun.[16] The perfect participle, by contrast, may be classified as a first/second-declension adjective, to judge solely by its morphology.[17] We may represent the forms schematically as in table 2.3.

It is clear from table 2.3 that by judging from form alone, there is no way to choose either one of the supine or the perfect participle as underlying the other or to choose either one as underlying the future participle (in Bloomfield's sense of *underlying*), since they are the same morphome, identical in all constant aspects of their sound forms (up to and including the -*T*-).[18] In fact, the grammar books are just about evenly divided as to whether they derive the future participle from the perfect participle or the supine. Older grammars (e.g., Allen and Greenough 1894) tend to speak in terms of the supine (presumably because the supine is neutral with respect to voice), while newer grammars tend to derive the future participle from the perfect participle. Some modern school grammars (e.g.,

Table 2.3
Schematic form of the supine and the perfect participle

Supine scheme

$$[[\text{root or derived stem}_i]_V + (\text{theme vowel})_j + T]_N + \begin{bmatrix} 4 \text{ decl.} \\ \text{masc.} \quad \text{case} \\ \text{sg.} \end{bmatrix}$$

Perfect participle schema

$$[[\text{root or derived stem}_i]_V + (\text{theme vowel})_j + T]_A + \begin{bmatrix} & \text{num.} \\ 1/2 \text{ decl.} & \text{case} \\ & \text{gender} \end{bmatrix}$$

Note: The final brackets hold the case, number, and gender suffix. Within each pair of brackets, the left column represents the constant properties of the form in question, while the right column holds the variable properties, fixed in any given case by agreement or government. All the (morphosyntactic) properties within this pair of brackets are abstract, with a given combination triggering affixation of a particular unit suffix. For example, in the supine, because it is always fourth declension, masculine, singular, in the accusative case we will find the suffix -*um*, which is triggered by fourth declension, masculine, singular, accusative. Note that this suffix is also triggered by other combinations of morphosyntactic features.

Wheelock 1960) do not even mention the supine, which brings us to one possible argument in favor of choosing the perfect participle over the supine: frequency. The supine is infrequent in the classical period (enough so that an elementary textbook can get by without mentioning it) and many common verbs are not attested in the supine. Hence the choice of the perfect participle in the more modern elementary grammars. But this argument, though pedagogically sound, has no theoretical validity.[19] I conclude that the existence of the supine form casts doubt on any analysis that derives the future participle from either the perfect participle or the supine. That is why, so as not to prejudice the case, I refer to what is common to all three forms as the *third stem*, rather than using either of the traditional terms (past participle or supine stem). I have chosen the ordinal *third* to designate this stem because it is the third stem that Latin verbs have and because, unlike the other two stems, it cannot be associated reliably with a morphosyntactic property like *present* or *perfect*.

2.2.3 The third stem

Besides the three form types discussed so far, the third stem of verbs appears regularly with three derived noun suffixes and three derived verb types. The noun suffixes are the *-or* (feminine *-rix*) agentive suffix and two abstract nominal suffixes, *-iō(n)* and *-ūr-*.[20] The verb types are the desiderative *-ur-ī-*, the intensive (no overt suffix, but with theme vowel always *-ā*) and the iterative *-it-* (also with theme vowel *-ā*).[21] Examples of each are given in table 2.4.[22] Of special interest are doubly derived forms, in which one third-stem derivative is built on another, as in Table 2.5.

We now have a total of nine reasonably productive form types built on the third stem of verbs. The obvious question to ask is whether any one of these types can be said to be systematically based on another, in a lexeme-formation sense. Semantically, the answer is decidedly no, except in one case: there are a number of *-ūr-* nouns that correspond systematically to *-or* nouns with the special sense of 'office held by *X* or'. Some examples are *censūra* 'office of the censor' and *quaestūra* 'office of the quaestor'. But not all *-ūr*-nouns follow this pattern, so we are probably dealing here with morphological potentiation (Williams 1981) or Spencerian analogy (Spencer 1988) rather than with semantics pure and simple. In the case of the doubly derived third stems in table 2.5, the noun types are simply deverbal in their semantics and not restricted semantically by the third stem of the base. A fairly exhaustive search reveals a good number of morphological types built on the third stem but no semantic or morpho-

Table 2.4
Form types derived from third stems

Derived form	Base verb, third stem	Gloss
-or nouns		
cantor	canō, cant-	'singer'
vector	vehō, vect-	'carrier'
petītor	petō, petīt-	'candidate'
victor	vincō, vict-	'winner'
tonsor	tondeō, tons-	'hair-cutter'
-io(n) nouns		
cogitātio	cogitō, cogitāt-	'thought'
conventio	conveniō, convent-	'meeting'
mūnitio	muniō, mūnit-	'fortification'
dēpulsio	dēpellō, dēpuls-	'defense'
-ur- nouns		
scriptūra	scrībō, script-	'writing'
tonsūra	tondeō, tons-	'shearing'
pictūra	pingō, pict-	'painting'
Desiderative verbs		
ēsuriō	edō, ēs-	'be hungry'
empturiō	emō, empt-	'want to buy'
parturiō	pariō, part-	'be in labor'
Intensive verbs		
iactō	iaciō, iact-	'fling'
volūtō	volvō, volūt-	'tumble about'
tractō	trahō, tract-	'drag'
Iterative verbs		
scriptitō	scrībō, script-	'write often'
vīsitō	videō, vīs-	'see often'
iactitō	iaciō, iact-	'bandy'

Note: Each derived form is given in citation form. For nouns, this is the nominative singular, and for verbs, the first person, singular, present, indicative, active. In the second column appear the citation form of the base verb and the third stem.

Table 2.5
Doubly derived third-stem forms

haesitātio 'indecision'	<	haesitō 'stammer'	<	haereō 'stick'
iactātio 'tossing'	<	iactō 'fling'	<	iaciō 'throw'
cantātor 'singer'	<	cantō 'sing'	<	canō 'sing'

logical evidence that any one of them is basic to any other. I will therefore adopt the null hypothesis: that all third-stem types are based on the category *verb* (as their semantics dictates) and built on a particular morphomic form of the verb, the third stem.[23] We therefore must distinguish the syntactic category of the lexeme on which a lexeme-formation rule is based from the sound form of that lexeme on which the phonological form of the output is built.

2.3 The Stem and Related Notions

I will now show how such an analysis can be represented within a lexeme-based framework. What we need, and what the framework provides, is a distinction between the aspect of morphology that deals purely with the morphological determination of forms, or morphological spell-out (which, following Zwicky 1986, I am calling *morphological realization*) and a more inclusive definition of morphology that comprises both this morphophonological aspect and *morphosyntax*. This distinction lies at the heart of the lexeme-based approach that I outlined in chapter 1, in which morphosyntax (broadly or narrowly construed) and morphophonology are viewed as two separate phenomena.

While a lexeme has arbitrary properties on three dimensions—sound form, syntax, and meaning—as well as the usually arbitrary association among them, I will reserve the term *stem* for only the sound-form part of this trinity. A stem, in my use of this term, is a sound form. In particular, it is the phonological domain of a realization rule: that sound form to which a given affix is attached or upon which a given nonaffixal realization rule operates.[24] It is especially important to realize, however, that we cannot simply equate the two notions 'stem' and 'sound form of a lexeme'. There are several reasons for this. First, as I will show in detail later on, a lexeme may have more than one stem, not all of them necessarily listed. Second, there are several other well-established terms having to do with the sound form of a lexeme that must be distinguished from *stem*. Three of these—*base*, *root*, and *lexical representation*—are traditional

and useful. Another, *citation form*, is in need of clarification and is not,
I would contend, linguistically significant. Although in the end I am interested only in stems, nonetheless it is important to touch on all of the
others, if only to clarify *stem* by way of contrast.

Matthews notes that "In many discussions 'root' and 'stem' ... also
'base' ... are used in equivalent senses" (1972, 165, n. 4). The first two
differ from the last in that, while stems and roots are purely sound forms,
the base (in my own use, as defined in *WFGG*) is a complete lexeme or
syntacticosemantically defined set of lexemes. Thus the base of the word-
formation rule that derives abstract nouns of the form *X-ation* in English
is the set of English verbs, and the base of the single abstract noun PUL-
VERIZATION is the verb lexeme PULVERIZE, not simply the sound form of
this verb lexeme.

To turn to *root*, although *root* and *stem* both designate sound forms of
lexemes, the most important difference between them is that a root is
defined with respect to a lexeme, while a stem is always defined with
respect to a realization rule. One might say that *root* thus abstracts away
from all morphology. The most important thing about roots, in the sense
for which I wish to reserve the term, is that they be morphologically
unanalyzable. A root is what is left when all morphological structure has
been wrung out of a form.

Let me now turn to the term *citation form*. Here I will cite Lyons's
definition, which seems entirely satisfactory: "By the citation-form of a
lexeme is meant the form of the lexeme that is conventionally employed to
refer to it in standard dictionaries and grammars of the language" (1977,
19). The term thus refers to the sound form of a particular member of
the paradigm of a lexeme, and this sound form is conventionally used in
mentioning it. As such, *citation form* is a metalinguistic notion not necessarily meant to be of significance in a theory of language. Here the word
conventionally is important. Different traditions use different paradigm
members as citation forms. In classical Greek and Latin dictionaries, it is
always the first person, singular, present, indicative, active for verbs, while
in Semitic languages, it is the third person, masculine, singular, perfect
form. In Sanskrit, it is the root. In most other languages, it is the infinitive
for verbs. Sometimes, when there is no established scholarly tradition
for a particular language, different dictionaries may use different citation
forms. For example, as Robert Hoberman points out to me, one dictionary of modern Aramaic uses the infinitive, while another uses what
Hoberman (1989) calls the *J(ussive) stem*. For nouns, the nominative,
singular form is the one most commonly used for citation purposes.

The choice of a citation form is (at least originally) governed by a pedagogical principle. The idea is to pick a single full, surface form of a lexeme (and hence pronounceable in isolation) from which the rest of that lexeme's paradigm may be deduced and that conversely may be retrieved from any sound form of that lexeme. In theory, this allows learners to have an entire paradigm at their command by memorizing only one sound form and a small set of algorithmic principles. It also makes the use of a dictionary possible, since the dictionary user, native or nonnative, must know what paradigm member to look up in searching for a definition in a dictionary. The citation form thus also normally serves as the address of the lexeme in a dictionary.[25] In actual fact, a single full, surface form is not always sufficient for predicting an entire paradigm, even in regular cases, nor is the system always reversible (allowing for the recovery of the citation form from any other form of the lexeme). Hence the use in Latin dictionaries of three or four principal parts for verbs and two forms (nominative and genitive singular) for many types of nouns.

Within linguistic theory, the idea that there is, for any given lexeme, a single sound form in the mental lexicon from which an entire paradigm may be deduced, and furthermore that this form is the address of the lexeme whose paradigm is being generated, the idea, in short, of a *lexical representation* (Aronoff 1978b), has been tremendously important. The lexical representation, however, differs from the citation form in that it is (or may be) an abstract sound form, both phonologically and morphologically, that never actually occurs as a surface form of the lexeme.

2.4 Stems and the Permanent Lexicon

The term *stem* has been used for all of the notions that I have now distinguished with the terms *lexeme*, *base*, *root*, *citation form*, and *lexical representation*, not all of which are of interest to morphological theory. One property, however, sets stems apart from all the other entities that I have discussed. This is the fact that a given lexeme may have more than one stem, different stems being demanded by different realization rules. Traditional Latin grammar, for example, recognizes three stems for every verb; traditional Hebrew grammar recognizes two for simple (qal) verbs, an analysis that I will defend in chapter 5.

Certain recent theorists have accepted the possibility of multiple stems, but they have attempted to link this possibility to an entirely tangential entity, the (permanent) lexicon. Their idea is that a lexeme may have more than one stem just in case these stems are irregular and hence listed in the (permanent) lexicon. The most influential use of this idea is in Lieber 1981. Because Lieber deals specifically with Latin verb stems in developing her framework, I will discuss her work in some detail.

The clearest cases of needing more than one stem for a given lexeme come from suppletion. No one would say that *went*, the past tense form of the English verb *go*, is derived from the same stem as the present-tense forms. We therefore conclude that at least two stems must be listed for this verb, *go* and *went*. The question that naturally arises to the theoretically minded is whether this is the only circumstance under which a lexeme may have more than one stem. A common fallacy is to assume that the answer is positive. The fallacy is based on the confusion between the two largely unrelated senses of the term *lexical* that I discussed at some length in chapter 1. In one sense, *lexical* means 'idiosyncratic', while in the other major sense, it means 'having to do with lexemes'. In the case of stems, the confusion of the two senses leads one to conclude that if a lexeme (which is lexical in the 'having to do with lexemes' sense of the term) demonstrably has more than one stem, then all these stems must also be lexical in the idiosyncratic (hence listed) sense of the term *lexical*.

Let us see how this works in Lieber's analysis. According to Lieber, "The permanent lexicon consists of a set of all those terminal elements which cannot be decomposed into smaller parts" (1981, 38).[26] A class of rules that Lieber calls *morpholexical rules* operates on this set.[27] Lieber defines a morpholexical rule informally as follows. "A morpholexical rule is a relation defined between pairs of lexical items which are listed in the permanent lexicon" (1981, 39). Furthermore, the members of this pair are related to one another in a special way: they are what Lieber calls *stem variants or morpheme variants*. In other words, not just any two lexical items may be related by morpholexical rules, since morpholexical rules define only the special morphophonological relation of being variants.[28] Lieber thus claims that there is a special set of morphophonological rules that defines only *existing* variant forms of lexical items. Lieber discusses two such sets of rules in detail, one for German (later rejected in favor of another device, string-dependent rules) and one for Latin verb stems. In analyzing the latter, Lieber takes great pains to show that Latin verbs must have more than one stem (in addition to a root for each verb) and that these stems and roots must be related to one another by means of morpholexical rules. She provides a set of five such rules for present stems (root + theme vowel), a rule for nasal infixing of certain present stems, six rules for forming perfect stems, and two for (perfect) participles. Lieber argues that these rules are all morpholexical on the basis of the fact that it is not always possible to predict which stem form a given root will select for a given stem type (present, perfect, or third stem). In every case, Lieber argues that none of these morpholexical rules can be considered to be a productive rule, since it is arbitrary which rule will apply to a given lexical item. The inevitable conclusion is that all Latin verb stems must be listed in the permanent lexicon. Lieber then goes on to claim that all the variants that she has argued be listed are available for further word formation, which thus demonstrates (she feels) that word formation operates on existing stems.

But is it really true that we can never predict what stem type a given verb will have, that the stem allomorphs of Latin verbs are unpredictable? In the vast majority of cases, once we know the present stem of a simple verb (its theme vowel), it is possible to predict the other stems.[29] Consider the first conjugation (theme vowel $= -\bar{a}$), which is the largest. Allen and Greenough say that this conjugation has about 360 simple members, of which all but 16 are regular, which makes 96 percent of the members of this class regular (once the theme vowel is given). The number of derived members of this conjugation is very large, inasmuch as both large classes of intensive and iterative verbs are members of it, and all of these derived verbs are regular, so that the proportion of perfectly regular verbs of this conjugation is actually much higher.[30]

In the fourth conjugation, with theme vowel $-\bar{\imath}$, which is the smallest in number, having about 60 simple members, two thirds of the members are regular. This class also includes productively derived desiderative verbs. For the second conjugation, with theme vowel $-\bar{e}$, of which Allen and Greenough give 120 members, 75 percent form their perfect and third stems regularly. This conjugation is not, however, extendable by any regular word-formation rule. The third conjugation ($-e$ and $-i$ theme vowels) is the least predictable, but even here, of approximately 170 simple verbs, more than 35 percent form their perfect participles in s.

Thus, of the 700 or so simple Latin verbs, more than 75 percent are regular within their conjugation. This is a far cry from Lieber's characterization of the system as unpredictable, and it does not even take into account productive derivation, which would raise the predictability of the system even further. It is therefore disingenuous to conclude that Latin verb stems are essentially unpredictable and that they must all be listed in the permanent lexicon.

Latin therefore provides no evidence for a necessary connection between a verb's having more than one stem and those stems being listed in the permanent lexicon. Contrary to what Lieber claims, the majority of

verb stems are regular and hence most likely are nonlexical (in the idiosyncratic sense of the term). Being listed is therefore not a necessary criterion
for being a stem. Nor, conversely, is a stem's being listed in the permanent
lexicon a sufficient criterion for a stem's serving as an input to further
derivation. As Lieber notes (1981, 90), there are no cases in Latin of
derivational affixes building on the perfect (active) verb stem, regardless
of whether the perfect stem is idiosyncratic or not. Lieber calls this an
accidental gap, but it is no more accidental than the lack of derivatives
from past tense verbs in English.

I conclude that a given lexeme may have more than one stem and that
these stems are not necessarily arbitrary and hence listed in the permanent
lexicon (though they may be). We must remember, however, that the stem
in the sense that I have adopted is a purely morphophonologically defined
entity. If a given realization rule is viewed as a constant function from
a sound form (of a lexeme) to another sound form (of a possibly identical
lexeme), then the first sound form is the stem of the rule, the domain of the
morphophonological function. Put simply, the stem is the sound form on
which a particular form is built.

2.5 Empty Morphs

Within a simple theory, every sound form has a meaning, and when we
join meanings, we join forms. Morpheme-based theories are usually of
this simple sort. Lexeme-based theories allow for a more indirect relation
between form and meaning, inasmuch as they permit a separation between building a form and building its meaning.[31] In the case at hand,
there are nine form types morphologically built on the Latin third stem,
all of which are based semantically on the basic meaning of the verb. The
t (or *s* or whatever distinguishes a particular third stem) cannot be said to
have a meaning that is constant across all nine types (unless we arbitrarily
stipulate one meaning as basic and subtract it in forming the other types,
as Mel'čuk would do). Either it has nine separate meanings, or it has no
identifiable independent meaning at all. We can't tell which, and in fact
the choice between the two may be irrelevant. The morphomic function
that forms the third stem is the equivalent of what Hockett (1947) calls an
empty morph. The third stem occurs in a specific morphological environment but makes no detectable independent contribution to the meaning of
the whole form.

It has long been noticed that stem-forming morphs or operations may
be semantically empty. Bloomfield discusses a number of such cases in

compounds (1933, 229–231). In classical Greek, what he calls the *compounding stem* "may differ formally from all the inflections of its paradigm." In Germanic languages, Bloomfield notes, the first member of a compound often has a suffix that is semantically inappropriate in this particular environment. Botha (1968) has also discussed this at length.[32]

2.5.1 The theme vowel

Among the best-known examples of empty morphs are the theme vowels that characterize the various verb conjugations of Latin. As we will see, Latin theme vowels, in addition to being classic examples of empty morphs of a certain kind, also interact with verb stems in a complex manner. I will therefore explore them in some detail. Table 2.6 presents a close-to-traditional synchronic classification of the verb conjugations according to their theme vowels, which usually show up in the present active infinitive (this is not true of *i*, which is neutralized to *e*).

Let us see what happens if we assume that the theme vowels are ordinary meaningful verb suffixes, which is to say that they work in the same way that the English suffix -*ize* works, simply as derivational affixes. What sorts of problems arise under such an assumption?

One problem is that there will be only a handful of underived verbs in the language under this analysis, namely those few (but very frequent) verbs like *ferre* that have no theme vowel and are otherwise quite irregular in many respects. All other verbs will be formally derived. This is certainly unusual but not impossible. Bengali and other modern Indo-Aryan languages, for example, have only a handful of simple verbs, the rest formally being compounds.

Another problem is that the putative suffixes will be largely synonymous, marking only the category *verb* rather than having any additional

Table 2.6
Theme vowels of Latin verbs

Conjugation	Theme vowel	Present active infinitive	Gloss
first	ā	am-ā-re	'love'
second	ē	dēl-ē-re	'destroy'
fourth	ī	aud-ī-re	'hear'
third	e	leg-e-re	'pick'
third	i	cap-e-re	'take'
third	∅	fer-re	'carry'

significance. Again, this is not impossible. English, after all, has several suffixes with this same value (-*ize*, -*ate*, -*ify*).

A more serious problem is that actual meaningful derivational verb suffixes are quite common in Latin. We have already discussed a few of them in the context of suffixes that select for the third stem (see table 2.4 for examples). Each one of these suffixes forms verbs that have a sense associated with the suffix, each suffix belongs to a particular conjugation, and different suffixes belong to different conjugations. Because all these derivatives each belong to a particular conjugation, under the analysis of the theme vowel as a verb suffix, each one of these genuine derivational suffixes would have to be analyzed as complex, consisting of the derivational suffix followed by the theme vowel, which must also be a derivational suffix, but now one that derives verbs from "nonoccurring" verbs. This is very peculiar.

Table 2.7 contains a list of derivational verbal suffixes, with the theme vowel of each suffix indicated. The table very clearly reveals that the theme vowel is conditioned by the category of the immediately preceding morph: the theme vowel appears after the morph that carries the category *verb*, regardless of whether that morph is a root or an affix.[33] Furthermore, each category-carrying morph selects a particular theme vowel (idiosyncratically). The theme vowel is thus a marker of the category *verb* only in the sense that it is determined by the category *verb*, just as final devoicing is a marker of the word boundary. In itself, it has no significance. It is empty. Nonetheless, it is not useless. It has a use in the language, but that use is purely morphophonological: the theme vowel is the *conjugation vowel*, it serves to determine the conjugation of the verb stem, or which inflectional affixes will realize the various morphosyntactic properties that the verb bears in a particular instance.[34] The theme vowel is thus never referred to by any syntacticosemantic rule but only by the morphological rules that realize the various syntacticosemantic categories.

Table 2.7
Derivational verb suffixes

Suffix	Vowel	Meaning	Example	Gloss
-ur-	ī	desiderative	ēsurīre	'be hungry'
-it-	ā	iterative	vīsitāre	'see often'
-sc-	e	inceptive	calescere	'get warm'
-ess-	e	intensive	capessere	'seize'
∅	ā	intensive	iactāre	'throw hard'

2.5.2 Theme vowels and stems

It is usual to associate the choice of a conjugation class or theme vowel with the lexeme rather than with the stem, so that we speak of first or second conjugation verbs. However, the actual situation in Latin is more complex. From my perspective, it is also an enlightening example of the workings of pure morphology, form without meaning. I will deal with the simplest case first, that of the most regular conjugation, the one with the theme vowel -ā. This conjugation has the largest number of actual verbs and the greatest productivity. It is also the ancestor of the most productive conjugation in the Romance languages.

Latin verbs, unless they are defective (about which more later), have three basic stems, traditionally termed *present*, *perfect*, and *supine* or *perfect participle*. I am calling this last one the *third stem*. In regular verbs of the first conjugation (theme vowel -ā), it is easy to see that the theme vowel appears in all stems at the underlying phonological level, being deleted only before vowel-initial suffixes. Table 2.8 contains a sample of relevant regular verb forms of this conjugation. The same is true with regular verbs of the fourth conjugation (theme vowel -ī) except that the theme vowel is shortened rather than deleted before vowels, as shown in table 2.9.

Table 2.8
Sample first-conjugation verb forms and stems

Surface form	Underlying form	Stem	Gloss
armō	arm-ā-ō	arm-ā	'I arm'
armāmur	arm-ā-mur	arm-ā	'we are armed'
armābunt	arm-ā-b-u-nt	arm-ā	'they will arm'
armāvistī	arm-ā-u-istī	arm-ā-u	'you sg. armed'
armātus	arm-āt-us	arm-ā-t	'armed masc. nom. sg.'

Table 2.9
Fourth-conjugation regular verb forms and stems

Surface form	Underlying form	Stem	Gloss
audiam	aud-ī-am	aud-ī	'I may hear'
audīrēmus	aud-ī-rē-mus	aud-ī	'we might hear'
audīverat	aud-ī-u-er-at	aud-ī-u	'he had heard'
audīta	aud-ī-t-a	aud-ī-t	'heard fem. nom. sg.'

With the other conjugations, however, the theme vowel is not ubiquitous. In the second conjugation, with theme vowel -$\bar{e}$, the pattern parallel to those of the preceding tables (with the theme vowel in all stems), appears with only five roots, as shown in table 2.10.[35] These roots, however, share a singular property, which is that they must be analyzed as being vowelless if the seeming theme vowel is truly a theme vowel.[36] Latin verb roots otherwise are never less than a syllable in length. In other words, it is most likely that the $\bar{e}$ of these roots is a root vowel rather than a theme vowel. If we agree that the $\bar{e}$ of these five verbs is indeed part of their lexical form, then they are not really second-declension verbs at all, let alone regular. In that case, however, there are no true second-declension verbs that have the theme vowel -$\bar{e}$ in either the perfect stem or the third stem. The majority of second-conjugation verbs are like mon-$\bar{e}$- 'warn'. They form their perfect stem with u attached to the bare lexical form of the verb (e.g., mon-u-). They form their third stem with it (occasionally just t) attached also to the bare lexical form (e.g., mon-it-, doc-t-). The remainder form their perfect and third stems in various ways, but never with a theme vowel. The theme vowel -$\bar{e}$ is thus characteristic of only the present stem of second-conjugation verbs, where it occurs without exception. Here, then, is the first clear example of the association of theme vowels directly with particular stems, rather than with the entire lexeme.

The third conjugation is the most heterogeneous of all four. It includes verbs with no theme vowel, those with the theme vowel -e, and those with -i. Some have a nasal infix in the present stem. Others have reduplication or vowel lengthening in the present stem. What unites all these in one conjugation is the selection of particular suffixes by the present stem, to which I will return below. In the perfect and third stems, however, the members of this class are quite heterogeneous. They form the perfect stem in many different ways, including conversion of the root or the present stem, reduplication, root-vowel lengthening, ablaut, suffixation of s, suf-

Table 2.10
"Regular" second-conjugation verb roots

Root	Present stem	Perfect stem	Third stem	Gloss
(dē)lē	dēlē	dēlē-v	dēlē-t	'wipe out'
flē	flē	flē-v	flē-t	'weep'
nē	nē	nē-v	nē-t	'spin'
viē	viē	viē-v	viē-t	'weave'
-plē	-plē	-plē-v	-plē-t	'fill'

fixation of *v* or *u*, and combinations of these. The third stems are similarly various. All third-conjugation verbs do, however, share one property: the uniform absence of any theme vowel in the perfect and third stems, just as in the second conjugation. Since the methods of forming the perfect and third stems found in the second conjugation are a subset of those found in the third, the two conjugations can be seen to differ only in the formation of the present stem. The category *third conjugation* is therefore valid only for the present stem, just like the category *second conjugation*.

A less subtle type of evidence for the direct relation between conjugation or theme vowel and stems, rather than lexemes, lies in the fact that there are many verbs whose individual stems "belong to different conjugations." These are almost all verbs of the first or fourth conjugation that lack theme vowels in the perfect or third stem. Examples of each type are given in table 2.11. In these cases, it is simply impossible to say that a lexeme belongs to a conjugation or selects a theme vowel. Rather, we must say that an individual *stem* of a lexeme belongs to a particular conjugation, as we did above for verbs of the second and third conjugations in general.[37] This only reinforces my earlier remark that theme vowels are associated directly with stems of lexemes rather than with entire lexemes.

To what extent, however, can lexemes be said to have theme vowels? The following observations seem to be true:

Table 2.11
Verbs of mixed conjugation type

Present stem	Perfect stem	Third stem	Gloss
crepā	crepu	crepit	'rattle'
iuvā	iuv	iut	'help'
stā	stet	—	'stand'
reperī	repper	repert	'find'
venī	ven	vent	'come'
sancī	sanx	sanct	'hallow'
sarcī	sars	sart	'patch'
sentī	sens	sens	'feel'
sepelī	sepelīv	sepult	'bury'
aperī	aperu	apert	'open'
pete	petīv	petīt	'aim'
cupi	cupīv	cupīt	'want'

• All verbs except for a small number with very high-frequency have a theme vowel in the present stem.
• Second- and third-conjugation verbs never have a theme vowel except in the present stem.
• Almost all first- and fourth-conjugation verbs have a theme vowel in all stems.

It is clear that theme vowels appear consistently across conjugations only in the present stem. I will now argue that the presence of the theme vowels -$\bar{a}$ and -$\bar{\imath}$ in first- and fourth-conjugation nonpresent stems is a secondary phenomenon, with the result that we can see theme vowels as firmly rooted only in the present stem of verbs.

First we must review the formation of nonpresent stems. In the second conjugation, the most common method is to add u to the verb root of simple verbs for the perfect stem and it for the third stem. This pattern also appears with simple third-conjugation verbs, but more common is the addition of s to the root for perfect stems and t for third stems. Among the other methods of perfect-stem formation in the third conjugation is to form the perfect stem not on the verb root but rather on the present stem minus the theme vowel. This may be detected in cases where the present stem has a nasal infix. The nasal is sometimes absent in nonpresent stems, but sometimes it appears either in the perfect or both the perfect and the third stems. All these types are exemplified in table 2.12. The top section of the table contains verbs where the nasal is absent in nonpresent stems; the second section contains verbs that show the nasal in at least one nonpresent stem; finally, the last section contains roots that vary.

The first section of the table shows very nicely the variety of ways in which the nonpresent stems may be built on the verb root with simple third-conjugation verbs. We see clear examples of vowel lengthening, ablaut accompanied by lengthening, and suffixing of s and u in the perfect stem. In the third stem we see both t and s, sometimes accompanied by lengthening. In the second section we find the same phenomena, but accompanied by retention of the nasal. The pattern exemplified by *iunge* is the most common.[38] In the last section, we have two nice examples of how the same root may show nonpresent stems of different types in different lexemes, sometimes with and sometimes without the nasal.

Overall, the simplest analysis of the table would build nonpresent stems that retain the nasal on the present stem, while those without the nasal would be built on the lexical representation.[39] Within a lexeme-based framework, this is easily expressed. A given realization rule always selects

Table 2.12
Stems of verbs with nasal infixes

Present stem	Perfect stem	Third stem	Gloss
frange	frēg	fract	'break'
linque	līqu	lict	'leave'
line	lēv/līv	lit	'smear'
finde	fīd	fiss	'split'
funde	fūd	fūs	'pour'
(in)cumbe	cubu	cubit	'lie'
rumpe	rūp	rupt	'break'
temne	temps	tempt	'despise'
sine	sīv	sit	'allow'
sperne	sprēv	sprēt	'spurn'
iunge	iūnx	iūnct	'join'
pinge	pīnx	pīct	'paint'
lambe	lamb	—	'lick'
ungue	ūnx	ūnct	'anoint'
pange	pepig	pāct	'agree on'
pange	pānx	—	'fasten'
compinge	compēg	compāct	'confine'
punge	pupug	pūnct	'punch'
compunge	compūnx	compūnct	'prick'

as its stem some specified sound form of the lexeme, not necessarily the lexical representation. Normally, this sound form is specified by a constant function across lexemes for a given realization rule, but we see here that this function may be specified lexically in some instances.[40] We have already seen this sort of discontinuous function at work in the case of the English Past Tense and F_{en}.

In the second conjugation there are no verbs with a nasal infix, which makes it impossible to tell for the second conjugation whether any nonpresent stems are built on the present stem. Nor do we find nasal infixes in either of the other conjugations. In the first and fourth conjugations, however, the theme vowel appears quite regularly in nonpresent stems, in fact, almost overwhelmingly in the first, which is the most common and most productive conjugation. When the theme vowel is retained, the perfect is always formed by suffixation of u, and the third stem by suffixation of t. Since we have already seen that the simplest analysis of patterns of the less regular third conjugation permits at least some stems to be built on the present stem, we may most easily account for the most common forms by saying that the default method of building the perfect and third stems for all conjugations is by suffixing *u* and *t* to the present stem of the verb. The default method will operate almost without exception on first-conjugation verbs and on about two thirds of fourth-conjugation verbs. We also expect that, because it is the default method, it will operate on newly formed verbs unless their morphology specifically triggers another method. This prediction is borne out: newly coined verbs follow this pattern, except those formed with the suffixes *-ess* and *-esc*, both of which select special stems. We can also now accommodate the first- and fourth-conjugation irregular verbs in table 2.11. These are seen to be exceptions to the general pattern that first- and fourth-conjugation verbs follow the default pattern of stem formation.

I conclude that the theme vowel occurs basically in the present stem for all Latin verbs and that it occurs in other stems only when they are built on the present stem. In these other stems, the theme vowel does not necessarily fill any particular function.

As I have said, the function of the theme vowel is to select the verb endings. In those paradigm members built on the present stem, and in those paradigm members only, there is a variety of ways in which the morphosyntactic property arrays are realized morphophonologically (though they are always realized as suffixes, traditionally called *verb endings*). The choice among these verb endings is determined by the theme vowel. Table 2.13 shows how this works. Note that only a representative sample of verb endings is included in the table. Each of the other endings is similar to one of those found in the table. For ease of exposition, I have included the theme vowel along with the endings in a bundle, so that the form given is the surface form.[41]

There is much to say about this table, especially with regard to syncretism (Carstairs 1987). My concern, however, is only to show that the set of endings for each conjugation is unique, although some conjugations share more endings than others.[42] The table shows that knowing the theme vowel of a given verb will allow one to determine uniquely (and with no exceptions of any kind in the language) the entire paradigm of the forms of that verb that are formed on the present stem. The theme vowels can thus be understood just in purely morphological terms and in their interaction with the morphology of verb stems. Semantically, the theme vowels are empty.[43]

Table 2.13
Sample list of Latin verb endings by theme vowel

Category	Theme vowel				
	ā	ē	e	i	ī
Active					
pres. ind. 1 sg.	ō	eō	ō	iō	iō
pres. ind. 2 sg.	ās	ēs	is	is	īs
pres. ind. 3 sg.	at	et	it	it	it
impf. ind. 1 sg.	ābam	ēbam	ēbam	iēbam	iēbam
fut. ind. 1 sg.	ābō	ēbō	am	iam	iam
fut. ind. 2 sg.	ābis	ēbis	ēs	iēs	iēs
fut. ind. 3 sg.	ābit	ēbit	et	iet	iet
pres. subj. 1 sg.	em	eam	am	iam	iam
pres. subj. 2 sg.	ēs	eās	ās	iās	iās
pres. subj. 3 sg.	et	eat	at	iat	iat
imp. sg.	ā	ē	Ø/e	e	ī
imp. pl.	āte	ēte	ite	ite	īte
pres. inf. act.	āre	ēre	ere	ere	īre
pres. participle	āns	ēns	ēns	iēns	iēns
Passive					
pres. ind. 1 sg.	or	eor	or	ior	ior
pres. ind. 2 sg.	āris	ēris	eris	eris	īris
pres. ind. 3 sg.	ātur	ētur	itur	itur	ītur
impf. ind. 1 sg.	ābar	ēbar	ēbar	iēbar	iēbar
fut. ind. 1 sg.	ābor	ēbor	ar	iar	iar
fut. ind. 2 sg.	āberis	ēberis	ēris	iēris	iēris
fut. ind. 3 sg.	ābitur	ēbitur	ētur	iētur	iētur
pres. subj. 1 sg.	er	ear	ar	iar	iar
pres. subj. 2 sg.	ēris	eāris	āris	iāris	iāris
pres. subj. 3 sg.	ētur	eātur	ātur	iātur	iātur
pres. inf. pass.	ārī	ērī	ī	ī	īrī
fut. participle	andus	endus	endus	iendus	iendus

2.6 Semantics and the Latin Basic Stem Types

I will now turn to the semantic role of the three traditionally recognized basic verb stem types of Latin that I have discussed (present, perfect, and third stems).[44] Latin paradigms are remarkably rigid, by which I mean that a particular morphosyntactic property array is always realized within a given conjugation by a particular ending attached to a particular stem type. The imperfect past tense, for example, is always formed by attaching to the present stem of a verb the suffix *b*, preceded by an appropriate conjugation-determined vowel sequence (the vowel, V, before *b* is always long) and followed by the imperfect endings. The future is also formed on the present stem, with the same $\bar{V}b$ that we find in the imperfect tense (although with -*ā* and -*ē* verbs only) and the appropriate endings, which vary this time according to the conjugation of the verb. This same rigidity is found with other stem types: specific categories are always realized by certain endings on certain stem types for each conjugation.[45] Individual verb stems may be formed irregularly and indeed are irregular in a remarkably large number of cases. Nevertheless, we never find that a given category for a particular irregular verb is realized by attaching the endings to a different stem type or with endings different from the normal pattern. The only pervasive exception is the system of deponent verbs, which are syntactically active (and usually intransitive) but morphologically passive, which is to say that they show passive endings where we would otherwise expect active endings.[46] But even here the paradigm is rigid, except for the one fact that passive morphology systematically substitutes for active. Furthermore, when we find partially deponent verbs, of which there are a very few, whether a particular form of a verb is deponent varies entirely by stem type. So *dēvortor* 'turn in' and *rēvortor* 'turn back' are deponent only with the present stem but not with the perfect stem, where they show active rather than passive morphology. By contrast, *fīdō* 'trust' and its compounds—*audeō* 'dare', *gaudeō* 'be happy', and *soleō* 'be used'—are deponent only with the perfect stem.

Further evidence of the way in which paradigms are organized around stem types comes from so called *defective verbs*, verbs that lack one or more forms. Most defective verbs, of which there are quite a few, are defective in that they lack one or more stems, rather than individual forms. Inceptives with the suffix -*sce*- occur only in the present stem, as do desideratives with the suffix -*urī*-; similarly with many individual verbs such as *lacteō* 'suck', *tussiō* 'cough', and *glubō* 'peel'. Some verbs have only the perfect stem, such as *coepī* 'begin' and *meminī* 'remember'. Many verbs lack the third stem. In all these defective verbs, what is missing or what occurs is determined by the absence or presence of a stem.[47]

In light of the rigidity with which paradigms are organized around stem types, it is reasonable to look at the semantics of these stem types. Indeed, one might expect that the rigidity is due, in part at least, to stem semantics, that a particular ending always goes with a particular stem type because of the semantic relation between the two. I will now show that this is quite surprisingly untrue. A survey of the morphosyntactic properties realized on the three stem types reveals a constant value for one stem type but much less identifiable semantic value for the other two. It is therefore unlikely that paradigmatic rigidity can be attributed entirely to semantics. Instead, it seems to be in large part morphological. Table 2.14 contains a schematic representation of the inflectional morphosyntactic property arrays that are associated with each of the three verb stem types. I have included only inflection in order to strengthen the possibility of finding a uniform semantics for each stem type, since the inclusion of derivational categories would likely doom the exercise from the start.[48] The general categories of mood, tense, and voice are given in the order in which they are normally realized, although the categories are in actual fact seldom realized by distinct exponents. The table should be read in blocks across as follows: each block represents a set of mood, tense, and voice combinations. For example, the first block indicates that combinations of the indicative mood with present, future, or imperfect tenses and active or passive voices exist, all formed on the present stem. In the subjunctive, only present or imperfect is found with active or passive (which is to say that there is no future subjunctive), again all formed on the pesent stem. Similarly for the remaining blocks. In analyzing the table, we are seeking semantic uniformity for a given stem type in the sense that the stem type should realize a specific morphosyntactic property, such as *perfect* or *present*. Ideally, the uniformity should go two ways, so that a given property or property array is also always realized by the same stem type.

Traditional Latin grammar distinguishes two verb aspects, imperfect and perfect, called *infectum* and *perfectum*, associated with the present and perfect stem types respectively. Also, the perfect stem is found only with active verbs. One might therefore propose that the meaning of the present stem is 'imperfect', while the meaning of the perfect stem is 'perfect active'. The chart reveals that there is indeed a mutual implication between the complex syntactic category Perfect Active and the perfect

Table 2.14
Categories realized on verb stem types

Stem	Mood	Tense	Voice
present	indicative	present future imperfect	active passive
present	subjunctive	present imperfect	active passive
present	imperative	present	active passive
present	infinitive	present	active passive
present	participle	present	active
present	gerund(ive)	n.a.	n.a.
perfect	indicative	perfect pluperfect future perfect	active
perfect	subjunctive	perfect pluperfect	active
perfect	infinitive	perfect	active
third-stem PP	indicative	perfect pluperfect future perfect	passive
third-stem PP	subjunctive	perfect pluperfect	passive
third-stem PP	infinitive	perfect	passive
third-stem FP	participle	future	active
third-stem FP	infinitive	future	active
third-stem supine	infinitive	future	passive

stem type: all and only perfect active tenses are realized on the perfect stem (deponents aside). Similar relations for the remaining stem types and the remaining categories cannot, however, be so easily extracted from the table. Thus, although all perfect passive tenses are realized on the third stem, not all third-stem forms are perfect passives, since some nonfinite futures, active and passive, are realized on the third stem. These same categories also spoil the symmetry of the present stem, but in the other direction, from meaning to form. We can claim that the present stem goes only with imperfects (if we permit the gerund and gerundive to be imperfect, which they arguably are, being always incomplete in some sense), but then not all imperfects will be realized on the present stem (the nonfinite futures again being exceptional). The following list seems best to express what is going on:

- Perfect active tenses are formed on the perfect stem.
- Perfect passive tenses are formed on the third stem.
- Certain nonfinite futures are formed on the third stem.
- The remaining (imperfect) categories are formed on the present stem.

This list has two notable features. First, it only goes one way, from morphosyntactic property array to morphological form and not vice versa. Second, the present stem is a kind of default stem, in the sense of Zwicky (1986). It is difficult to see how any more generality could be extracted from the table without doing violence to the data, yet the schema does express, albeit indirectly, precisely the sort of semantic system that we expect to find if we espouse a lexeme-based framework with stems. Within such a framework, stems do not have meanings. Still, we may say that they are more or less semantically uniform on the basis of the syntacticosemantic categories realized on them. Thus the perfect stem is semantically uniform because the category *perfect active* is always and only realized on the perfect stem. The other stems are less semantically uniform because the morphological system of the language uses these stems in a less semantically homogeneous manner. This measure of semantic uniformity is not, however, central to the theory in any way.

As I noted above, stems are special entities within the morphological system of a language. Strictly speaking, stems are morphomic, because, as I have argued at some length, they are only sound forms of lexemes and not meaningful units. They may therefore not participate in the semantic calculus directly as meaning-bearing units. Stems must also be contrasted with those affixes that are introduced by realization rules as markers of morphosyntactic properties. Such markers, although they do not, strictly speaking, have meaning independent of the rules by which they are introduced, nonetheless are much more easily connected to the semantics of their rules. Thus we are able to say that the English suffix /z/ is a marker of the plural or "means" Plural, among other things, without being as misleading about linguistic semantics as we would be in assigning a meaning to the category *Latin present stem*.

Another difference between affixal markers and stem types is in their abstractness. With Latin affixal markers, there is usually a fairly direct connection between meaning and form. But the Latin categories *present stem* and *perfect stem* are neither meaning nor form. On the one hand,

they are similar to a morphosyntactic property array in being realized by
rules that spell out particular forms as the present stem or the perfect
stem, for example, by suffixing *u* or *s* to a verb root to form the perfect
stem. On the other hand, unlike morphosyntactic entities, they do not
directly reflect the semantic or syntactic system. Instead, they are morphomes, part of the abstract and unmotivated morphological machinery
of the language. In this respect, stems are much closer to theme vowels
than to more orthodox affixal markers of morphosyntactic properties.

2.7 Phonologically Specific Stems

My discussion so far has centered on the three traditionally recognized
basic stem types of Latin verbs. I have tried to show that these stems,
whether or not they are listed in the permanent lexicon, have three important properties. First, they are not meaningful. Second, the abstract elements present stem, perfect stem, and third stem enjoy a special status
in Latin grammar as independent parts of the morphological system of
the language. Realization rules of the language operate on these abstract
elements, and not on specific forms, when selecting forms on which to
operate. Finally, they are functions whose output may vary considerably
according to the verb to which they apply.

Many stems are of this abstract type, but some are much more concretely specified. Consider the following fact. In Latin verbs of the -$\bar{a}$ and
-$\bar{e}$ conjugations, the future and imperfect tenses are formed by adding
certain person and number suffixes to a stem of the verb that is itself built
on the present stem by means of the suffix $\bar{V}b$.[49] For the other conjugations, however, while the imperfect is formed on this same stem, the future
is formed with the vowel $\bar{e}$ attached to the present stem.[50] The relevant
forms are given in table 2.15.

Table 2.15
Future and imperfect forms

Conjugation	Future 2 sg.	Imperfect 2 sg.	Gloss
$\bar{a}$	laudābīs	laudābās	'praise'
$\bar{e}$	mordēbis	mordēbās	'bite'
e	acuēs	acuēbās	'sharpen'
i	capiēs	capiēbās	'take'
$\bar{i}$	mūgiēs	mūgiēbās	'bellow'

I want to say here that the imperfect of all verbs is formed on what I will call the *b stem*, while the future of only -$\bar{a}$ and -$\bar{e}$ verbs is formed on the *b* stem. The *b* stem thus has a status outside the rules that refer to it, since it is referred to by more than one realization rule. But the *b* stem is constant in sound form: it is always formed with the suffix $\bar{V}b$ on the present stem. However, it cannot be defined in terms of the inflectional system. It thus contrasts with the three basic stems, which are quite variable in their sound forms, sometimes arbitrarily so, but which can always be characterized in terms of the inflectional realizations whose domains they define.

We see in Latin, then, two very different kinds of stem types, those characterized in terms of a constant sound form and those characterized by their place in the morphological paradigm.[51] The two sorts of stem types seem to be quite widely distributed among the world's languages (a conjecture that I will not try to prove here), and Latin does not seem to be exceptional in having recourse to both sorts. As far as I know, the literature does not explicitly distinguish these two different kinds of stems, terminologically or otherwise. In my investigations I have not found any cases where the morphology distinguishes the two kinds, in the sense that rules that build on variable stems have different properties from rules that build on constant stems. Nor does morphomic theory provide any simple way to distinguish them. Nevertheless, the difference should be kept in mind, since it may have consequences that I am unaware of.

Chapter 3
Gender and Nominal Inflectional Classes

In Navaho ... some terms belong to the round (or roundish) class, others to the long-object class, others fall into classes not dependent on shape .... I doubt that such distinctions, at least in Navaho, are simply linguistic recognitions of nonlinguistic, objective differences ...; they seem rather to be covert grammatical categories. Thus one must learn as a part of learning Navaho that 'sorrow' belongs in the "round" class.

B. L. Whorf, "Grammatical Categories"

Important points bear repeating. Alfred Ernout, on the first page of his classic study of Latin morphology (1974, [1914]), makes the observation that gender, and by extension other morphosyntactic properties and categories, are reliably detected not on the word that inherently carries the gender feature but rather on the lexemes that receive the feature by way of the syntax.[1] So, although there are three genders in Latin, it is not always possible to tell the gender of a given noun by inspection:[2]

Thus *nauta* is masculine, but *fāgus* feminine, although in general the final -*a* characterizes feminine nouns and the final -*us* masculine ones.

It is the adjective alone that indicates in an unambiguous manner the masculine or feminine gender of the noun: a masculine noun is one accompanied "by the masculine form of the stem of the adjective that agrees with it," and a feminine noun, "one that calls for the feminine form of the adjective" (Meillet 1964 [1937] 169).

Meillet (1964) notes that it is a general property of Indo-European languages that the distinction between masculine and feminine gender is reliably correlated not with inflectional noun classes but rather with the form of the adjective. More generally, across all languages, we may say that the inherent morphosyntactic properties of a word do not always serve as a valid predictor of its inflectional class. To put the point even more strongly, Meillet and Ernout have shown that it is not true, as many linguists believe, that inflectional classes are simply exponents of morpho-syntactic properties. Instead, inflectional classes have a life of their own, existing as independent parts of the grammatical engine.[3] My purpose in this chapter is to explore inflectional classes in some detail by way of supporting this last claim. In doing so, I also reinforce the basic idea that morphology has a place of its own in language.

I will treat morphosyntactic categories and properties (specifically gender) from the same perspective. Here I have two main points to make. First, if inflectional classes are not simple direct exponents of morpho-syntactic properties, then the inverse also needs to be emphasized: mor-phosyntactic properties are not directly detectable from the form of an utterance, including the inflectional classes of the lexemes, but are instead always abstract syntactic elements. Second, although we tend to think of morphosyntactic properties as reflections or at least descendants of se-mantic categories like sex and animacy, a linguistic theory in which syn-tax, semantics, and morphology are distinct makes no claim that this should be the case. In such a theory the morphosyntactic categories and properties of a language can always be semantically arbitrary, since their place in the theory is between syntax and morphology and not between syntax and semantics. Athough I have not found any examples of (histori-cally or synchronically) totally unmotivated morphosyntactic properties, in the next chapter I will discuss in detail two languages where member-ship in a given morphosyntactic class seems to depend for the most part on phonological shape—surely the reverse of what we expect under the "normal" assumption that morphosyntactic categories are rooted in ref-erence or at least in conceptual structure. On the other hand, once we understand the role of these morphosyntactic categories and properties in morphology, which I will discuss in more detail below, their frequent lack of semantic motivation becomes more understandable.

For rhetorical coherence, this chapter and the next treat only gender and the associated inflectional category of nominal declension. However, my conclusions are meant to extend beyond gender and declension to other morphosyntactic categories and their corresponding inflectional classes. In chapter 5, I deal with verb conjugations from the same gen-eral perspective. I should also note that my discussion of gender focuses largely on its distinctiveness from inflectional class. For a much more comprehensive discussion of gender from a fairly similar perspective, you should consult Corbett's masterful (1991) survey.

From this perspective, syntax and morphology are autonomous linguis-tic levels, in the sense of Z. Harris (1960) and Chomsky (1975).[4] By *auton-*

omous, however, I do not wish to imply the radical autonomy of the post-Bloomfieldian structuralists, who deplored all mixing of levels.[5] Instead, I mean only that an autonomous level is not entirely reducible to another level and follows principles of its own, in addition to broader principles that may apply to other levels as well.

Note that autonomous levels of the sort that I have in mind may be related to one another or similar in their organizations. Aspects of one may influence or even determine aspects of another. So, within a framework of autonomous levels, it is perfectly legitimate to expect to find similarities or correlations between levels. I will explore such correlations in this chapter, and I will express them in the traditional manner, which is to say in terms of rules or mappings from one level to another. But the claim of autonomy predicts that these mappings between levels are seldom perfect, since the levels are autonomous. For example, in describing Spanish nominal gender, it is perfectly reasonable to have a rule according to which nouns that denote males will have masculine gender. This rule relates two levels: conceptual structure (which is probably not strictly linguistic) and syntax (gender being a syntactic notion, a point that I will discuss below). Yet the mapping is not perfect in either direction: there are nouns denoting males that are not masculine, and there are masculine nouns that do not denote males. The two are correlated, but imperfectly. We expect such a state of affairs if syntax is autonomous from semantics. Similarly, we may write a rule according to which masculine nouns in Spanish belong to an inflectional class that I call class 1. Membership in class 1 is indicated formally by means of a rule feature. This feature will in turn trigger a realization rule that results in members of this class receiving the suffix *o*. This system relates syntax (gender) and inflectional morphology, which are autonomous levels, but once again we find that the correlation is not perfect, because the levels are autonomous: there are masculine nouns that do not belong to class 1 and vice versa.

Although the mapping is not perfect, we should not doubt its validity. Inflectional classes are almost always partially determined by gender, just as genders may be partially determined by denotational properties of nouns. There may be exceptions, but experience tells us that the mappings between levels are normally partial, and I will use the partial nature of such mappings as a diagnostic tool throughout what follows. Where we find a partial correlation, we may use it as evidence of autonomy. I will call the partial mappings between levels of this type *implicational rules*.

3.1 Terminology

3.1.1 Inflectional classes

I would like the term *inflectional class* to cover the traditional senses of the terms *conjugation* and *declension*. *Webster's Third* gives the sense of the Latin term *conjugatio* as a "class of verbs having the same type of inflectional forms." For *declension* they give the corresponding sense: "a class of nouns or adjectives having the same type of inflectional forms." Let us interpret *inflection* broadly as a synonym of *accidence*, to cover all morphophonological realization of morphosyntactic properties (as opposed to the narrow sense, in which inflection is opposed to agglutination). By combining the two definitions from *Webster's*, we come up with the definition of an inflectional class as a set of lexemes whose members each have the same type of inflectional forms. If we substitute for the term *inflectional form* the slightly broader term *realization*, so that we may include nonaffixational morphology, we then arrive at the following final informal definition:

Definition An *inflectional class* is a set of lexemes whose members each select the same set of inflectional realizations.

Matthews (1991) also uses the term *inflectional class*, and although he does not define it directly, his use seems to agree with the sense that I have given it.

According to my definition, a language will have inflectional classes when there is more than one realization for a given morphosyntactic property array.[6] In Latin, for example, where case and number are always jointly realized, there is almost always more than one suffix by which a particular case and number array may be realized.[7] For a given noun or adjective, we must therefore know, for each case and number array, which of its realizations will appear.[8] Let us call the pairing of a morphosyntactic property array and a realization a *realization pair*. The set of realization pairs for all possible morphosyntactic property arrays of a given lexeme is the inflectional class of that lexeme. A priori, each lexeme could select its own set from among all possible realization pairs. For example, in Latin, if we minimally assume five cases[9] and two numbers (singular and plural) and if there were two ways phonologically to realize each of the ten combinations of number and case values, then we might have to specify for each noun or adjective which of the two ways is appropriate for each combination, which results in 2^{10} different classes. However, as Carstairs (1987) has shown, normally the total number of classes is minimal: it is equal to the highest number of choices of phonological realizations available for a single morphosyntactic property array. So if no array allows more than two choices, then Carstairs's paradigm economy principle would predict that there are only two inflectional classes of nouns and adjectives. I will return below to Carstairs's principle and its instantiation with an example that appears to contradict it. For the moment, though, let us assume that the number of inflectional classes for any language is determinately minimal.[10] We still need to know, for a given lexeme, what set of realization pairs it has. We must assure that a given lexeme will pair a particular phonological realization with a given array of morphosyntactic properties. For instance, how do we assure that the genitive singular of Latin *naut-* 'sailor' will be *nautae*, while the genitive singular of *dom-* 'house' is *domi* and that of *ac-* 'pin' is *acus*? In each of these instances, it happens that syntactic gender is not a valid predictor of inflection (the gender of each of these nouns is contrary to the normal gender for the class in question). The lexical entry for the noun must therefore bear some sort of flag to assure that it will manifest the appropriate set of inflections. This flag is the inflectional class of the noun. Membership in a given inflectional class will guarantee that the noun has exactly the realization pairs of that class: nouns of class 1 will take the accusative plural suffix *-ās*, the genitive singular suffix *-ae*, and so on; nouns of class 2 will take a different set of suffixes. Mechanically, as a way of insuring that all the realization pairs of a given class will be linked to members of that class, I add the class name to the first member of each realization pair. The class thus acts as a rule feature or rule trigger, and the realizations characteristic of a given class or paradigm will all be conditioned by that class name or class flag or rule trigger. Alternatively, we may say that the realizations realize the inflectional class and the morphosyntactic property arrays. In the cases under discussion, where the declension must be lexically specified, the inflectional class is part of the lexical entry for each lexeme. Where the inflectional class is predictable from other properties of a lexeme, as it often is, the inflectional class will be assigned to the lexeme by rule, rather than being lexically specified.

3.1.2 Gender

The term *gender* is often understood as being essentially connected to sex. For example, *The Shorter Oxford English Dictionary* gives the following definition of the grammatical use of *gender*: "Each of the three (or two) grammatical 'kinds,' corresponding more or less to distinctions of sex (or absence of sex), into which sbs. are discriminated according to the nature of the modifications they require in words syntactically associated with them." Etymologically, this association between gender and sex is partly correct. The Latin term *genus* 'kind' (and indeed the English word *kind*) is derived historically from the Indo-European root *gen/gon* 'be born', and the connection between reproduction and sex is well established. However, the definitional restriction of grammatical gender to sex-based gender seems to have arisen more from the fact that Indo-European gender systems are rooted in sex distinctions than from any principle. When we inspect a wider range of gender systems, it becomes clear that the more important part of the definition is instead the second. The special property of genders as grammatical kinds of substantives is that they are distinguished from one another with respect to agreement and not that they are sex-based. *Webster's Third* makes the second point explicit by including shape and animacy along with sex as examples of the kinds of "distinguishable characteristics" that may serve as the basis of gender. I will therefore use the term *gender* in this work in this sense of 'nominal agreement class', as discussed in detail by Corbett (1991). A language will have gender if and only if we find in that language (1) some form of agreement with nouns that (2) involves a distinction among noun classes, no matter what the semantic basis of the distinction may be. Indeed, since agreement and gender are syntactic phenomena, the question of the nature of the substantive basis of a gender is in principle irrelevant to our present concerns, which are syntactic and morphological. I must also stress that gender as I have defined it is manifested solely in agreement *with* nouns. A language may have morphologically distinct noun types, but so long as we do not see signs of agreement, we do not have gender, again following Corbett.

An important question, which I will not address here, is the relation between gender and classifier systems of the sort commonly found in languages of southeast Asia and adjacent areas (see Dixon 1982 for some discussion). Another important question that I will not address is why gender is a nominal property. What prevents verbs from having genders? These are both fascinating questions, but exploring them would take me too far afield.

3.2 Two Simple Examples of the Relation between Gender and Inflectional Class

In recent work Greville Corbett (1991), Morris Halle (1990), and James Harris (1991a, 1991b) have provided several nice examples of the relation between gender and inflectional class. I will briefly review two of these here by way of introduction to the subject and to my particular treatment of inflectional classes, which involves the use of rule triggers. There are differences between the theoretical frameworks of these authors and mine, but they are not germane to the issue at hand.

3.2.1 Spanish

Harris (1991a) shows that the simple view of Spanish gender morphology, according to which feminine words end in *a* and masculines in *o*, is incorrect. To consider nouns first, a large number of masculine nouns (approximately 600) end in *a* and a fair number of nouns of both genders end with no final vowel or only an epenthetic *e* (which is inserted by late phonological rule and has no morphological value). We may therefore say that Spanish has three inflectional classes of nouns, *o suffixed* (which I will call class 1), *a suffixed* (which I will call class 2), and *suffixless* (which I will call class 3). Some examples of these three classes, with nouns from various genders, are given in table 3.1.

Adjectives are similar to nouns, except that adjective lexemes are inherently unspecified for gender and acquire their gender syntactically from the noun that they modify or are predicated of. We therefore find three basic classes of adjectives, just as we do for nouns, but one class is different. The similar classes are class 2, which comprises adjectives that always end in *a* regardless of gender, and class 3, adjectives that have no suffix (or only epenthetic *e*) regardless of whether they agree with masculine or feminine nouns. The largest class, a class of adjectives that vary their inflectional class according to gender, naturally does not exist for nouns.[11] There is also a fourth class, which Harris calls geographical/national/

Table 3.1
The relation between gender and noun class in Spanish

Marker	Class	Gender	Example	Gloss
-o	1	masculine	muchacho	'boy'
-o	1	feminine	mano	'hand'
-a	2	masculine	dia	'day'
-a	2	feminine	muchacha	'girl'
$\emptyset$	3	masculine	Cid	'Cid'
$\emptyset$	3	feminine	sed	'thirst'
$\emptyset$ (*e* inserted)	3	masculine	padre	'father'
$\emptyset$ (*e* inserted)	3	feminine	madre	'mother'

ethnic (GNE), whose peculiarities I will discuss below. Examples of each type are given in table 3.2.

What is the relation between gender and noun or adjective class, since it is not a perfect correspondence, as Harris has shown? In particular, is there still a sense in which *a* is the feminine suffix and *o* the masculine suffix in Spanish? The major generalizations concerning the relation between gender in nouns and inflectional classes seems to be the following:

Generalization 1   Feminine gender nouns may be idiosyncratically specified as belonging to class 3. Otherwise, they belong to class 2.

Generalization 2   Masculine gender nouns may be idiosyncratically specified as belonging either to class 2 or to class 3. Otherwise, they belong to class 1.

How do we encode these generalizations into a morphological theory? If we view each inflectional class as a rule trigger that is a morphosyntactic property of each lexeme belonging to that inflectional class,[13] then there must also be realization rules for these features to trigger.[14] I express this triggering effect of inflectional classes by pairing a morphosyntactic property array that includes the inflectional class with a realization rule, as illustrated in table 3.3. The property array is enclosed in square brackets

Table 3.2
The relation between gender and adjective class in Spanish

Class	Marker	Gender	Example	Gloss
2	-a	masc./fem.	belga	'Belgian'
3	Ø	masc./fem.	azul	'blue'
3	*e* (inserted)	masc./fem.	posible	'possible'
variable	-a	fem.	alta	'tall'
	-o	masc.	alto	'tall'
GNE	-a	fem.	española	'Spanish'
GNE	Ø	masc.	español	'Spanish'

Table 3.3
Pairings of rule triggers (morphosyntactic property arrays) with realization rules

Morphosyntactic array	Realization rule	Realization pair
[N, class 1]	$X \rightarrow Xo$	$\langle$[N, class 1], $(X \rightarrow Xo)\rangle$
[N, class 2]	$X \rightarrow Xa$	$\langle$[N, class 2], $(X \rightarrow Xa)\rangle$
[N, class 3]	$X \rightarrow X$	$\langle$[N, class 3], $(X \rightarrow X)\rangle$

and represents the syntactic conditions under which the realization rule that it is paired with operates, i.e., the rule trigger. The realization rules each operate on a particular stem of a lexeme, which is represented by the variable X in the realization rules. The rule triggers and realization rules form realization pairs, which I represent as in table 3.3.

Because no noun can belong to more than one inflectional classes and because each realization rule is triggered by only one inflectional class, the realizations will be disjunctive.[15] The realization of class 3 is described in terms of the identity rule. One might say instead that class 3 is indeclineable, that it is outside the morphological class system. On this view, suffixless nouns do not actually belong to any morphological class. Masculine nouns that take *a* will be specified individually in the lexicons as belonging to class 2.[16] Feminine nouns that take *o* (of which there are only a handful) will be specified individually in the lexicon as belonging to class 1. All class 3 nouns of either gender will have to be specified lexically. Regular masculine and feminine nouns will be unspecified for their inflectional class and will receive their class by means of rules assigning inflectional classes on the basis of gender, as follows:

(1) Masculine → class 1

(2) Feminine → class 2

Class 3 is never assigned by rule. What the rules say, then, is that masculine-gender nouns go into class 1, and feminine-gender nouns go into class 2, except for those that are specified otherwise. Class membership may also be idiosyncratically specified for a given noun.[17] There is a small residue of nouns with what may be thought of as peculiar suffixes. Examples given by Harris include *torax* 'thorax', *heroe* 'hero', *metropoli* 'metropolis', *sintesis* 'synthesis'.[18] According to the analysis I have given, these would also be included in class 3 and treated as being suffixless.

Adjectives have no idiosyncratic gender syntactically but receive masculine or feminine gender by way of the syntax. Morphologically, there are four types: adjectives that are suffixless regardless of gender; those that always end in *a*; those that end in *a* or *o*, depending on the gender that they have been assigned; and a small set of geographical/national/ethnic adjectives with *a* when feminine but no suffix when masculine. Let us assume that adjectives, like nouns, may be idiosyncratically specified for membership in class 2 or 3.[19] Adjectives with no idiosyncratic marking, if they acquire feminine gender syntactically, will undergo the rule that assigns feminines to class 2. If an adjective receives masculine gender from its syntax, then it will be assigned to class 1. This accounts for all but the geographical/national/ethnic adjectives. These are anomalous in having no suffix in the masculine but a normal feminine suffix *a*. As I noted above, adjectives have no inherent gender. Correspondingly, most adjectives in Spanish can be assumed to have no inherent specification for a particular inflectional class either when they bear a specific gender. For this small class, however, we may assume that the form of the masculine *only* is specified in the lexicon as being class 3.

The specification of one gender form of an adjective is unusual, but it is certainly found in other languages. French, for example, has three types of adjectives whose masculine form ends in *-eur*, as shown in table 3.4. If we assume that the regular class is the one that simply adds *e* in the feminine, then we must somehow indicate in the lexicon that the other two classes have irregular feminine forms. In classical Greek, as Mel'cuk points out, the lexeme for 'one' is suppletive, masculine *heîs*, but feminine *mia*. The numbers 'one' and 'two' are similarly irregular in Hebrew: the masculine for 'two' is *šne* but the feminine is *šte*, with a replacive *t* that is not found elsewhere. The Spanish situation is similar but a little more systematic.

We see then that the morphological system needed for class markers in Spanish adjectives is the same as that needed for nouns. The entire system calls for five distinct types of entities:

1. Two mutually exclusive syntactic gender properties: Masculine and Feminine
2. Two rules that map the syntactic gender of a lexeme onto an inflectional class
3. Three inflectional classes
4. Three realization rules: one for suffix *a* and another for suffix *o* and one identity rule
5. The phonological forms that result from these realizations

Table 3.4
Feminine forms of French adjectives ending in *-eur*

Masculine	Feminine	Gloss
menteur	menteuse	'lying'
protecteur	protectrice	'protective'
extérieur	extérieure	'outside'

Table 3.5 presents a picture of how the five types of entities figure in the mapping from syntactic representation to phonology.

Let me now comment on each level and entity. Gender is a syntactic category that is either specified lexically for a lexeme or assigned by rule. For nouns, so far as we have seen, gender is specified lexically. In the case of gender in adjectives, it is distributed syntactically by agreement. Some nouns most likely acquire their gender by rule, though not by syntactic rule. For example, there is arguably a conceptual rule that assigns Masculine and Feminine to words for biologically male and female referents that are not prespecified for gender. Such rules, however, are beyond the scope of my study. In any case, the syntactic gender properties, however they are determined, are not usually determined by morphology in Spanish, although they are in other languages. We have seen, though, that genders play a (somewhat indirect) role in morphology, which is why they are usually called *morphosyntactic* properties. Their role is to trigger the (morphosyntactic) rules that assign inflectional classes to nouns and adjectives (if the lexemes are not already specified as belonging to any such class).

The realization rules, like the morphosyntactic rules, are rules that mediate between morphological entities and other entities. In this case, the other entities are phonological.

The inflectional classes, however, neither mediate between morphology and another linguistic level nor have any substantial properties characteristic of another. They are purely morphological. Of the five types of entities, we may say that the three central ones (2–4) constitute the morphology per se of inflection. The outer two (1 and 5) are what the morphology maps between.

Table 3.5
The mapping from syntax to phonology through morphology

Level	Entity
(morpho)syntax	(morpho)syntactic properties (gender)
(morpho)syntax to morphology	morphosyntactic rules (gender to inflectional class)
morphology by itself	inflectional classes realization pairs
morphology to phonology	realization rules
phonology	phonological forms

Spanish thus shows us that the relation between gender and its phonological representation is quite complex and indirect. Words of the same gender may bear different phonological markers or none at all, and the same phonological marker (or none at all) may appear on words of different gender. Furthermore, at least on the account I have given, the notion of an inflectional affix is not directly applicable to all gender-bearing words in Spanish, in the sense that there does not exist for all Spanish words a phonological label for its gender. On the other hand, what my account does show is that there is a well-behaved, albeit complex, mapping from syntactic gender to phonological form through inflectional classes, for nouns and adjectives. This mapping constitutes the morphology of Spanish gender.[20]

I should note finally that Harris emphasizes that the inflectional classes are so independent of gender that they also play a role outside the gender system of the language. Thus Harris points out that adverbs show the same word-final patterns as nouns and adjectives (e.g., *solo* 'only (adv.)', *fuera* 'outside', *delante* 'ahead'). I have not given rules for adverbs, but they will map subclasses of adverbs onto the three inflectional classes. For example, the fact that there is a class of adverbs ending in *mente* and none in *mento* or *menta* shows that this adverbial suffix places its bearer in class 3.

3.2.2 Russian nouns

Russian has three genders—feminine, masculine, and neuter—and three inflectional classes of singular nouns.[21] All plural nouns are inflected in the same way, so that one may say either that the noun class system operates only in the singular or that plurals are assigned to a fourth class (Beard, to appear). The case endings of the three singular noun classes and the plural are given in table 3.6. Because Russian, unlike Spanish, has

Table 3.6
Suffixes for Russian noun declensions

	Class 1	Class 2	Class 3	Plural
Nominative	Ø/o	a	Ø	i/a
Accusative	a/o	u	Ø	i/a/Ø/ov/ej
Genitive	a	i	i	Ø/ov/ej
Dative	u	e	i	am
Instrumental	om	oj	ju	am'i
Locative	e	e	i	ax

Note: Based on Jakobson 1984.

overt case markers, each class is associated with a paradigm, a set of realization pairs, rather than a single realization, as in Spanish. Remember that each realization pair consists of a morphosyntactic property array paired with the realization rule that it triggers. No noun may be specified for individual case endings from different paradigms, because nouns are specified only for inflectional classes and not for single realization pairs.

The relation between gender and noun class in Russian is at once simpler and more complex than in Spanish.[22] First, class 1 has no feminine members, and class 3 has only one masculine member *put'* 'way' and only a small number of neuter members (e.g., *imja* 'name'). Class 2 is thus the only one where gender and class diverge significantly: most of its members are feminine, but a relatively small number are masculine. For masculine and neuter nouns, then, we lexically specify *put'* and a few neuters as belonging to class 3 and a relatively small number of masculines as belonging to class 2.[23] Otherwise, a general rule applies that assigns nonfeminine nouns to class 1. For feminines, though, there is a choice between class 2 and class 3. Statistically, class 2 is much larger; class 3 comprises about 70 individual nouns and a number of noun suffixes, some of them productive.[24] One should therefore posit a general rule assigning feminine nouns to class 2, with class 3 nouns being exceptional. The implicational rules assigning noun classes on the basis of gender for Russian are given below:

(3) [N, Feminine] → [class 2]

(4) [N] → [class 1][25]

These rules are exactly analogous to the rules given above for Spanish. Each class marker will define a unique set of realizations pairs, the set of all pairs that contain that class marker, and hence may be used to name the set. A simple example is given in (5), which contains the set of realization pairs defined by class 2:

(5) $\langle$[N, class 2, Nominative], $(X \to X\text{a})\rangle$
    $\langle$[N, class 2, Accusative], $(X \to X\text{u})\rangle$
    $\langle$[N, class 2, Genitive], $(X \to X\text{y})\rangle$
    $\langle$[N, class 2, Dative], $(X \to X\text{e})\rangle$
    $\langle$[N, class 2, Instrumental], $(X \to X\text{om})\rangle$

Some arrays will be more complex. For example, although both masculine and neuter nouns appear in class 1, only neuters have a nominative suffix

(-o). The property array for this suffix must therefore include the gender of the noun, as well as its inflectional class.

Among the inflectional classes, the most interesting one is class 3. As I noted above, this class is feminine, with only one exception. I also noted that it is small. Because of its size relative to class 2, one treatment would simply assign all class 3 words and affixes lexically, with no rule mentioning the class. But this treatment obscures the fact that class 3 is overwhelmingly feminine. What we need to express this generalization about class 3 is an implicational rule that is opposite in direction to the ones above. This rule is given below:

(6) [N, class 3] → Feminine

This rule implies that all feminine class 3 nouns and suffixes will indeed be individually stipulated in the lexicon as belonging to this class (there is no rule assigning class 3 membership), but that these nouns and suffixes will be inherently unspecified for gender, unlike other nouns, and receive their gender by rule (6). This type of rule is intuitively peculiar. Linguists tend to assume that gender (being syntactic) is prior to inflectional class in the same way that syntax is prior to morphology, so that rule (6) appears to be inverted. We will see in the next chapter, however, an entire system (that of the Papua New Guinea language Arapesh) in which most rules involving noun classes are of this inverted sort. I conclude, therefore, that inverted morphosyntactic rules like (6) are universally available, though admittedly less common than the normal sort exemplified in Russian by (3) and (4) and in Spanish by (1) and (2).

A final noteworthy feature of Russian noun inflection is that the inflectional classes are distinct only in the singular. In the plural, there is only one noun declension type. We may handle this fact by providing a rule for plurals:

(7) [N, Plural] → [class Plural]

Must we then say that the remaining inflectional classes are restricted to the singular? This could be done by modifying rules (3) and (4) to (8) and (9):

(8) [N, Feminine, −Plural] → [class 2]

(9) [N, −Plural] → [class 1]

However, if we assume that the syntactic feature [−plural] is unmarked and if unmarked features are unspecified, then rules (3) and (4) will fail to operate on plural nouns in any case.

3.3   Hebrew, a Language without Nominal Inflectional Classes

Hebrew, like Spanish, has two genders, masculine and feminine.[26] Like Spanish, Hebrew also has no cases but only number and gender for nouns and adjectives. Unlike Spanish, which has only one plural marker, *s*, that follows the suffix of the singular inflectional class (if there is one), Hebrew has two plural markers, both of which are cumulative in their exponence.

I will begin with the singular. The Hebrew nominal gender is reliably revealed, like Latin gender, in agreeing adjectives and, unlike Latin, in finite verbs and participles, which agree in gender with their subject.[27] This allows us to detect the gender of a noun, regardless of its class marker, in exactly the manner that Ernout (1974) prescribes. In traditional Hebrew grammar, no distinction is made between genders and inflectional classes, because the two types of entities are not normally distinguished. In fact, the notion of inflectional class does not easily extend to Hebrew, which is what makes it interesting.

In my exposition of the facts of Hebrew, I will introduce rules directly as a means of presenting the data. I do this for two reasons. First, I hope that the reader is now familiar enough with the general method to follow it. Second, I believe that this manner of exposition is much easier to follow in the case of Hebrew.

Masculine nominals are much simpler morphologically than feminines. In the singular, masculine gender has no morphological marker associated with it.[28] Within the framework adopted here, the formal analogue of this absence is a realization rule whose form is an identity rule triggered by Masculine Singular. One might assume that, Masculine and Singular both being unmarked values, Masculine Singular nominals formally have no syntactic gender or number feature associated with them, which entails the lack of a corresponding realization rule. I prefer, however, to follow Jakobson's (1971) original observations that formal marking is correlated with semantic markedness (see also Battistella 1990) and to believe that the realization of this particular array in terms of identity follows from the unmarked nature of the syntactic property array Masculine Singular.[29]

Masculine nominals normally take the plural suffix *im*. We may express this by means of a realization pair directly relating syntactic representation to realization without any specification of inflectional class, a move that I will justify shortly:

(10) $\langle$[N, Masculine, Plural], $(X \rightarrow X$im$)\rangle$

There are, however, approximately 80 masculine nouns in current use that take instead the normally feminine suffix *ot*. Table 3.7 contains a sample of masculine nouns with both plural markers. Some generalizations can be made about the form of masculine nouns that take the *-ot* plural, but none are watertight. For example, half of them have *o* as their final vowel (but not all words of this form take *-ot*); most nouns ending in *e* (but not all) take *-ot*. In any case, the class is more or less closed, so its members must be individually stipulated as undergoing the *-ot* plural rule, as indicated below (where membership N_i is stipulated):

(11) $\langle$[N_i Plural], $(X \rightarrow X\text{ot})\rangle$

Nouns stipulated to undergo this rule will be exempted by the elsewhere condition from the default pairing (10) of masculine plurals with the [suffix *-im*] rule.[30] Note also that we do not need to specify that the stipulated nouns that undergo this rule are masculine, since only masculine nouns need to be individually stipulated for it. Feminine nouns will undergo this rule simply because they are feminine, since this same *-ot* is the normal feminine, plural suffix. We may pair regular feminine nouns with this same realization in a fashion parallel to the pairing for regular masculines (10):

(12) $\langle$[N, Feminine, Plural], $(X \rightarrow X\text{ot})\rangle$[31]

However, there are thirty or so feminine nouns that take the *-im* plural suffix. These must be specified as taking this suffix in the same way that I specified certain masculines as taking the *-ot* suffix. The class of nouns in (13), where N_i is stipulated, is thus parallel to those in (10):

(13) $\langle$[N_i Feminine, Plural], $(X \rightarrow X\text{im})\rangle$

Table 3.7
Hebrew masculine nouns with *-im* and *-ot* plural markers

Singular	Plural	Gloss
yeled	yeladim	'boy'
nigun	nigunim	'melody'
santer	santerim	'chin'
mazleg	mazlegot	'fork'
yitron	yitronot	'advantage'
'av	'avot	'father'
sade	sadot	'field'
zug	zugot	'pair'
nahar	naharot	'river'

Feminine singulars may take either no suffix or any one of a number of feminine suffixes. Those that take no suffix will be idiosyncratically stipulated for the (normally masculine) identity rule. Of the suffixes, the most common is *-a*. The remaining feminine suffixes all end in *t* (*-it*, *-ut*, *-et*), but they cannot be reduced to a single suffix.[32] I will assume that the default form for feminine singular nouns contains the suffix *-a*. This is expressed in rule (14):

(14) $\langle$[N, Feminine, Singular], $(X \rightarrow X\text{a})\rangle$

Other feminine nouns will be specified as undergoing one of the other suffix rules. Table 3.8 contains a sample of feminine nouns with various singular and plural form types.

Interestingly, although participles are nominals in terms of their morphology (not showing agreement in person as verbs do, even in predicate position), they do not (except in one binyan) have the *-a* suffix. Instead, they have *-t*. The presence of this *-t* cannot be attributed to any phonological factors but is due entirely to the fact that these items are participles. Furthermore, there are no individually exceptional feminine participles. We may therefore give the following realization pairs for feminine participles:

(15) $\langle$[N, Participle, Feminine, Singular], $(X \rightarrow X\text{t})\rangle$

(16) $\langle$[N, Participle, Feminine, Singular, hif'il], $(X \rightarrow X\text{a})\rangle$

This particular pattern shows how complex the distribution of morphs may be: *a* is the default feminine singular for nominals in general, but *-t* is

Table 3.8
Hebrew feminine nominals with various singular and plural endings

Singular	Plural	Gloss
mila	milim	'word'
erec	aracot	'land'
galut	galuyot	'exile'
iša	našim	'woman'
ir	arim	'city'
tavit	taviyot	'label'
zimra	zimrot	'melody'
šomeret	šomrot	'watch' (part.)
mazkira	mazkirot	'remind' (part.)

the default for participles, with *-a* appearing only with a restricted subset of these.

Adjectives too are interesting. The feminine singular suffix depends on the adjective suffix to a great extent. For example, the very common adjective suffix *i* (e.g., *carfati* 'French') always takes the feminine singular suffix *-t* (*carfatit*). When adjectives are used as nouns, however, this restriction is lost, so that the word for Frenchwoman is *carfatiya*, with the default *a* suffix, because we are now dealing with a noun and the generalization about *-i* is restricted to adjectives.

To conclude this section, I note that the following general pattern emerges when we look at number and gender morphology in Hebrew nominals. There are two major patterns:

Generalization 3   The largest number of masculine nominals show no suffix in the singular and the suffix *-im* in the plural.

Generalization 4   The largest number of feminine nominals show the suffix *-a* in the singular and the suffix *-ot* in the plural.

It seems wrong, however, to call these two patterns inflectional classes, because the distribution of affixes in the language is not paradigmatic: individual nouns are almost always exceptional in terms of individual affixes, rather than in terms of sets of affixes. Thus masculine nouns take the *-ot* plural suffix much more readily than they take the *-a* singular. Indeed, only one word, *layla*, pl. *lelot*, 'night' is masculine and appears to occur with both the singular suffix *-a* and the *-ot* plural suffix; no other masculine word takes *-a* at all. Also, feminine nominals may take a variety of singular suffixes or no singular suffix; in the plural, they take either *-ot* or *-im*, with no correlation between the singular and the plural suffix.

In other languages, as we have seen in the case of Russian, for instance, exceptional nouns are designated exceptionally as members of an inflectional class. Certain Russian masculine nouns thus belong exceptionally to the normally feminine class 2, as we have seen. This means that they will show the entire class 2 pattern in their inflection. In Hebrew, nothing of the sort happens. Instead, exceptional individual nouns are specified for individual singular and plural suffixes *independently*. There are no noun paradigms in the language. This is important for the general theory of inflection. I said above that inflectional classes identify *sets* of pairings of morphosyntactic property arrays with realizations, which makes inflectional classes a secondary rather than a basic entity. The basic entities are the realization pairs that map morphosyntactic property arrays onto real-

Table 3.9
Realization pairs for Hebrew nominal gender and number suffixes

Morphosyntactic property array	Realization
[N, Masculine, Singular]	$X \rightarrow X$
[N, Feminine, Singular]	$X \rightarrow X$a
[N, Masculine, Plural]	$X \rightarrow X$im
N, Feminine, Plural]	$X \rightarrow X$ot
[N, Participle, Feminine, Singular]	$X \rightarrow X$t
[N, Participle, Feminine, Singular, hif'il]	$X \rightarrow X$a

izations. Hebrew supports this claim, since the simplest description of the nominal inflection and the exceptional items must incorporate these pairs directly, without recourse to inflectional classes. This is not to deny the reality of inflectional classes, merely their necessity.

For convenience, I now repeat in table 3.9 the realization pairs for Hebrew nominals that I have given so far. This set of realization pairs is not complete (the feminine singular suffixes other than -*a* are not treated in any detail), but it should provide an idea of how the system is meant to work. I have given the rules in order of ascending specificity. However, their application is not meant to be ordered extrinsically but rather governed by a general elsewhere condition that assures that a realization whose conditions are a subset of another realization will take precedence over that other realization.

Remember that these pairs are not rules of affixation but rather trigger the affixation rules (realization rules). This abundance of devices may seem superfluous, but it makes sense if we think of the realization pairs as analogues of statements like "Feminine, plural nominals take the suffix -*ot*." Such statements involve not affixation itself but rather the *distribution* of affixes. They specify the conditions under which the particular affixes appear. That is what these realization pairs do: they distribute the affixes, or more precisely, the realization rules.[33]

3.4 Latin Nominal Inflection

3.4.1 Neuter
I have shown that we must distinguish between gender (and other morphosyntactic properties) and inflectional class and that the relation between inflectional class and realization rules can be profitably treated in terms of sets of realization rules: an inflectional class is a paradigm of

pairs of particular morphosyntactic property arrays and particular realizations. The distinction among gender, inflectional class, and realization rule that has been established and their independence from one another make it possible for there to be other relations among these levels than the normal ones that I have described up to this point. I will now provide examples of direct mappings between an inherent morphosyntactic property (Latin gender) and both morphosyntactic cases and realizations.

First we must briefly review the system of nominal declension in Latin. Traditionally, five declensions or inflectional classes are distinguished for all nominals. The last two classes are small and include only nouns. Tables 3.10 through 3.14 contain examples of nouns from each class inflected for all common cases in both singular and plural. For each class where neuter words are found (classes 2, 3, and 4), I have given a neuter example along with a masculine, so that the reader may see exactly where the neuters differ.[34]

My discussion will be confined mostly to nouns. Adjectives and participles differ only minimally from nouns. As Halle (1990) has noted, although inflectional class is invariable for nouns, adjectives that do not belong to class 3 vary between class 1 and class 2, according to the noun

Table 3.10
Class 1, the Latin noun *mens-* 'table' fem.

	Singular	Plural
Nominative	mensa	mensae
Accusative	mensam	mensas
Genitive	mensae	mensārum
Dative	mensae	mensīs
Ablative	mensā	mensīs

Table 3.11
Class 2, the Latin nouns *domin-* 'master' masc. and *regn-* 'kingdom' neut.

	Singular		Plural	
	Masculine	Neuter	Masculine	Neuter
Nominative	dominus	regnum	dominī	regna
Accusative	dominum	regnum	dominōs	regna
Genitive	dominī	regnī	dominōrum	regnōrum
Dative	dominō	regnō	dominīs	regnīs
Ablative	dominō	regnō	dominīs	regnīs

Table 3.12
Class 3, the Latin nouns *custōd-* 'keeper' masc. and *mari-* 'sea' neut.

	Singular		Plural	
	Masculine	Neuter	Masculine	Neuter
Nominative	custōs	mare	custōdēs	maria
Accusative	custōdem	mare	custōdēs	maria
Genitive	custōdis	maris	custōdum	marium
Dative	custōdī	marī	custōdibus	maribus
Ablative	custōde	marī	custōdibus	maribus

Table 3.13
Class 4, the Latin nouns *fluctu-* 'wave' masc. and *cornu-* 'horn' neut.

	Singular		Plural	
	Masculine	Neuter	Masculine	Neuter
Nominative	fluctus	cornu	fluctūs	cornua
Accusative	fluctum	cornu	fluctūs	cornua
Genitive	fluctūs	cornūs	fluctuum	cornuum
Dative	fluctuī	cornū	fluctibus	cornibus
Ablative	fluctū	cornū	fluctibus	cornibus

Table 3.14
Class 5, the Latin noun *rē-* 'thing' fem.

	Singular	Plural
Nominative	rēs	rēs
Accusative	rem	rēs
Genitive	reī	rērum
Dative	rei	rēbus
Ablative	rē	rēbus

that they are in agreement with (this is parallel to Spanish adjectives). I will follow Halle in assuming that these adjectives, like their Spanish counterparts, have no inherent class but rather acquire their class from nouns in the following manner: first, they acquire gender by feature passing or percolation; second, they undergo the following rules:[35]

(17) [N, Feminine] → [class 1]

(18) [N] → [class 2]

Other differences between adjectives and nouns are found in the third declension, where certain adjectives show differences due to gender. I will deal with these in more detail below.

I now return to the main issue at hand, the existence of other relations between morphosyntactic properties and realizations. Let me start with the special characteristics of neuter nominals. The basic facts are very well known and can be stated quite succinctly, as I have done in generalizations 5 and 6:

Generalization 5 The nominative and accusative case forms are identical for all neuter words.

Generalization 6 In the plural, the neuter nominative and accusative suffix is always -*a*.

Let me note first that generalizations 5 and 6 are absolutely without exception. I therefore assume that they are not accidental but must be stated somewhere in the grammar of the language. What is most remarkable about these generalizations is that they cut across inflectional classes completely, applying as they do to *all* neuter nominals. Our job is to show how these generalizations can be accommodated in an explicit treatment of Latin nominal inflection.

Generalization 5 is the more difficult one to state formally. Halle (1990) handles it by means of what he calls a "readjustment rule," which he states as follows:

(19) [Acc] → [Nom]/[+ Neut] + Number + ____

There are two problems with this rule. First, it is not clear at what linguistic level the rule is meant to apply. It should not be syntactic, since that would entail having neuter accusatives become syntactic nominatives, which would cause problems. For examples, in conjunctions, the rule might give us a neuter nominative (former accusative) conjoined to a masculine accusative, resulting in an otherwise impossible conjunction of unlike cases. The proper level for such rules (if they exist) is the one that I called *morphomic* in chapter 1. Whatever we call the level, it must be made clear that it is morphological and not syntactic. Zwicky and Pullum (1989) call rules of this sort "referrals." In such cases, the realization of one morphosyntactic property for a given inflectional class is accomplished by referring to the realization rule for another such property. For example, Zwicky and Pullum say that the default rule for the past participle of a verb in English refers to the rule for the past form of the same verb. But this solution shares a weakness with Halle's, which is its directionality. Why should the past form of an English verb be "prior" to the past participle? There is no morphological or other evidence for any such priority, just as there is none for Latin third stems, as shown at length in chapter 2.

Similarly, rule (19) as stated rewrites the accusative as nominative. Zwicky and Pullum's equivalent would refer accusative to nominative in the case of neuters. Is there in fact any support for this directional claim? The only possible support that I can find is in present participles and class 3 adjectives "of one ending," where the identifiably nominative, singular suffix *s* appears on both nominative and accusative neuter forms (e.g., *regens* 'ruling'). Class 3 neuters normally take no nominative or accusative suffix, and -*s* is the most common nominative singular suffix for nonneuter class 3 nominals but is never the accusative suffix (which is usually -*m*, e.g., masc. *regentem*). One might therefore conclude from this class of neuters that the nominative form is indeed prior to the accusative, as the rule seems to say it should be.

On the other hand, class 2 singular nominals might seem to provide evidence to the contrary. Here, the suffix -*um* that is found with nonneuter accusatives, and never with nonneuter nominatives, is found with both cases in neuters, which leads me to give the accusative priority. In no other instances is there any evidence for the priority of either nominative or accusative: in class 3 nouns, and probably in class 4 nouns, the neuter, singular nominative and accusative is suffixless and other genders are usually suffixed, which provides no opportunity for evidence;[36] in the plural, the fact that the nominative and accusative neuter suffix in all classes is always -*a*, which never appears with other genders in the plural, makes for a similar lack of evidence. Given all of this, it seems best to state the rule (at the morphomic level) without any direction, as follows:[37]

(20) [Acc] = [Nom]/[Neuter]____

The problem with this rule is that I don't quite know what its status is. The simplest way to interpret it is as a metarule governing the spelling out of these particular features, so that it is equivalent to saying something like "Accusative and nominative neuter nominals are always spelled out in the same way, however these properties are realized," I give another one below for dative and ablative plural. If more rules like this are found, then we may be better able to understand their exact nature. For the moment, I will assume that rule (20) entails that all realization rules spelling out neuter accusative or nominative will be paired with disjunctions of morphosyntactic properties of the following form, regardless of class, and that such disjunctions are generally permitted by the theory of realization pairs:

(21) [N, Neut, Acc or Nom]

One might wish to think of (20) and (21) in terms of neutralization: the distinction between morphological accusative and nominative cases is neutralized for neuter nominals.

The second generalization about neuters, generalization 6, depends in part on the first, since the identity of nominative and accusative here presumably follows from the first generalization.[38] According to generalization 6, the neuter nominative/accusative plural is realized with the suffix -a, regardless of the inflectional class of the lexeme. In other words, in this instance, an array of morphosyntactic properties is paired with a realization rule for all nouns of a given gender, rather than being restricted by mediating inflectional classes, as we find elsewhere in the language. We encountered phenomena like this in the description of Hebrew, but there, I argued, there are no inflectional classes. The existence of such a phenomenon in Latin, where inflectional classes are very robust (all nominals belong to some inflectional class) is therefore interesting. Among other things, it seems to contradict at least the spirit of Carstairs's (1987) paradigm economy principle. He deals with the problem by invoking a new notion of *macroparadigm*, discussion of which would take us too far afield. In any case, my own interest is not in paradigm economy but rather in what sorts of mappings are permitted in a morphological rule system. I will therefore assume that we may have a pair like (22) to handle this generalization:

(22) $\langle$[N, Neuter, Plural, Acc or Nom], $(X \rightarrow X\mathrm{a})\rangle$

The major import of this pair is that it shows that inflectional classes and pairs relating morphosyntactic representations directly to realizations can coexist in a language. On reflection, what we find here seems reasonable. One particular array of morphosyntactic properties is always realized as the same form; the remaining arrays are more varied in their realizations and are routed through inflectional classes. However, it is not clear why there are no exceptions to rule (22). Exceptions should be possible in the same way that we find exceptional plurals in Hebrew. I will leave the answer to this question as a puzzle for future research.

3.4.2 Dative and ablative plural

Completely parallel to the syncretism of neuter nominative and accusative forms is the syncretism of dative and ablative plural in all nominal genders and classes, as Carstairs (1987) points out. There are three suffixes. classes 1 and 2 share the suffix -*īs*, classes 3 and 4 share the suffix -*ibus*, and the suffix for class 5 is -*ēbus*.[39] The identity of ablative and dative extends also to pronouns, which have various suffixes (all reminiscent of the nominal suffixes) but always show identical dative and ablative plural forms.[40] Again, it is not clear exactly how this generalization should be expressed, although its existence strengthens the belief that generalizations of this type are not simply spurious. Note that these two morphosyntactic property arrays are clearly the most marked in the language, so it is intuitively understandable that they might be subject to neutralization. But why should they be neutralized with each other, and what is the formal mechanism for accomplishing this?[41]

3.4.3 Phonological form and gender in Latin

We are used to the idea that words belonging to a certain morphological class might consequently have a certain form. For example, we conventionally think of Latin class 1 nominals as ending in -*a* and class 2 nominals as ending in -*us*, hence *mensa* 'table' and *dominus* 'master'. Of course, because of the inflected nature of the language, nominals belonging to these classes will not always show these forms, but in a language like Spanish, where nouns are uninflected for case and hence have a more constant form, inflectional class does determine nominal form to a great degree: -*a* class nominals will always have an -*a*, and -*o* class nominals will have an -*o*. Here the inflectional class of the lexeme determines the phonological form of the word.

In a language with template morphology, the effect of inflectional class on phonological shape is even more dramatic: in any Semitic language, verbs are narrowly restricted in their form, and this form is determined by inflectional class. I will return to a detailed discussion of Semitic verb classes in chapter 5, but for now I will mention only a few cases. A Hebrew verb must fall into the shape determined by one of five inflectional classes for verbs, and there are no exceptions to these five patterns, even among recent borrowings. Late Aramaic dialects (e.g., Syriac and Talmudic) show three classes (Costaz 1964, Levias 1900), and Hoberman (1989) analyzes one modern Aramaic dialect as having only two strict inflectional classes into which all verbs must fall.

The reverse situation, where the inflectional class of a lexeme is determined by its phonological shape, seems counterintuitive at first. After all, in rules that we have seen so far, more abstract properties trigger realization rules, and not usually vice versa. However, if we put the question a little differently, then the possibility that I have raised will not seem so peculiar. The question is, What sorts of factors determine what gender a given lexeme will belong to? In a language where gender is partially based on sex, conceptual and "natural" factors other than sex may also sometimes play a role. In Latin, names of plants are typically feminine, even when they belong (as many do) to the typically masculine class 2 (nominative in -*us*). Kuhner and Holzweissig (1912, 265) list some fifty lexemes for plants that follow this pattern of feminine gender and class 2 inflection.[42] Names of rivers and mountains are typically masculine, again with a few notable exceptions like *Lethe* and *Alpēs*. Letters of the alphabet and linguistic expressions, when mentioned, are usually neuter, as are most indeclinable words.

In a climate of reliable generalizations like these, which can be found in most Latin grammars, it is not so odd to find similar generalizations based on phonological form. While they are not as robust as those just discussed, they can be found in Latin, mostly in class 3 nouns. Some of the more significant ones follow:

Generalization 7   Stems ending in *el, al, us, os,* and *ūs* are usually neuter, e.g., *mel* 'honey', *animal* 'animal', *opus* 'work', *corpus* 'body', *rūs* 'countryside'.[43]

Generalization 8   Stems ending in stops are rarely neuter. The only examples are *lac* 'milk' and *caput* 'head'.

Generalization 9   Stems ending in C*r* are usually masculine, e.g., *imber* 'shower', *venter* 'belly'.[44]

The last class extends into adjectives in a complex but interesting fashion. Although most class 3 adjectives do not distinguish masculine from feminine forms, there is one small subclass containing about a dozen members that does (in the nominative only): the stems of these all end in this same C*r*. Thus an adjective like *ācr*- 'sharp' has three nominative forms: *ācer* (masc.), *ācris* (fem.), *ācre* (nent.). The *-e* nominative marker is quite characteristically neuter, but the *-is* is not especially feminine as opposed to masculine, which makes this class very peculiar indeed. But once we see that nominal stems ending in C*r-* are particularly masculine, which makes a nominative form ending in C*er* notably masculine, then we have some understanding of what is going on here: the nominative masculine form of these adjectives doesn't need the nominative suffix *-(i)s* that we normally find with class 3 nonneuter adjectives, because the C*er* is sufficient to indicate its gender and case. Furthermore, to have a feminine noun ending in C*er* might be jarring, so such words will receive the *-is* nominative suffix, which leaves C*ris* for feminines only. I am not presenting this analysis as a formal explanation of this small though strikingly anomalous class, but it does seem clear that the peculiarity of these adjectives in having "three endings" can only be understood in terms of the connection between C(*e*)*r-* and masculine gender.[45]

I will now turn to two languages where the relation between phonology and gender is much more robust and where gender and inflectional class operate almost in tandem. Nonetheless, we will see that all three must still be kept separate, so that overall, the general picture that has emerged of gender, phonological form, and inflectional class as belonging to distinct linguistic levels related by implicational rules will still hold.

Chapter 4
Gender, Inflection, and Phonological Form in Two Languages of Papua New Guinea: Arapesh and Yimas

Man speaks, and no brute has ever uttered a word. Language is our Rubicon, and no brute will dare to cross it.

Max Müller

Arapesh is a language of the Torricelli family, spoken near the north coast of Papua New Guinea. Yimas is a member of the unrelated, geographically adjacent and much smaller Lower Sepik family. Foley (1986) notes that these two families have noun-class systems that depend largely on phonology. Foley says, "As far as I know, this feature is unique among the languages of the world" (1986, 85). As I have just shown for Latin, we can find in other languages instances of phonology influencing the choice of noun class (gender), but the extent to which phonology determines noun class in these languages of Papua New Guinea and the complexity of the systems are certainly startling.[1]

My discussion of Arapesh is based on R. F. Fortune's (1942) grammar, a volume in the celebrated series Publications of the American Ethnological Society, edited by Franz Boas, which included many of the great descriptive works of early American linguistics.[2] Throughout the grammar, Fortune uses the term *noun class* in a fashion that does not discriminate between syntax and morphology. However, it is clear from the grammar, as I will demonstrate, that the distinction between syntax and morphology is crucial to the operation of these classes in the language. I will therefore use the two terms *gender* and *inflectional class* to distinguish the morphosyntactic and morphophonological classes in the same way that I have done in the previous chapter.

The reader should beware that the system is complex and of an unfamiliar type. The data must therefore be presented in considerably more detail than I have given heretofore. Nonetheless, I believe that the reward will be commensurate with the effort and that Arapesh shows in sometimes striking ways the validity of two major points. The first is that the distinction that I have emphasized between gender and inflectional classes extends well beyond the standard languages for which it has been posited. Indeed, if morphology is not syntax, then the distinction must be universal. Evidence for it will not always be forthcoming, though, and the Arapesh evidence, for example, is often quite subtle. The second point is that the defining property of a morphosyntactic class of lexemes (gender) may be phonological, which shows conclusively that there is no essential link between gender and conceptual categories, even at the most abstract level.

My discussion of Yimas will be much briefer and based entirely on the work of Foley (1986, 1991). The two languages differ in the extent to which the gender system is phonologically driven and are worth contrasting in this regard. The individual inflectional classes of Yimas are also somewhat more complex than those of Arapesh.

4.1 Arapesh Gender as Revealed through Agreement

Fortune lists thirteen noun classes. I will show that these classes are agreement classes or genders and not inflectional classes, of which there are quite a few more than thirteen. Fortune uses roman numerals for the genders. I will retain Fortune's numbering, i through xiii, and use arabic numerals by way of contrast for the corresponding inflectional classes; I will append lower case letters where more than one inflectional class corresponds to a single gender. For example, corresponding to Fortune's class iv, which I will call gender iv, there are six inflectional classes, which I have numbered 4a through 4f. I will begin with a very brief exposition of the inflectional classes. These classes are distinguished in terms of the singular and plural forms of their members. Table 4.1 contains one representative member of each inflectional class in each form.

As we see, although most of Fortune's noun classes (which I am now calling genders) correspond to only one inflectional class, there are four genders that each correspond to two inflectional classes and one gender (iv) with six corresponding inflectional classes. I will return to the actual inflectional classes below. For the moment, my concern is to establish the fact that there is a distinction between inflectional classes and genders. The distinction emerges very clearly when we look at agreement, for here the differences between the purely inflectional classes disappears, and we are left with Fortune's thirteen original noun classes (my genders). Since I have claimed that gender is syntactic but that inflectional class is not, this state of affairs is exactly what we expect, agreement being purely

Table 4.1
Arapesh inflectional noun classes

Class	Alternation	Singular	Plural	Gloss
1	by̥/bys	agaby̥	agabys	'back'
2	bør/ryb	ñibør	ñiryb	'belly'
3a	ag/as	aijag	aijas	'leg'
3b	g/gas	aweg	awegas	'seed'
4a	ky̧/meb	iloky̧	ilameb	'a bird'
4b	ky̧/rib	yahaky̧	yaharib	'a fruit tree'
4c	ky̧/ib	unuky̧	unib	'teeth mother'
4d	ky̧/guhijer	aniky̧	aniguhijer	'rattan species'
4e	ky̧/ijer	barahoky̧	barahijer	'granddaughter'
4f	ky̧/u	amagoky̧	amagou	'fly'
5	m/ipi̧	irum	iripi̧	'breadfruit'
6	n/b	narun	narøb	'wave'
7	n/m (masc.)	araman	aramum	'man'
8a	iñ/iš	kobiñ	kobiš	'ditch '
8b	V/Vhas	bode	bodehas	'stone axe'
9a	py̧/gwis	barupy̧	barugwis	'mountain track'
9b	py̧/s	apapy̧	apas	'banana'
10	r/guh	jur	juguh	'snake'
11a	t/togy̧	alit	alitogy̧	'shelf'
11b	t/gy̧	nybat	nybagy̧	'dog'
12	uh/ruh	nauh	naruh	'tooth'
13	ah/eh	atah	ateh	'ear'

syntactic and hence capable of passing on only syntactic information. A noun will pass on its gender but never its inflectional class, and agreeing categories will be differentiated by gender and not by inflectional class.

The alternations exemplified in table 4.1 are not confined to nouns but are mirrored in three types of agreement: adjective, verb, and proword.[3] Readers familiar with Bantu will recognize a striking similarity to the normal Bantu agreement pattern. I will discuss each type of agreement in some detail.

4.1.1 Adjective agreement

For each gender (i–xiii) we find corresponding suffixes, singular and plural, that are obligatory on modifying adjectives and numerals. These correspond closely to some of the alternations given in table 4.1 (a fact that I

Table 4.2
Arapesh adjective agreement

Gender	Singular	Plural
i	bagara-bi	bagara-bysi
ii	bagara-børi	bagara-røbi
iii	bagara-gi	bagara-gasi
iv	bagaro-kwi	bagara-ui
v	bagara-mi	bagare-ipi
vi	bagara-ni	bagara-bi
vii	bagara-ni	bagara-mi
viii	bagare-ñi	bagare-ši
ix	bagara-pi	bagara-si
x	bagara-ri	bagara-ruhi
xi	bagara-ti	bagara-gwi
xii	bagaro-whi	bagara-ruhi
xiii	bagara-hi	bagare-hi

will return to later), but they are followed by the adjective suffix *i*, with re-sultant deletion of the final vowel of the inflectional class suffix if there is one. The relevant forms of the adjective *bagara-* 'big' are given in table 4.2.

As predicted, there is only one inflectional class of adjectives for each gender. All gender iv nouns, for example, trigger the same set of adjective suffixes, although there are six inflectional subclasses of gender iv nouns. The adjectives thus reveal quite clearly that the noun classes designated with roman numerals are syntactic agreement classes, genders, while their subclasses are purely inflectional.

4.1.2 Verb agreement

Verbs also obligatorily mark the gender of their subjects, but with a prefix rather than a suffix. This prefix varies with the gender of the subject noun in the same fashion as the adjective suffix varies, as shown in table 4.3. However, there is some unexpected syncretism in the subject prefixes. For example, in gender ii, which shows the markers *bør* (singular) and *røb* (plural) for adjectives, we find *ba-* for both singular and plural subject prefixes. Also, the gender vii plural marker is *ha-* instead of the expected *ma-*.[4] These peculiarities show that it would be difficult to derive the subject prefixes on verbs by brute-force copying of the inflectional class marker of the subject (in those cases where the inflectional class of a given gender is unique) or by direct morphological incorporation of a pronoun.

Table 4.3
Arapesh subject prefixes on verbs

Gender	Singular prefix	Plural prefix
i	ba-	sa-
ii	ba-	ba-
iii	ga-	sa-
iv	kwa-	wa-
v	ma-	pa-
vi	na-	ba-
vii	na-	ha-
viii	ña-	ša-
ix	pa-	sa-
x	ra-	wha-
xi	ta-	gwa-
xii	wha-	ha-
xiii	ha-	ha-

Some more complex morphology must be involved. Exactly what mechanism is responsible for verb-subject agreement is a syntactic question. Whatever the mechanism, though, it is clear that verb-subject agreement is closely related to pronominal anaphora in Arapesh, as it is in many languages, since both verbs and pronouns are sensitive to noun genders in exactly the same fashion, as I will now show.

4.1.3 Intensive pronouns

The independent third-person pronouns, which Fortune calls *intensive*, are listed in table 4.4. Again, as with verb-subject agreement, these pronouns correspond closely to class alternations in their organization and form. Unlike nonintensive pronouns, which are clitics, as we will see immediately below, intensive pronouns pattern syntactically like full NPs: subjects precede the verb and objects follow. I assume that the syntax guarantees that individual pronouns are in their proper gender and number. The actual forms of the independent pronouns can be analyzed as follows: begin with the gender marker; this is preceded by a vowel if it has none of its own (only *ipị* has a preceding vowel). This vowel is usually *a*, but it can be *e* or *u* for phonological reasons, which I will not discuss here. The vowel is then preceded by a copy of the least sonorous segment of the marker, which is itself preceded by *a* (never by another vowel).[5] A sample derivation is given in table 4.5.

Table 4.4
Arapesh intensive pronouns

Gender	Singular	Plural
i	abab	ababys
ii	ababør	abarøb
iii	agag	agagas
iv	akwokų	awau
v	amum	apeipį
vi	anan	abab
vii	anan	amum
viii	eñeñ	ešeš
ix	apapų	asas
x	arar	agwaguḥ
xi	atat	agwagų
xii	awhoh	aharuh
xiii	ahah	aheh

Table 4.5
Morphological derivation of a sample independent third-person pronoun

Form	Description
bys	base form (class i plural)
abys	prefix *a*
babys	reduplicate least sonorous segment
ababys	prefix *a*

Non-third-person independent pronouns are quite different. First, they do not vary according to gender; each has a single constant form. Second, this form is quite different from the pattern just described. There is no reduplication; instead we find the suffix *-ak* attached to a morph that otherwise appears as a subject marker on the verb. If we assume that gender is carried only by nouns in Arapesh, then non-third-person pronouns, which do not dominate nouns, will simply not participate in the gender system of the language. Similarly with verb agreement.[6] I will assume that third-person pronouns in this language are actually determiners of phonologically null nouns, so that they do show gender.

4.1.4   Object pronouns

Nonintensive pronominal objects appear as affixes.[7] The distribution of these affixes is somewhat complex. Depending on the class of the verb, they are either prefixes or suffixes.[8] If they are suffixes, then third-person forms resemble the gender alternations, except that they are preceded by a vowel, usually *a*. If they are prefixes, then they are followed by *a* but are otherwise largely identical to the suffixes. The forms of the third-person object pronouns are given in tables 4.6 and 4.7. As predicted, they show forms for the thirteen genders.

4.1.5   Demonstrative prowords

There are three types of demonstratives, translatable roughly as 'this', 'that near you', and 'that over there'. These also show distinct forms for the thirteen genders in both singular and plural. I will not list the forms here, since they are not crucial to my discussion. Demonstratives will be brought up again in connection with first- and second-person pronouns, where they have especially interesting properties.

4.1.6   Possessive prowords

Possession is indicated by means of the morph *i*, to which is added a suffix that corresponds to the gender and number of the head (possessed) noun, just as in the Romance languages, for example. Fortune lists examples for every gender, but I will give only a few, listed in table 4.8. The interrogative possessive works in the same way, although Fortune gives only two examples, which I repeat here:

(1) amwiet ulypat
    whose house

(2) amwień batauiń
    whose   child

All of the foregoing phenomena demonstrate that gender agreement is endemic in this language. To quote Foley's conclusion about a similar system in Yimas, "[It] is all pervasive, and much of the grammar revolves around the presence of such an elaborate system" (1986, 88). But a review of the agreement system shows that it is restricted to the thirteen genders; the inflectional classes are never mentioned, as predicted by strict separation of syntactic gender and morphological inflectional classes.

Table 4.6
Arapesh object pronoun prefixes

Gender	Singular prefix	Plural prefix
i	ba-	bysa-
ii	børa-	røba-
iii	ga-	gasa-
iv	kwa-	wa-
v	ma-	pa-
vi	na-	ba-
vii	na-	ma-
viii	ña-	ša-
ix	pa-	sa-
x	ra-	guha-
xi	ta-	gwa-
xii	wha-	ruha-
xiii	ha-	he-

Table 4.7
Arapesh object pronoun suffixes

Gender	Singular suffix	Plural suffix
i	-ab	-abys
ii	-bør	-røb
iii	-ag	-agas
iv	-okų	-ou
v	-am	-eipį
vi	-an	-ab
vii	-an	-um
viii	-eiñ	-eiš
ix	-ap	-as
x	-ar	-aguh
xi	-at	-agų
xii	-oųḫ	-aruh
xiii	-ah	-eh

Table 4.8
Selected Arapesh possessive prowords

Gender	Possessive singular	Possessive plurval
i	ib	ibys
iii	ig	igas
iv	iku	iu
vi	in	ib
vii	in	im
viii	iñ	iš

4.1.7 Default agreement

The most dramatic demonstration of the separation between gender and inflectional class comes from a phenomenon that I will call *default agreement*, which is important enough in the language that Fortune calls special attention to it in several places.

Default agreement is quite simple in concept: when an element bears an agreement marker and the gender of that marker cannot be determined for whatever reason, the marker always has the form that it would have if the head noun that determines its agreement were a member of gender viii, which I therefore call the *default gender*.[9] I will show that this default "agreement" arises syntactically in several distinct ways. In the first type of example, when an element must bear a gender marker but the proper gender of that marker cannot be determined because the head noun from which that gender would normally be determined is null, then the default gender marker is used. In the second type of example, there is a gender clash between coordinated nouns, so that the gender of the entire coordinate NP cannot be determined by normal means from the head (there presumably being none). Here again we find gender viii agreement. In this case, though, the reason for the failure is conflict rather than lack of information. In the third type of example, if a noun does not fit into one of the thirteen genders (for any reason), then it is placed in the default gender viii. Finally, default gender sometimes arises through complete absence of syntactic agreement, when the head is genderless because it is first or second person. All of these cases are covered by a fairly straightforward analysis in which members of certain lexical categories (nouns, adjectives, verbs, and prowords) obligatorily bear gender features. Normally, all of these elements, except for nouns, will receive a gender feature by agreement or feature passing from a head noun. However, in cases such as those just surveyed, there is no head noun, with the result that the

Table 4.9
Arapesh demonstrative prowords of (default) gender viii

Singular	Plural	Gloss
eñuda'	ešuda'	'pro-near-me'
neñuda'	nešuda'	'pro-near-you'
ñeiñuda'	šeišuda'	'pro-over-there'

agreeing elements do not receive a gender feature. They are therefore provided with the default gender viii. Examples of default agreement follow.

Headless noun phrases   Let us begin with the unknown, cases of null heads. As noted above, there are three sets of demonstrative prowords, translated roughly as 'this', 'that near you', and 'that over there'. As also noted, the demonstrative is like other prowords in agreeing in gender and number with its antecedent or head. However, if the demonstrative has no readily identifiable antecedent or has a null head, the form of the default gender viii is used, as shown in table 4.9. The solution is clear: since no gender feature is provided by matching the antecedent or head, the default gender is invoked.[10] Number is provided by context. Gender viii singular or plural is subsequently spelled out on the determiner by the morphology.

Interrogative prowords are similar. The proword for 'what/which' is *mal* (subject) or *man* (object). When the head noun or antecedent is given, the suffix appropriate to the gender of this noun will follow the proword. But if it is not given, the suffix *eš* is found, which is the gender viii plural suffix. Fortune cites the following example:

(3) neña   nene' man-eš
     you.sg do   what-viii.pl
     'What do you do?'

The gender will be assigned by the mechanism just described. In order to get the plural suffix, I will assume that the null interrogative head is inherently plural.[11]

The form for 'who/which person' is *amwi*. To judge from Fortune's two example sentences, when this form is used as a subject and the gender of the antecedent is unknown, the gender marker *ña*, which is the default gender viii marker, appears as the subject agreement marker on the verb, as in the following example from Fortune:

(4) amwi-ña di   ep
    who-viii plucked them.v
    'Who plucked them?'

This instance of gender viii is especially interesting, since the word for
'who' is animate in meaning (contrasting with the word for 'what', discussed in the last paragraph). As I will show below, all animate nouns fall
into two genders, masculine and feminine, and so we might expect one or
the other of these genders to show up in the case of the animate interrogative pronoun. The fact that neither one does attests to the robust character
of the default system.[12]

Conjoined noun phrases   In any language with gender, problems will arise
when two or more nouns of distinct gender are conjoined in a single NP
(Corbett 1991). What is the gender of the entire NP? Sometimes there is a
dominant (or unmarked) gender. In most Indo-European languages, the
dominant gender in conjoined NPs is masculine. Often, though, even in
languages with a dominant gender, the verb will agree with the nearest
member of the conjunction by a sort of attraction. In many languages
there is a great deal of variance, almost as if the grammar could not decide
in these cases.

In Arapesh, the pattern of agreement with conjoined NPs is clearcut:
whenever the conjoined members of an NP disagree in gender, the NP as
a whole is given default gender viii. This fact follows directly from the
general proposal that any gender slot not filled by normal mechanisms is
filled with the default gender. Fortune is very clear on this point, and I will
therefore quote him in full:

Noun class viii presents an interesting phenomenon linguistically. The plural, intensive, pronominal form, *ešeš*, is used as a blanket plural form. Thus the plural,
intensive pronominal form of *aramagoụ*, women, is *awau*; of *nubagụ*, dogs, is
agwagụ, of *juhurøbys*, eggs, is *ababys*. But the plural intensive pronominal form
for a mixed reference to women, dogs, and eggs as a compound subject is *ešeš*.
Similarly cockatoos and fowls as a compound subject would be referred to as *ešeš*,
where cockatoos alone would be referred to as *aharuh* and fowls alone as *agwagụ*.
Men and women are referred to pronominally as *amum* and *awau* respectively,
but a mixed company as *ešeš*. The plural pronoun of Class VIII thus refers either
to a plural noun of Class VIII, or to a plural made up by reference to two or more
singulars of disparate noun classes, or to two or more singulars or plurals of
disparate noun classes.

Similarly subclasses of nouns that do not follow the formal rules governing the
classes are assimilated to the *ñ-š* class for syntactical reference. The *ñ-š* class exists

in its own right, and is extended to cover formal discrepancies to the rules of the noun classes, and also to cover exigencies in meaning such as compound plurals made up from disparate noun classes. (1942, 30–31)

Default gender assignment in nouns   Default agreement is different from default gender assignment, which Fortune hints at in the last paragraph above and which I will now discuss. With default gender assignment, the noun itself shows the default gender, rather than an agreeing element. Nonetheless, default gender assignment is syntactic, inasmuch as the gender assigned is a syntactic element and there is no reason to assume that the assignment of the gender viii feature to these nouns takes place anywhere but in the syntax. Furthermore, the general syntactic mechanism that I have assumed for default gender, which assigns the default gender feature to all unfilled gender slots in agreeing elements, will also automatically fill such slots in nouns if they happen not to have a gender. Of course, spelling out the feature is done morphologically, but that will always be true.

There are several types of default-gender-bearing nouns. All are exceptions to the general pattern of gender, which is that the gender and inflectional class of a noun are functions of its final segments, as shown in table 4.1. Furthermore, all these exceptions may be analyzed as instances of rule failure—failure of the rule that assigns gender to nouns on the basis of their final segments—with the result in all cases that a noun enters the syntax without a gender. The grammar then fills the empty slot with the default gender viii feature.

The simplest type of exception is the noun whose final segments lie outside the system. For example, Fortune notes that only two nouns in the language end in *b*. They are *kwagesab* 'croton' and *mib* 'thigh'. Similarly, only *bobok* 'ogre' and *ñibiok* 'sacred flute' end in *k*. These nouns are syntactically placed in gender viii. They also fall into the default inflectional class, a fact that I will take up later. If we assume that gender is normally a function of inflectional class and that inflectional class is normally a function of phonological form, a point that I will also elaborate on later, then since their aberrant phonological forms assign these nouns to no inflectional class, they will receive no gender by rule, and the default gender will automatically be invoked by the general principle that I have established.

A second type of exception consists of nouns that conform to a normal class morphologically but that exceptionally do not have the gender generally associated with that inflectional class. For example, nouns ending in *g* form their plurals in *as*. They make up Fortune's gender iii syntactically and inflection class 3 morphologically. There are, however, four nouns that fit the inflectional class exactly but have default gender viii instead of gender iii. Similarly, the noun *diliat* 'side post that supports eaves of a house', pl. *diliatogu*, is a perfectly well-behaved member of inflectional class 11 morphologically but has default gender. We may analyze these items as lexically marked exceptions to the general rule that maps inflectional class onto gender. They thus belong to an inflectional class, but do not undergo the rule that maps inflectional class to gender. If this last rule does not operate, they will not receive any gender, and so their gender value will be filled by the default gender.

Still another type of exception has the appropriate singular form of a given inflectional class but, for mysterious reasons, does not have the corresponding plural form. In my terms, it is an exception to the rule that assigns nouns to inflectional classes on the basis of their terminal segments. Because it thus has no inflectional class, such a noun will receive no gender by the general rule and will therefore receive default gender. Two examples are *lim* 'roller for launching a canoe' and *sam* 'taro and coconut croquettes', which should belong to inflectional class 5 on the basis of their form but do not have a plural of inflectional class 5 and have default gender. Other examples that Fortune gives end in *n* (class 6) and *r* (class 10).

A final type of morphological exception is a group of nouns ending in *gør*. Nouns ending in *r* normally belong to inflectional class 10 and have a plural ending in *guḥ*, except for nouns ending in *bør*, which belong to class 2. But nouns ending in *gør* have a plural in *gu* (which we may analyze as formed by subtraction of the final *r*, with subsequent automatic phonological adjustment of the vowel). I will assume that these nouns form a well-defined inflectional class, which seems reasonable, since they share a plural form that belongs to no other inflectional class and are otherwise analogous to class 2. Let me call this inflectional class 14. What is exceptional about this class within my framework is that it is purely morphological and has no corresponding gender, as the other inflectional classes do. All its members will thus receive the default gender.

One set of words may be analyzed as receiving default gender for semantic rather than morphological reasons; this is the set of sex-neutral terms for persons. Two genders in the language have nonphonological correlates. These are gender iv, which contains most of the nouns that designate female persons, and gender vii, which contains all and only the nouns that designate males persons and the exclusively male roles of warfare and male initiation ceremonies. Words that designate persons in a sex-neutral fashion cannot belong to either of these genders. They are therefore given the default gender viii. Words of this sort include *arapeñ* 'friend', *ašukeñ* 'elder sibling', and *batauiñ* 'child'.

In conclusion, I have shown in this section that there are various types of exceptional nouns, all of which are given the same treatment with respect to gender: they receive default gender because, for any one of a number of morphologically or semantically well-defined reasons, the mechanisms that normally assign gender to nouns fail to operate. The main point is that, whatever the reason, the syntactic result is the same. Gender, which is syntactic, is thus insulated from the lexical and morphological vagaries of these exceptional cases.

4.1.8 Genderless persons

A slightly different case comes from the first and second persons, which lie completely outside the noun and gender system, so I have called them *genderless*. They differ from the nouns just discussed, which do not receive gender by normal means but, being nouns, must have gender in the syntax and are therefore supplied with default gender, which then passes on the agreeing elements. The genderless status of the first and second persons reveals itself first in the fact that the first- and second-person pronouns, unlike the third, do not have as many forms as there are genders; more strikingly, verbs with first- and second-person subjects do not distinguish gender but agree instead in person. However, gender does interact with these genderless persons in one instance: there are separate demonstrative forms for the first- and second-person pronouns, and these consist of the normal pronoun followed by a gender viii demonstrative.

The demonstrative obligatorily bears a gender marker, as we have already seen in table 4.9. However, if the first and second persons do not belong to the gender system, then they have no gender to assign to their modifying demonstratives in this construction. The default gender is therefore invoked on the demonstrative, as it is when the antecedent is unknown. Table 4.10 shows the normal intensive first- and second-person pronouns and their demonstrative counterparts, which consist of this same pronoun followed by a gender viii demonstrative. The approach to the distribution of the default gender that I have already taken will have gender viii fill any slots for unspecified gender features. The gender slot must belong only to the demonstrative and not to the entire NP. This must be so for two reasons. First, the NP must echo the genderless status of its first- or second-person head, inasmuch as the agreeing verb shows

Table 4.10
Arapesh first- and second-person demonstratives

Category	Intensive pronoun	Demonstrative	Gloss
1 sg.	eik	eñuda'	'I here'
1 du.	awhok	eñuda'	'we two here'
1 pl.	apak	eñuda'	'we here'
2 sg.	ñak	eñuda'	'thou here'
2 sg.	ñak	neñuda'	'thou there'
2 pl.	ipak	eñuda'	'you here'
2 pl.	ipak	neñuda'	'you there'

person instead of gender. Second, it is clear from the table (and Fortune explicitly remarks) that the demonstrative *in this construction alone* appears "in singular form only, whether used with 1st or 2nd person pronoun in the singular or in the plural, indifferently" (1942, 49). In the cases where there is a phonologically null head, discussed above and exemplified in table 4.9, we find both singular and plural forms of the demonstrative. Why? The answer is that in the cases exemplified in table 4.9, the phonologically null head, although unspecified for gender, may be either singular or plural, so that the entire NP will in turn be made either singular or plural by feature passing. The specification for singular or plural, together with the default gender viii feature on the phonologically null head, will then pass on to the rest of the members of the NP, which gives the forms in table 4.9. The forms in table 4.10, by contrast, do not have a null head unspecified for gender, as in table 4.9, but rather have a head specified as being outside the gender system. As a result, the NP as a whole has no gender, rather than the default gender, and no syntactic number either (syntactic number being inextricably bound up with the gender system).[13] There is thus no way for the demonstratives in table 4.10 to acquire gender and number from the heads of their NPs. But the demonstrative must, by its very nature, have its gender slot filled. The result is that it is supplied with both the default gender and number: gender viii singular. We thus see that the syntactic distribution of default gender, which is complex and interesting, can always be insulated from its morphological spelling out and from other morphological vagaries. Overall, this is because the distribution of gender in Arapesh, as in all languages, is syntactic rather than morphological.

4.2   Inflectional Classes by Themselves

So far we have not looked in any detail at inflectional classes. I will
remedy this oversight now. First, I will look again at the distinction between gender and inflectional class, but this time from the opposite van-
tage point. Then I will look at the relation between inflectional class and
phonological form.

4.2.1   Inflectional class versus gender

According to my general framework, inflectional class and gender, belonging as they do to distinct levels, must be distinct.[14] But this is a
theoretical claim that must be substantiated empirically. One simple empirical reason for distinguishing inflectional class and gender in Arapesh
is the fact, already noted in section 4.1, that there is sometimes a one-to-
many mapping from gender to inflectional class. As Fortune himself says
of gender iv, "The linked plural end-forms are several, and each may be
considered as forming a subclass. These sub-classes are, however, not of
any separate syntactical significance" (1942, 17) In other words, a single
gender may map onto more than one inflectional class.

Some of Fortune's inflectional classes are reducible by phonological
means. For example, Fortune says that gender vi has two subclasses,
those in which a final *n* changes to *b*, and those in which *ab* is suffixed.
Contrast *narun* 'wave', pl. *narøb*, with *uman* 'a fruit', pl. *umanab*. But all
of the items in the first subclass have *u* before the final *n*, while none of
those in the second subclass do. We may therefore assume that the plural
in both subclasses is the suffix *b*. A phonological rule will delete *n* in the
context *u____b* (and then *u* will go to *ø* by another phonological rule).
Elsewhere, an epenthetic *a* is inserted between *n* and *b* (*a* apparently being
the default epenthetic vowel in the language, to judge from other data). I
thus reduce the inflectional classes corresponding to gender vi to a single
one.

But this reduction is not always possible. In gender iv, the plural
morphs *meb*, *u*, and *hijer* of the different inflectional classes are not relat-
able by any plausible phonological means. We must therefore set up
several inflectional classes, at least one for each of these three morphs.
Nonetheless, all fall together in gender iv (as evidenced by agreement facts).

It is important to note that we find only one-to-one mappings from
inflectional class to gender (if we discount simple exceptions, which I will
discuss shortly). Each inflectional class maps onto a single gender (which
is not true in the other languages that we have looked at). We can thus

predict gender from inflectional class in Arapesh by positing implicational rules going from inflectional class to gender, some of which converge on a single gender (as in gender iv). This predictability runs counter to common ideology, but no more so than positing rules that assign nouns to inflectional classes on the basis of their final segments, which also seems correct for most (though clearly not all) nouns in the language. I will therefore adopt a doubly inverted system in which not only is the gender of a noun determined from its inflectional class by an implicational gender-assigning rule (as I argued should be done for Russian class 3 nouns) but also the inflectional class of a noun is determined by an implicational inflectional-class-assigning rule on the basis of its phonological form (which I will discuss in more detail in section 2.3). The only major anomalies for such a system are the sex-based genders, to which I will also return below. In any case, it is clear that gender and inflectional class are not isomorphic.

Further evidence of the lack of isomorphism is the fact, noted in my discussion of default gender, that not all nouns follow the general implicational patterns from inflectional class to gender. The most interesting exception to these rules is the class of nouns ending in *gør*, which form their plurals in *gu*, and which I have analyzed as comprising the new inflectional class 14. According to this analysis, these nouns fall into gender viii, but not because a rule assigns gender viii to inflectional class 14. Instead, there is no gender-assigning rule for inflectional class 14, and so its members receive gender viii by default rather than by rule.

Another type of exception that I have mentioned comprises nouns, like *diliat*, that belong to an inflectional class but do not have their gender normally assigned by that class. They will thus be lexical exceptions to the implicational gender-assigning rule system. There are also words that must be analyzed as not belonging to any inflectional class. These will be asgned to the default inflectional class, which I will now discuss.

4.2.2 Default inflectional class

Just as there is a default gender, so too there is a default inflectional class. If gender and inflectional class are distinct, then so too should their defaults be. This is indeed true: there are nouns that belong to one but not to the other. The diagnostic for membership in the default inflectional class, class 8b, is the plural marker *ehas*. The most obvious members of this class are those nouns whose terminal segments do not fit any of the normal inflectional classes. These are at least those ending in *k*, *b*, and *s*, all of which form their plurals in *ehas*. Examples include *mib* pl. *mibehas* 'thigh' and *bokok* pl. *bokokehas* 'cannibalistic ogre'. Fortune mentions only one word whose singular ends in *s* (*pas* pl. *pasehas* 'taro pounder'). He points out that *s* is a common plural morph, so that final *s* is not phonologically unusual in the language. This would seem to strengthen my point that these words are exceptions to the morphology, although most of them are also phonologically odd.[15] The analysis of these items is clear. Since their singular forms do not fall under the scope of any inflectional-class-assigning rules, they cannot be assigned membership in any inflectional class, and so they will automatically fall into the default class if every noun must bear an inflectional-class feature.

Other items fall into the default class because they are genuine exceptions to inflectional-class-assigning rules. I mentioned above the exceptional gender of words like *lim* 'roller for launching a canoe' which should belong to gender v on the basis of its final segment but instead receives the default gender. Not noted was the fact that exceptions of this sort also have the plural marker *ehas* (*limehas*, etc.) rather than their expected plural form. Both of these facts (default gender and default plural) follow from the exceptionality of these items to inflectional-class rules. If they are exceptions to the inflectional-class-assigning rules, then they will not only automatically fall into the default inflectional class but will also automatically have no gender (gender being assigned on the basis of inflectional class) and so will receive the default gender. The aberrant items discussed in the last paragraph will also receive the default gender because their forms do not confer any inflectional class on them.[16]

Default gender, though, is not always dependent on default inflectional class. I noted above that items like *diliat* 'side post' are morphologically normal but exceptional with respect to gender only. Similarly, class 14 nouns, which end in *gør*, have default gender but do not show default inflection. There are also a few morphologically odd items that do not receive default inflection. For example, Fortune lists five words ending in *n* that should belong to gender vi and should be members of inflectional class 6, since they have their plurals in *b* (*waiaun* pl. *waiaub* 'modern beads' is a regular case). Instead, these show the inflectional class 1 plural *bys*: *gun* pl. *gunabys* 'sago pounder of stone'. They also have default gender. These are very peculiar items, and it is intuitively understandable that they should have default gender, although providing them with default gender is tricky.[17] Regardless of the formal problem, though, they still show default gender and no default morphology.

I have found no examples of default plural forms without default gender, although one can easily imagine such words, a priori. They would have the gender normally predicted on the basis of their singular form, but their plural form would show the default suffix *ehas*. Instead, the *ehas* plural always goes hand in hand with the default gender. This gap follows straightforwardly from the claim that gender is based on inflectional class rather than directly on the singular form, even though inflectional class is itself usually based on the singular form.[18] The argument is simple: if form directly determined gender, independently of inflectional class, we would expect to have nouns whose gender corresponded to their form, even though they were exceptions to the independent inflectional-class-assignment rules. This is precisely the sort of nouns that we do not find. Let us now take a closer look at the relation between form and inflectional class.

4.2.3 Inflectional class and phonological form

What determines the membership of a noun in its inflectional class? I have already argued at length that it is not gender, for a variety of reasons. It is also clear that it is generally not lexical semantics, a topic to which I will return. The most obvious candidate is phonological form. As I have already noted, Foley says quite directly, "In these languages, the assignment of the bulk of noun-stems to their corresponding class is on the basis of their phonological stem" (1986, 85). Fortune himself says, "The noun falls into classes marked by coupled conventional endings for singular and for plural, respectively" (1942, 6) and "The noun class terminals are, as far as the usage of the noun is concerned, an integral part of the root form of the noun" (1942, 9).

I will attempt to provide a more explicit version of Fortune's analysis within the framework developed here, one that differentiates among phonological form, inflectional class, and gender. The core of this analysis is the idea that the singular form of a noun is morphologically unanalyzable and determines its inflectional class directly. The plural form and gender of a noun are determined in turn by its inflectional class. Consider nouns ending in *by*. These are of inflectional class 1. We may therefore write a set of rules as follows:

(5) a. N, $X$by → class 1
    b. class 1 → gender i
    c. $\langle$[N, class 1, Plural], $(X \rightarrow X$s$)\rangle$

An agreeing element that acquires gender i by agreement, feature passing, or percolation will in turn be assigned to class 1 by the inverse of (5b), which is given in (6), below. This feature-filling rule will operate only on words that have a gender but do not have a inflectional class.[19]

(6) gender i → class 1

Realization pairs similar to the inverse of (5a) will spell out the appropriate phonological forms for the inflected singulars of agreeing elements. I say "similar" because, as I noted in section 4.1, in addition to the fact that there are many more inflectional classes of nouns than there are of agreeing elements, there are also sometimes differences between the endings of the singular nouns that determine their class (and gender) and the corresponding endings on singular agreeing elements, as well as differences among the classes of agreeing elements. Realization pairs similar to (5c) will operate on the plurals of agreeing elements.

Other nouns will undergo similar rules for inflectional class and gender: the form of the (singular) noun will determine its class, which will in turn determine its plural form and gender. For some inflectional classes, the rule for the form of the plural will be not simply additive but rather replacive. For example, class 5 in the singular ends in -*m* and the plural ending is -*ipį*, without the *m* (*warum* pl. *waripį* 'sprouting coconut'[20]). The realization pair for the plural will therefore be as follows:

(7) ⟨[N, class 5, Plural], (*X*m → *X*ipį)⟩

The realization-rule half of this pair expresses Fortune's claim that the singular-noun terminals are an integral part of the root of the noun. A more conservative treatment of these classes would instead have it that inflectional classes are characterized by a singular and plural suffix pair. The "real" noun stem would therefore consist of the forms containing these suffixes minus the suffixes (*war* in the example at hand). The problem with this treatment is that after morphological segmentation, these classes with paired singular and plural endings have no phonological or other property of the extracted stems that is predictive of inflectional class or of anything else: the stem of the example will be *war-*, but other stems of this same class will be *but-*, *jaha-*, *uluku-*, and *šubarie-*, to name only a few. Under this analysis, all the members of this class and other similar classes will have to be assigned lexically to the class that they belong to because they have no defining characteristics. The remaining classes must have no singular suffix under any treatment, since their plural is formed by suffixing or infixing on the singular and not by adding a different suffix. Thus the default class 8b has the plural marker *ehas* suffixed to the singular (*pas* pl. *pasehas* 'taro pounder'), while class 12 has an infixed plural marker *r* (*aroy̨ḩ* pl. *araruh* 'sugar cane'). For these latter classes a phonological definition is always correct, since the final segments of the stem do in fact provide necessary conditions for predicting which plural suffix will be added to a given noun and no other factors have any predictive value.[21] The conservative analysis thus has us posit phonological predictors of inflectional class but just in case the segmentation procedure results in a zero singular suffix for a given noun stem. The remaining nouns, those that have singular suffixes in this treatment, must all be lexically assigned to their inflectional classes, which in turn are realized through suffixes for both singular and plural. Allowing replacive rules along the lines of (7) permits us to define these singular "suffixed" classes phonologically in the same way that the singular "unsuffixed" classes are defined, in terms of the final segments of the singular form of the noun, inasmuch as the particular replaced segments of the singular serve as the signal of the inflectional class of a noun. It also means that we have inflectional classes whose members are assigned arbitrarily only where the singular members of two or more classes have the same terminal segments. I will therefore permit replacive rules like (7) where appropriate, which is in about half of the classes. Note that the analysis also depends on the assumption that the singular form of a noun bears no inflectional marker and is therefore equal to the noun stem. On this analysis, Arapesh is like English in having no singular marker, while the plural of a noun will be morphologically complex, just as in English. The various noun plurals are produced by realization rules that vary with the inflectional class of the stem of the base, as is true in most languages. What makes Arapesh distinct is that these Arapesh inflectional classes are (for the most part) determined phonologically.

Earlier in this work, I introduced the definition of an inflectional class in terms of realization rules (a lexeme is a member of a given class if it undergoes the realization rules that define that class). This definition fits this analysis of Arapesh very nicely: a given noun belongs to a given inflectional class just in case it undergoes the realization rule that defines the class. In Arapesh, membership in a given class will be assigned phonologically in most cases, which makes this language and its neighbors so distinctive, but otherwise the inflectional classes of the language are quite normal.

A problematic case   We may now look at a case that is problematic within the picture I have drawn, according to which inflectional class is determined phonologically and gender in turn is determined implicationally from inflectional class. The inflectional classes that map onto gender iv are troubling. These all end in *ky* but show various plurals, some with and some without *ky*. Because all share the same domain phonologically, we must mark all members individually for each class, no matter what our theory. More troubling is the fact that all *ky* classes are assigned to the same gender. On the analysis that I have adopted, whereby Arapesh gender is a function of inflectional class and not directly of phonological form, this is accidental. An analysis that reads gender directly off of phonological form, independently of inflectional class, would predict the gender unity of all *ky* classes, which is what we find. Further support for a purely form-based view of gender iv comes from three morphologically irregular members of this gender, listed in table 11. Fortune (1942, 19) singles out these three nouns as being irregular, because they show this peculiar plural termination.[22] Nonetheless, their syntax shows that they belong to gender iv, a fact predicted by a phonological account of this gender.

On the other hand, a pure phonological account of *all* genders predicts a type of exception that we do not find (see section 4.2.2 above). Also, a phonological account cannot be extended to all genders, because it fails to accommodate the difference between gender-class vi/6 and gender-class vii/7. These two gender-classes both end in *n* in the singular. Which gender-class a given noun belongs to can be determined by the fact that gender-class vii/7 can be defined conceptually as denoting male persons (as discussed in section 4.3 below). A direct phonological definition of all genders cannot distinguish the two. In addition, the direct phonological definition of gender would not rid us of inflectional classes, because we must posit a set of six inflectional classes precisely for those nouns whose gender does seem to be determined phonologically, under any analysis. I will therefore posit a direct mapping from form to gender for *ky* nouns alone. To do so is to admit that the mapping among phonological form, inflectional class, and gender is not uniform for the language, but this is no great admission, since it is also clear that gender iv differs from most

Table 4.11
Irregular gender iv Arapesh nouns

Singular	Plural	Gloss
babweky	babwekomi	'grandmother'
jameky	jamekomi	'mother'
amakeky	amakekomi	'mother's sister'

of the other genders in the language and is more normal in having an exceptionless conceptual correlate in addition to the phonological correlate that is usual in Arapesh. I will now turn to this conceptual issue and its relation to morphology.

4.3 Sex, Gender, and Inflectional Class

Fortune is very explicit in pointing out that what he calls the noun classes and what I am calling genders and inflectional classes are for the most part free of any conceptual basis. I quote Fortune in full:

The wide question of the noun classes in relation to meaning can best be answered after an examination of the actual membership of the noun classes. Only one definite rule appears. The noun class which has singular termination *n* and plural termination *m* implies masculine gender, although masculine gender is not rigidly confined to that noun class. Feminine gender is contrasted by inclusion in the noun class that has singular termination *kų* and various plural terminations, although singular termination *kų* does not imply feminine gender. The completeness of the *n-m* class in non-admission of non-masculines secures a possibility of feminine contrast in the *kų*-various plural terminations class, without that class being exclusively or even predominantly feminine.

The system of noun classes is not a division of meaningful objects on any recognized principle of meaning, or of the form of things meant. Sex is indicated in two classes, but does not absorb them, and is sometimes indicated outside them. Similarly, but on a lesser scale, fruit and leaf are indicated in two separate classes, but do not absorb them, and are sometimes indicated outside them. (1942, 11)

Fortune makes it quite clear that two genders do have at least partial conceptual bases; these are genders iv and vii, which are both sex-related. Gender vii is simpler, so I will discuss it first. This gender comprises terms for "persons of the male sex." Fortune also says that it covers terms used in warfare and mens' initiation ceremonies, but the examples he gives of these categories are terms for roles of male persons in these activities (e.g., terms for 'enemy' and 'leader in initiation ceremonies') and so are in fact covered by the first category if we broaden the definition to include roles of persons of the male sex.[23] This broadening will also cover male kinship terms, which are roles or relations. Thus modified, the definition also covers all and only members of the masculine gender, so that we may predict membership in this one gender solely on conceptual grounds. Fortune claims that "masculine gender is not rigidly confined to that noun class" (1942, 25), but I have been unable to find any terms for male *persons* and their roles that lie outside gender vii, so I will assume, contrary to Fortune, that sex does "absorb" this one gender.

Gender iv is different in that it includes but is not restricted to female persons and roles of female persons. Fortune demonstrates this fact in great detail, pointing out that "the class itself has more members with no such [female] implication, than with it" (1942, 20) We may thus say that terms for female persons belong to gender iv but that female personhood is not a necessary condition for membership in this gender, as male personhood is for gender vii. Furthermore, although gender iv corresponds to many inflectional classes, none of these is restricted to terms for women, as Fortune also explicitly shows. In other words, the various *ku̧* inflectional classes are all purely based on sound, as are all other inflectional classes but the male inflectional class 7. Inflectional class 7 and gender vii thus stand alone in being completely conceptually based.

We are now in a position to understand the exceptionality of gender vii and its correlated inflectional class. Here alone is a gender that is not eventually rooted in phonology. We should therefore be not surprised but instead pleased that the account given for the rest of the genders and inflectional classes doesn't work here. It shouldn't. The gender is exceptional, and this is reflected in my account of it. For this gender alone, it seems reasonable to assume that the conceptual system drives the morphology and the syntax quite directly. I will therefore adopt the following rules:

(8) a. 'male person or role' → Male (gender)

    b. $\langle$[Male, Singular], $(X \to X\text{n})\rangle$

    c. $\langle$[Male, Plural], $(X \to X\text{m})\rangle$

For female persons, by contrast, we may posit a derivational suffix *-ku̧*. This suffix will then be part of the stem of nouns denoting females and, as part of the stem, will act like other instances of the phonological sequence *ku̧*.

4.4 Word Formation

Fortune tries to demonstrate that certain terms are morphologically complex. Oddly, though, we see in these forms another phenomenon, which Fortune calls *intervocalic change*, and to which he devotes a section of the grammar.

Fortune notes that in many words there are "intervocalic changes between singular and plural forms, in addition to the regular terminal changes of the noun classes" and that "the lines of such changes are the same as the lines of the terminal changes" (1942, 39). For example, corresponding to singular *mañin* 'pigeon' we find the plural form *mašøb*. The entire word belongs to inflectional class 6 and gender vi, but it also shows the intervocalic alternation of *ñ/š* of inflectional class 8a. Fortune provides a table listing some fifty examples of such intervocalic changes.

The obvious question, which Fortune asks, is whether these changes are "a residue of the results of word building" (1942, 41). Among Fortune's fifty examples, there are unfortunately very few whose putative components can be recovered. The clearest cases are derived members of the conceptually based gender vii. For example, consider the term *aramatokwin* pl. *aramagowem* 'male woman' or 'effeminate man'. These forms clearly consist of the singular and plural forms for 'woman', *aramatokų* and *aramagou*, followed by the characteristic male terminations (*i*)*n* and (*e*)*m*. Similar is *arapeñin* pl. *arapešim* 'male friend'.

More often, the first component is recognizable, but not the last. For example, the terms for male and female infants are *aramaniñ* pl. *aramumwiš* and *aramatokwiñ* pl. *aramagoweš*. We can easily see that the first components are the terms for 'man' and 'woman', but the final component, although found in the term for infant or child (*batauiñ* pl. *batauiš*), is not identical to that term.

Also, even if these words are morphologically complex, they are very peculiar. Normally, in all languages, only the head of a complex word undergoes further morphology: *doglovers* pl. **dogslovers*. This fact follows from the basic mathematics of function composition (Raffelsiefen 1992). Counterexamples are rare.[24] In Arapesh, by contrast, pluralization of both the first and second components is the norm in the plurals of these words. The only examples that I have been able to find of the normal pattern are the words *batauišin* 'male child' and *batauišikų* 'female child', whose plurals are *batauišim* and *batauišijer*. But even here we find the internal plural *batauiš* throughout, rather than the expected singular *batauiñ*.

Let us assume, on the basis of the morphological evidence, that these words are the result of word formation. Whether this is compounding or derivation is not easily discernible. It may be that there is a 'male person' suffix *in* pl. *im* and a 'female person' suffix *ikų* pl. *ijer*. Either way, as long as we assume some sort of morphological complexity, we see an interesting difference between inflection and gender, as follows.

In terms of gender, the normal prediction about feature passing holds: the derived or compound noun as a whole always retains the gender of the rightmost (and presumably head) element. This fact is clear from agreement, as Fortune shows. There is thus a difference between inflection (which goes on both elements) and gender (which is passed on only from one). Although I still have no understanding of why we find these peculiar morphological facts, the difference is at least consonant with the general position that I have adopted, which is that morphology and syntax, being distinct, should sometimes operate differently. We also expect any discrepancies from the patterns that a compositional structure predicts to appear in the morphology and not in the syntax, and this is indeed what we find.

4.5 Yimas

Foley emphasizes the fact that the Papuan languages, although genetically very diverse, have been in close contact over a period of millenia. This proximity has resulted in extensive convergence of a sort unknown to early comparatists but increasingly documented in other areas where distinct languages have remained in close contact over long periods, the best known of which are probably the Balkans (Joseph 1983) and South Asia (Masica 1976). As I noted at the outset of this chapter, the Torricelli and Lower Sepik families, though unrelated, share the peculiarity of having most nouns assigned to genders on the basis of phonology.[25] From our perspective, the differences between the two languages help to bring out several important points of general interest, and for that reason I now turn to Yimas. Foley (1991) provides a detailed description of Yimas morphology. This section is based entirely on this work and on a shorter description in Foley 1986.

4.5.1 Gender

The most striking difference between the two languages is the number of conceptually based genders in Yimas. Foley puts the number at four: for human males,[26] for human females, for higher animals,[27] and for plants. The human-male and higher-animal genders also differ from all Arapesh genders in having no phonological correlates at all. We thus find in Yimas the peaceful coexistence of two very different gender types: the conceptually and phonologically based. In my treatment of Arapesh genders iv and vii, both of which are at least in part sex-related, I noted that neither one could be dealt with in the same way as the other genders of the language, by mappings from phonology to inflectional class and from inflectional class to gender. The resulting nonmonolithic character of the genders is even more apparent for Yimas, in which almost half of the genders are conceptual (two of them with no relation of any sort to phonological form), and the remainder are phonologically based, in the manner of Arapesh. On a very general level, this sort of mixed-gender system is expected in a framework where gender is explicitly recognized as a syntactic phenomenon with no necessary basis in the categories of any other linguistic level: Yimas gender is perfectly normal in its diversity.

The relation between the conceptual and the phonological genders is also worthy of note. Phonological gender is the default choice, which means that any noun not assigned to a gender on conceptual grounds will have its gender assigned on the basis of its phonology, with the result that the phonological genders comprise nouns for lower animals and inanimate things, but only by accident, as it were, because these classes constitute a conceptual residue. Foley notes that a noun may sometimes vacillate between the higher-animal gender and its expected phonological gender, depending on the role of the animal in a particular discourse. He calls this phenomenon "elevation." From my point of view, *elevation* is precisely the correct term: unless a noun is elevated into the higher-animal gender, it will fall into the default phonological gender.

Among the conceptual genders, two, like the Arapesh male gender, have associated markers in the singular: the female suffix *maŋ* and the plant suffix *um*. The other two have no singular suffix. There are six or seven phonological genders, depending on the details of analysis. As in Arapesh, these are distinguished by their singular word-final segments (consonants or codas), as shown in table 4.12. As in my analysis of Arapesh, it appears that these finals are not suffixes but rather simply the final segments of the basic stems. There are therefore only two genders with suffixes in the singular: the female and plant genders. Evidence for this analysis comes from the dual and plural forms of female nouns and the plural form of plant nouns. In these forms alone, the singular gender

Table 4.12
Yimas phonological genders

Gender	Final segments of nouns
v	p, k, m, n, ŋ, nt, r, l, i, y, c
vi	ŋk
vii	mp
viii	i, y
ix	aw
x.a	uk
x.b	uŋk

suffix is lost and replaced by another. So the dual and plural of *macawk-maŋ* 'mother-in-law' are *macawk-mprum* and *macawk-mput*; the plural of *pawn-um* 'tree species' is *pawn-uŋi*. Foley describes this last type as being formed "by replacing *-um* with *-uŋi*." But if these two genders alone have singular suffixes, as I have claimed, then the seemingly replacive nature of the dual and plural suffixes for these genders alone becomes perfectly normal: with all other genders, there being no singular suffix or gender suffix, there will never be any seeming replacement; with these two, the apparent replacement is simply the plural or dual suffix instead of the singular. Yimas is therefore more normal than Arapesh in lacking true replacive suffixes.

Among the phonological genders, six are characterized by unique final segments or features. Thus gender viii is characterized by the phonetic feature Front, while gender vii is characterized by the segments *-mp*. Gender v is the default. Foley lists the following finals for it: *-p, -k, -m, -n, -ŋ, -nt, -r, -l, -i, -y, -c.*[28] Inspection reveals an overlap with gender xiii (which Foley says is the smallest and which he also describes as having lost ground to gender v) and with gender x, which is also very small. The members of genders xiii and x must therefore be listed.[29] The following rules characterize the assignment of nouns to the various phonologically based genders, all of which stand in a default relation to conceptual genders:[30]

- Certain nouns ending in *uŋ* belong to gender x.a.
- Certain nouns ending in *uk* belong to gender x.b.
- Certain nouns ending in a segment with the phonetic feature Front belong to gender viii.
- Nouns ending in a segment with the phonetic feature Round are assigned to gender ix.
- Nouns ending in *ŋk* are assigned to gender vi.
- Nouns ending in *mp* are assigned to gender vii.
- All other nouns are assigned to gender v.

The relations among these gender assignments are all governed by the elsewhere or proper-inclusion principle.

4.5.2 Agreement

As in Arapesh, the gender system in Yimas shows widespread agreement: with adjectives, possessives, numerals, deictics, and verbs. Foley is careful to point out that agreement is determined by the gender of a noun and not by its form. For example, although male-gender nouns show various allomorphs in the dual and plural, both lexically and phonologically determined, the corresponding agreement suffixes never vary with the form of the head noun. The same is true for agreement with all other genders: for any given morphosyntactic property array, there will always be one and only one realization rule for agreement with a given gender, although there may be alternative realizations for the same property array on a head noun.

The morphology of agreement markers has some notable peculiarities. First, as in Arapesh, there are both prefixes and suffixes, with adjectives taking suffixes and verbs taking prefixes. Also as in Arapesh, the verbal prefix can often be characterized as a metathesized CV version of the corresponding VC adjective suffix. But the verbal prefixes enjoy a somewhat peculiar distribution in all genders. They occur with the numerals for 'two' and 'three', while the adjective suffixes occur with the numerals for 'one' and 'four'. The verbal prefixes also show up with the proximal and far-distal deictic stems, while the adjective suffixes appear on the near-distal deictic stem.

4.5.3 Morphology

Yimas differs greatly from Arapesh in the degree of morphological syncretism that we find among the various genders. For example, in genders iv and vi through x, the dual suffix on both head nouns and agreeing elements is always -*l*. In genders iv, v, vii, viii, and x.a, the plural suffix on agreeing elements is -*ra* and the plural prefix on agreeing elements is *ya*-, although the plural suffix on head nouns is quite diverse.

Foley comments on the minimal differences among the affixation patterns of the major genders: i (male), ii (female), iii (higher animals), and v (elsewhere). I reproduce in table 4.13 the affixes of gender iii as an illustration. All are identical to either a gender i or a gender v equivalent. Next to each form, I have put a i or v in parentheses to indicate the nature of

Table 4.13
Yimas gender iii affixes and deictics

	Singular	Dual	Plural
Adjective affix	-n (i, v)	-ntrm (v)	-ump (i)
Possessive affix	-kn (i, v)	-ntrm (v)	-ump (i)
Verb affix	na- (i, v)	tma- (v)	pu- (i)
Proximal deictic	na-k (i, v)	tma-k (v)	pu-k (i)
Near-distal deictic	m-n (i, v)	m-rm (i, v)	m-ump (i)
Far-distal deictic	na-n (i, v)	tma-n (v)	pu-n (i)

the identity. It is easy to see that the singular affixes are shared among genders i, iii, and v, while the dual affixes of gender iii are identical to those of gender v and the plurals of genders iii and i are identical. I do not, however, want to deny that gender iii is morphologically distinct, even though it has no affixes of its own.[31] What is distinct is the particular combination of affixes by means of which this gender is realized, rather than any single affix.[32]

Gender and inflectional class in Yimas   This remark brings us to the question that dominated my discussion of Arapesh: what is the relation between gender and inflectional class in the language? Unlike Arapesh, Yimas presents no striking evidence of separating inflectional class from gender: there are no nouns that show clear discrepancies of the sort we found in Arapesh between an identifiable inflectional class and an identifiable gender. Nonetheless, we still see evidence of the distinction. The major clue is the diversity of dual and plural forms of nouns. In all other instances, which is to say when we are dealing with agreeing elements like adjectives, verbs, etc., only one affix is possible for any morphosyntactic property array in a given gender, as I noted above. But with nouns, whose gender and inflectional class are inherent, there is a fairly wide choice, especially among plural suffixes, and this choice cuts across gender.

Let us disregard suppletive plurals, which seem to be fairly common for highly familiar words, as predicted by Anshen and Aronoff (1988) and others. The noun plural marker varies in all of the nonphonological gen-

Table 4.14
Yimas noun plural suffixes

Gender	Form
i	-um, -i, -ŋkat, -ntt
ii	-um, -i, -mput, -ntt
iii	-i, -ŋkat
iv	-uɲi, -ŋkat
v	-ŋkat, -i, -ra, -t
vi	-ŋki
vii	-mpat, -i, -a
viii	-Cmpt, -i, -a
ix	-ut
x.a	-at
x.b	-uŋkwi

ders and in three of the phonological genders, including the default gender v. Table 4.14 contains a list of all the plural markers by gender.

I will analyze the distribution of these markers by gender. For gender i (male and unmarked human), Foley says that -*i* is conditioned phonologically, occurring after *p* and *k*. The other suffixes are distributed lexically.

For gender ii, those nouns with the singular suffix -*maŋ* that is characteristic of this gender will have the corresponding suffix -*mput*. Otherwise, the distribution of suffixes is the same as for i.

For gender iii, Foley lists two suffixes, of which one, -(*w*)*i*, is phonologically conditioned, occurring after *a*. The other suffix, -*ŋkat*, is the elsewhere variant with nouns of this gender. It is also found in genders i, iv, and v. Interestingly, the only two gender i nouns that Foley lists with this suffix are for 'spirit' and 'mask carving', certainly not core human concepts, while one of the two gender iv nouns with this suffix is for 'black beetle', which Foley calls "quite unexpected for this gender" (which otherwise designates plants). In gender v, though, -*ŋkat* is clearly the default, as I will show below. I will therefore assume that -*ŋkat* is the default noun plural suffix for the language. It is important to note that this suffix is restricted to nouns and never occurs on such agreeing elements as adjectives or verbs. If the distribution of affixes for adjectives and verbs depends on the syntactic distribution of gender through the operation of agreement, then it seems clear that -*ŋkat* is independent of syntax and gender. It is a *noun* plural suffix.

The gender iv plural suffix is -*uŋi*, which replaces the singular marker -*um*. The velar nasal is unexpected and is also peculiar in other ways. Given that the sequence *umi* does not seem to occur, I will assume that the plural suffix for this gender is -*i* and that a phonological rule takes *m* to *ŋ* here.

Gender v nouns show the most complex distribution of plural suffixes. There are four. Of these, -*ra* occurs only with nouns ending in *n*, where it is the normal suffix. It never occurs with nouns of any other gender. Remember that this -*ra* is the plural agreement suffix for this and four other genders. The contrast between its highly limited distribution with nouns and its general distribution under agreement is striking. The suffix -*i* occurs after *k*, as it does in genders i and ii, although there are nouns ending in *k* that do not take -*i*, for complex phonological reasons. The suffix -*t* occurs normally with nouns ending in *nt* and sporadically with final *n* and *ar*. The suffix -*ŋkat* occurs everywhere else and also when a speaker is unsure of the proper plural form, another indication that it is the default form.

The gender vi plural marker is -*i*, which is expected, since the characteristic final consonant of the gender is *k* and -*i* is the normal plural suffix after *k*.

For gender vii, the normal plural is -*at*. We may assume that this is derived from -*ŋkat* by phonological means, with *ŋk* being absorbed into *mp*. The suffix -*a* occurs only once, and -*i* occurs in a few nouns whose singular ends in *mp* but whose plural stem loses the *mp*, which leaves exposed a final *k*, *p*, or *a*, the segments to which -*i* is usually suffixed. It is a mystery why the *mp* (and sometimes other segments in addition) should be lost, but the subsequent -*i* suffix is not.

Gender viii is very small and also largely irregular in its plurals. The most common plural suffix, -*Cmpt*, ends with a segment (*t*) also found in the plurals of genders ii (-*mput*), ix (-*ut*), and x.a (-*at*). This *t* shows up under agreement only with gender ix, however, where the adjective suffix is also -*ut*.

The gender x.a plural marker is -*i*, which is expected from the fact that the characteristic final consonant is *k*.

Looking at the noun plural suffixes individually, we see that -*i* and -*ŋkat* are the most productive and that their distribution cuts across all gender divisions, with -*i* being distributed phonologically and -*ŋkat* being the default plural suffix. We also see that the distribution of all noun plural suffixes is almost completely unrelated to that of plural agreement suffixes. We can conclude that nouns have genders and they have plural forms, but the two are independent of one another. The same cannot be said of the plural form of agreeing elements. This is entirely gender-dependent: a noun of a given gender will always trigger a particular suffix characteristic of that gender on agreeing plurals. This fact follows from the syntax of gender: what passes on to the agreeing element is the gender of the head noun, not its inflectional class, which makes the inflection of the agreeing element entirely dependent on gender.

Inflection under agreement also differs in form from noun inflection. For example, I noted above that the plural adjective suffix for genders iv, v, vii, viii, and x.a is -*ra*, and the corresponding verbal prefix *ya*-. As I noted above, -*ra* is highly restricted as a noun plural. The prefix *ya*- never appears on nouns. This wide distribution would also seem to indicate that these are the default realizations for these categories, but this distribution is entirely different from that of the default noun plural suffix -*ŋkat*. In other words, there is a distinction in this language between noun inflection and the inflection of agreeing elements of a sort that we have not seen before, and this distinction is rooted in the fundamental difference between gender and inflection.

We are now in a position to sort out the relations among phonological form, gender, and inflection in Yimas. For agreeing elements, gender determines inflection. In other words, no agreeing element has its own inflectional class (unlike Latin, for example, where adjectives can belong to declensions independent of the gender that they receive by feature passing, but like Arapesh). For nouns that fit into the conceptual genders, inflection (plural and dual markers) is determined by a complex of factors; the one thing that seems reasonably clear is that inflectional class does not play a large role here. For nouns in the phonological genders, it is clear that gender is phonologically driven, but it is also clear that the inflection of these nouns too is not closely tied to any independently identifiable inflectional classes.

4.6   Conclusion

Both gender and inflection are elaborate in Arapesh and Yimas. They are also intimately related. But close examination of both reveals that this relation is neither simple nor direct. Instead, gender and inflection operate as independent systems related both to each other and to phonology and conceptual structure.

Chapter 5

Binyanim as Inflectional Classes

It is the manifest form that is never twice the same, for this form, which we call linguistic morphology, is nothing more than a collective *art* of thought, an art denuded of the irrelevancies of individual sentiment.

E. Sapir

5.1 The Term *Binyan* and Its Meaning

The Hebrew word *binyan* is first recorded in the book of Ezekiel in the concrete sense of 'building' or 'structure', which it still retains today. In traditional Hebrew grammar, this same term is used for the various distinct patterns that verb roots can fall into (in a way that will be clarified shortly). The grammatical sense of the term has been variously translated into English as *conjugation, formative, verbal pattern, modification, theme,* and *verbal stem.* I will argue that from a purely morphological point of view, a binyan is an inflectional class, a conjugation.[1] What makes it different from a Latin or Greek verb conjugation is not anything morphological but rather differences in the relation between morphology and other components of the grammar.

Hebrew is not alone in having a verb morphology based on binyan. All Semitic languages do, though they differ greatly in the number of binyanim and in their relations to other aspects of the grammar. I will review a number of Semitic languages, as well as some fascinating data involving language loss in a young child, all of which point to the same conclusion, but I will begin with Hebrew. Once again, as in chapter 3, I use the term Hebrew panchronically, since there is strikingly little material change in the binyan system across the recorded history of the language. Indeed, Rosén, in his insightful overview of Israeli Hebrew, notes, "The morphological system of Israeli Hebrew tallies with that of Biblical Hebrew to an

extent hardly ever experienced with different stages of the same language"
(1977, 26).

5.2   The Hebrew Binyan System

A Hebrew verb can be conjugated according to one or more of seven
traditionally recognized binyanim.[2] Of these, two are found only as passive analogues of two others and are clearly not conjugations in the sense
that I have adopted. I will put them aside for the moment. That leaves us
with five truly major binyanim. In table 5.1, I give the root *qtl* in each of
these five binyanim in the standard citation form of third-person, masculine, singular, perfect. In the first column are the traditional names of
the binyanim. The glosses are from Gesenius and Kautzsch 1910.[3] Within
each binyan, an entire paradigm of forms is found: two tenses (prefixed
and unprefixed),[4] an imperative, a participle (two in *qal*), two infinitives,
a jussive, and an optative.[5] In the tenses, verbs are inflected for person,
number, and gender of the subject; in the imperative, only number and
gender are indicated. For each binyan, then, there is a paradigm of about
thirty forms.[6] These paradigms are almost always full for any given verb,
and they are highly regular. Semantically too, there are no idiosyncratic
forms within these paradigms. In other words, within a binyan, we are
dealing with a straightforward case of inflection, with full and regular
paradigms.[7]

By contrast, the simple picture of the binyan system presented in table
5.1 is highly misleading, as discussed most cogently by Berman (1978,
chap. 3). First, the system is filled with holes: few if any roots actually
occur in all five major binyanim. Indeed, if we restrict ourselves to the
Biblical text for the moment, some 71 percent of verb roots occur in *qal*,
28 percent in *nif'al*, 27 percent in *pi'el*, 32 percent in *hif'il*, and 11 percent in
hitpa'el. I know of no reliable method of determining, for any given root,

Table 5.1
Hebrew active-verb binyanim

Binyan name	3, masc., sg., perf.	Gloss
qal	qâtal	'to kill'
nif'al	niqal	'to kill oneself'
pi'el	qittel	'to massacre'
hif'il	hiqtil	'to cause to kill'
hitpa'el	hitqattel	'to kill oneself'

which binyan or combination of binyanim it will occur in. Because of these gaps, one might characterize the binyan system as overall much less productive than the system of tense, aspect, and mood. Waltke and O'Connor present binyanim as "a system of derivational morphology" (1990, 350), and this does at first seem to be a fair categorization. Certainly the gaps and differences in productivity among the binyanim that we find are characteristic of a derivational system as opposed to an inflectional one. Semantics too would seem to support a derivational treatment of the binyanim, for here again the simple picture of table 5.1 is highly misleading (again, Berman [1978] provides the best discussion). There are almost no roots that show the semantic pattern exemplified in table 5.1, while many roots have highly lexicalized meanings in various binyanim. This is especially striking in contrast to the system of tense, aspect, and mood, which, in addition to not showing gaps, is completely invariant semantically, as I noted above.

To judge from what we have seen so far, the proper treatment of Hebrew verb morphology thus seems quite straightforward: binyanim are derivational or lexeme-formational categories, while the paradigms of tense, aspect, and mood forms within a binyan are inflectional. Most investigators of Israeli Hebrew morphology (Bolozky 1978, 1982, 1986; Ornan 1971; Schwarzwald 1973, 1981) would agree with this general position, and it may be correct for earlier stages of the language than those for which we have texts. The inflectional status of tense, aspect, and mood morphology seems incontrovertible, and I will assume it, but there is one major problem with the claim that the binyan system is simply word-formational, which is that it is obligatory: no Hebrew verb form exists outside the binyan system. Analogous claims hold generally in all Semitic languages across time. Lexeme formation, by contrast, of which derivation is one morphological type, is never obligatory: there are underived lexemes in all languages. How do we reconcile obligatoriness with the clearly lexeme-formational nature of the binyanim?

Obligatoriness is usually seen as a hallmark of inflection. It is akin to being paradigmatic. Consider inflectional noun classes, as discussed in chapters 3 and 4. In a language with inflectional noun classes, every noun in the system must have or somehow be provided with an inflectional noun class, from which its entire inflectional paradigm follows, as Carstairs (1987) and Wurzel (1989) have emphasized. In languages with noun classes, we do sometimes find (usually borrowed) nouns that do not belong and, unlike the Arapesh examples I discussed, do not get assigned to any morphological class. What happens to such nouns is striking: they are indeclinable, lacking the entire inflectional paradigm. This happens in Greek, where foreign words like *Adam* or the (borrowed) letter names are indeclinable. Similarly in Russian, where over three hundred nouns in common use and a large number of technical terms and proper nouns, all recently borrowed, show no distinct inflected case forms. Ungebaun (1967) provides a reasonably complete discussion of the phonological predictors at work in determining whether a borrowed Russian noun will be indeclinable. Those ending in consonants are usually declinable. Most vowel-final borrowings are indeclinable, except for some common nouns ending in [a], e.g., *sofa*. In other words, borrowings that do not fit the phonological pattern of any noun class are likely to be indeclinable. The gender of indeclinables is usually assigned on conceptual grounds. Some Russian examples are given in (1):

(1) a. [viski] 'whiskey'
     b. [kafe] 'cafe'
     c. [bordo] 'claret'
     d. [tabu] 'taboo'
     e. [ura] 'hurrah'
     f. [flamingo] 'flamingo'

The notion that a noun class is an inflectional class predicts exactly what we find with indeclinables: nouns that cannot be assigned to a noun class will not show any case forms at all, because the inflectional class names a set of instructions for constructing inflected forms. If a noun is not assigned to any inflectional class, we have no instructions, and no rules will apply.[8] Note that Russian indeclinable nouns are not outside the syntax but only outside the morphology, since they have gender. To conclude this brief excursus, membership in an inflectional class is obligatory for nouns that are part of the inflectional system of the language.[9]

I have worked my way into a paradox: the binyan system shows clear signs of being both derivational and inflectional. It is inflectional because it is obligatory and determines the inflected forms of all verbs, but it is derivational because the distribution of the binyanim is not itself paradigmatic and because it is not always semantically compositional. This paradox is false, though, arising, as it does, from a common misunderstanding of the relation between derivation and inflection on the one hand and morphology on the other. We must first remember that derivation and inflection are not kinds of morphology but rather uses of morphology: inflection is the morphological realization of syntax, while derivation is the morphological realization of lexeme formation. Morphology can be put to either derivational or inflectional ends, and the same morphology can sometimes serve both.[10] In the simple sort of case usually adduced as evidence for the unity of derivational and inflectional morphology, we find examples of a single realization that is sometimes derivational and sometimes inflectional. A good example would be English -*ing*, which has a multiplicity of uses (Quirk, Greenbaum, Leech, and Svartvik 1985). The case at hand is more complex, though, since we are not dealing with mere morphological homophony, as with -*ing* and similar cases. Rather, we are dealing with a phenomenon that is *simultaneously* derivational and inflectional, serving both ends at once: a lexeme-formation rule may *assign* membership in a given binyan (inflectional class) to its output verb lexeme; the morphological (derivational) realization of this lexeme-formation rule is therefore the abstract binyan or inflectional class; the binyan in turn will serve, as all inflectional classes do, to *determine* the inflection of that lexeme. The binyan thus has a dual role: it serves as the abstract morphological mark of the lexeme-formation rule and, as an inflectional class, it dictates the phonological form of the verb.

To see how the system works, we must also remember the relation between derivation and inflection within syntax, broadly conceived. Derivation is the morphological reflex of lexeme formation: lexeme formation produces lexemes, which are complex symbols, inasmuch as a given rule of lexeme formation will simultaneously have syntactic, semantic, and morphological effects.[11] By contrast, inflection interprets or is matched against a morphosyntactic representation (in the sense of Anderson 1992) and provides the various forms that lexemes take in different morphosyntactic environments. In other words, lexeme formation intrinsically feeds inflection.[12] Lexeme formation *has* morphological effects. Inflection *consists of* morphological effects. The morphological effect of lexeme formation is often more abstract or indirect than inflection: it may sometimes provide a lexeme not only with phonological information directly (in the guise of an affix or template) but also with abstract morphological (morphomic) properties that themselves have no direct phonological repercussions but can be detected only in their subsequent effects on inflection. Sometimes the assignment of an abstract morphological property will be the only morphological effect of a rule of lexeme formation.[13] Clearest and most dramatic among the abstract morphological properties that may be assigned by a rule of lexeme formation is inflectional class.

Let me give an example that I touched on earlier. In Latin, as noted in chapter 2, there are three types of verbs formed on the third stem. Examples of each type are repeated here in table 5.2. As is clear from the table, two of the types have identifiable suffixes (-*it* and -*ur*), but one of them (the intensive verb) has no suffix of its own. The only morphological effect of the lexeme-formation rule that produces intensive verbs, aside from the selection of the third stem of the base as the stem of the lexeme-formation rule, is the assignment of the verbs to a particular inflectional class, first conjugation, as shown by the presence in these verbs of the theme vowel -*ā*, which is characteristic of this conjugation. As I argued in chapter 2, Latin theme vowels are assigned to verb stems from the abstract inflectional class, rather than directly, so that we cannot even say that the theme-vowel suffix -*ā* is a direct morphological effect of the lexeme-formation rule. It is rather an effect of the inflectional class, which, in the case of intensive verbs, is the only morphological effect of the lexeme-formation rule. The other lexeme-formation rules exemplified in table 5.2 assign to their output verbs both a suffix and membership in an inflectional class.

In general, in languages with inflectional classes of verbs, each lexeme-formation rule that produces verb lexemes will assign membership in a given inflectional class to all its output verbs, in addition to other more

Table 5.2
Latin verbs derived from third stems

Citation form	Infinitive	Base verb[a]	Gloss
Desiderative Verbs			
ēsuriō	ēsurīre	edō, ēs-	'be hungry'
empturiō	empturīre	emō, empt-	'want to buy'
parturiō	parturīre	pariō, part-	'be in labor'
Intensive verbs			
iactō	iactāre	iaciō, iact-	'fling'
volūtō	volutāre	volvō, volūt-	'tumble about'
tractō	tractāre	trahō, tract-	'drag'
Iterative verb			
scriptitō	scriptāre	scrībō, script-	'write often'
vīsitō	vīsitāre	videō, vīs-	'see often'
iactitō	iactitāre	iaciō, iact-	'bandy'
dormitō	dormitāre	dormiō, dormit-	'dream'

a. Here in the base-verb column, I give the present, active, indicative, first person, singular and the third stem.

concrete morphological markers, if there are any. To return to table 5.2, we see that two of the lexeme-formation rules assign first conjugation, but one assigns fourth conjugation (theme vowel -*ī*). Other lexeme-formation rules assign their output verbs to the third conjugation, as shown in table 5.3.

Nominal derivation is similar. In languages that have inflectional class and gender, productively derived nouns will be provided with both by their lexeme-formation rule.[14] Sometimes generalizations about gender can be made across lexeme-formation rules. For example, in Latin, as in most Indo-European languages with gender, the great majority of abstract noun suffixes denoting action or quality are feminine; similarly, the great majority of instrument suffixes are neuter. But not all suffixes can have their gender predicted in this conceptual way. Thus the abstract suffix -*or*/-*os* is masculine (*furor*, *pallor*, *amor*) rather than the expected feminine.[15]

To return to Hebrew, the solution is now clear. Each binyan is an inflectional class and every verb in the language will therefore belong to a binyan in the way that every verb in a language like Latin belongs to an inflectional class. At the same time, the lexeme-formation rules for forming verb lexemes each assign membership in a binyan (inflectional class) to their output lexemes. What is peculiar about Hebrew, on this account, is the fact that most of the verb-lexeme-formation rules carry no affix, only an abstract inflectional-class marker. Note also that the nature of inflectional classes dictates that a given lexeme can belong to only one binyan,

Table 5.3
Latin derived verbs of the third conjugation

Citation form	Infinitive	Base verb[a]	Gloss
Intensive verbs			
capessō	capessere	capiō, capere	'seize'
incessō	incessere	cedō, cedere	'assail'
facessō	facessere	faciō, facere	'do eagerly'
Inceptive verbs			
dormēscō	dormēscere	dormiō, dormīre	'fall asleep'
calēsco	calēscere	caleō, calēre	'heat up'
liquēscō	liquēscere	liquor, liqui	'melt'

a. Here in the base-verb column, I give the present, active, indicative, first person, singular and the present, active infinitive.

with the result that the newly assigned binyan in deverbal verbs drives out the old binyan, which leaves behind no trace of its former occupation.

I cannot give here a detailed account of the exact nature of Hebrew verb-lexeme-formation rules. The best accounts for Israeli Hebrew are in Berman 1978 and Bolozky 1978, 1982, 1986. For Biblical Hebrew, the task is made more difficult by the lack of native speakers. So as an example I will summarize the account of denominal verbs in Israeli Hebrew given in Bolozky 1982. Bolozky notes first of all that the *qal* binyan, although numerically the largest, plays no role at all in the formation of new verbs in Israeli Hebrew. Nor does *nif'al*. The most important binyan for forming new verbs is *pi'el*, followed by *hitpa'el*. The most surprising of Bolozky's findings is the extent to which phonological factors play a role in determining the choice of binyan. For example, with roots of more than three consonants, with triconsonantal roots whose middle consonant is a glide, and with biconsonantal roots, *pi'el* or *hitpa'el* is selected simply because the use of *hif'il* would lead to an unpronounceable word. Phonological factors aside, new causative verbs are usually *hif'il*, as are intransitive inchoative verbs of color and physical human quality (e.g., verbs for 'become white' or 'become fat'). Other intransitive inchoatives are *hitpa'el*, along with reflexives, reciprocals, and middles. All other denominal verbs, including other intransitives and most transitives, are *pi'el*.

5.2.1 Are there noun classes in Hebrew?

Parallel to the binyan system for verbs is a similar system for nouns, traditionally called the *mishkal* (literally 'weight') system. The two systems are identical in general form, consisting of templates (sometimes with a prefix or suffix as well). A few examples drawn from Berman 1978 are given in table 5.4. Grammars, however, traditionally draw a sharp distinction between them, generally without any explicit justification. The *mishkalim* also generally get much less space than the binyanim in grammar books.[16] It is quite possible to study Hebrew grammar for years without touching at all on the *mishkalim*, while the binyanim are part of any basic introduction. What lies behind this disparity in emphasis?

The only clearcut difference between the two systems is in their obligatoriness. The *mishkalim* are not obligatory in any sense. There are many native nouns that do not belong to any identifiable *mishkal*, and nouns are and have always been freely borrowed without being placed in any *mishkal*. The *mishkalim* are also usually said to be less regular semantically and less productive than the binyanim, but the difference here is one of degree and may in fact not be as great as is usually assumed. I have

Table 5.4
Hebrew mishkal patterns

Mishkal	Example	Gloss	Root	Gloss
CaCCan	rakdan	'dancer'	rkd	'dance'
	batlan	'loafer'	btl	'loaf'
	saxkan	'player'	sxk	'play'
CaCiC	parix	'crumbly'	prk	'crush'
	săvir	'breakable'	šbr	'break'
	kari	'readable'	kr'	'read'
maCCeC	mašpex	'funnel'	špk	'pour'
	mafteax	'key'	ptx	'open'
	maghec	'iron'	ghc	'press'
miCCaCa	mispara	'barbershop'	spr	'cut'
	mirpaa	'clinic'	rp'	'heal'
	minhara	'tunnel'	nhr	'flow'
CACeCet	ademet	'measles'	'dm	'red'
	xazeret	'mumps'	xzr	'return'
	kalevet	'rabies'	klb	'dog'

taken obligatoriness as a sign of inflection. It is therefore reasonable to conclude that the *mishkal* system is not obligatory because it is not inflectional: the *mishkalim* are not inflectional classes. This conclusion is supported by the fact that Hebrew nouns, unlike verbs in Hebrew, have no paradigms. First, Hebrew has no case affixes. The only possible case marker, which precedes definite objects, is a separate word. Second, as I have already shown in chapter 3, although there are markers for both gender and number and although the morphology of these markers is complex, the markers cannot in any sense be said to be arranged as inflectional classes. In other words, we already have independent evidence, having nothing to do with *mishkalim*, against nominal inflectional classes in Hebrew.

What, then, are *mishkalim* if they are identical in general form to binyanim but are not inflectional classes? Here we must remember again the distinction between morphology and its place in a grammar. I analyzed binyanim as inflectional classes to which lexemes are assigned by lexeme formation rules. *Mishkalim* too must be assigned by lexeme-formation rules, since, like binyanim, they are clearly derivational in nature. But they differ from binyanim simply in that they have no further function as inflectional classes, there being no inflectional classes of nouns in the language. As a consequence, they are not obligatory.[17] The notion of inflectional class thus allows me to account fully for the differences between the two systems, but only if we understand properly the subtle relations among derivation, inflection, and morphology within the grammar of a natural language.[18]

5.2.2 Forms of the passive

I noted above that there are seven common binyanim in Hebrew, but that two of them are restricted to the passive. I will now discuss the morphology of the passive and show that syntax too can play a role in the assignment of inflectional classes. I will assume that the passive is a syntactic construction rather than a lexemic one (i.e., that it is not sublexemic), although I will not assume or depend on any particular analysis of its syntax. The morphology of the passive is quite regular, although complex. Table 5.5 shows that the system consists of a set of correspondences between certain active binyanim and their passive counterparts.[19]

Some preliminary observations are in order. The history of the passive counterparts of *qal* verbs is complex. Originally Hebrew had a distinct binyan that was solely a passive of the *qal*, and there is evidence for it in the unpointed Biblical text. However, the Masoretes (who provided the vowels for and otherwise annotated the original consonantal text of the Bible from about 600 to 1000 C.E.) clearly had no knowledge of such a binyan, so they pointed the forms that were *qal* passives in such a way that they looked like *pu'al*, *h$\overset{\circ}{u}$f'al*, or *nif'al* forms, depending on their consonantism.[20] The majority of the forms in question appear in verse, and it is clear that this passive binyan was moribund in Biblical times (ca. 1000–200 B.C.E.). In any case, most verbs in the Bible that are clear passives of *qal* verbs are *nif'al*. One may therefore assume that the passive counterpart of *qal* was replaced by *nif'al* at some point during the Biblical period.[21] *Nif'al* has had and continues to have other uses throughout the history of the language, uses that are not relevant here. Also, some verbs are lexically specified as *nif'al* (e.g., *nixnas* 'enter').

Table 5.5
Hebrew active and passive binyan pairs

Active binyan	Passive binyan
qal	nif'al
pi'el	pu'al
hif'il	h$\overset{\circ}{u}$f'al

With the other two normally transitive binyanim, the situation is much clearer. Here, for each binyan$_i$, there has always been a corresponding binyan$_j$ in which the verb of binyan$_i$ will be in the passive. Furthermore, these two passive binyanim, *pu'al* and $h^o_u f'al$, have no other use besides being the passive counterparts of their respective actives.[22] In this way, they are truly secondary. They also lack certain forms found in all other binyanim: the infinitive and the imperative, both of which occur in all other binyanim (including the *nif'al* passive), so that one cannot attribute the lack of these forms to syntax alone.

In analyzing the morphology of the passive, it is convenient to separate Biblical and Israeli Hebrew. In both stages, transitive verbs may appear in three binyanim, but the rules that I will give for the passive differ slightly from one stage to another, because of the history of $h^o_u f'al$. Following most grammars, I will assume that the productive passive of *qal* is *nif'al* in Biblical Hebrew. I will also assume that *hof'al* and *huf'al* are in some sort of complex variation with one another, which is why I call this binyan $h^o_u f'al$. The morphological realization of the passive will then consist of a mapping from each active binyan to its passive counterpart (given in table 5.5) and replacement thereby (unless another binyan is lexically specified as the passive of a given lexeme, which rarely occurs). In Israeli Hebrew, the vowel variation in the $h^o_u f'al$ binyan is neutralized to *huf'al*. Thus, at this stage of the language, we may analyze the passives of both *pi'el* and *hif'il* as consisting morphologically of a vocalic melody *u a* that replaces the melody of the active verb stem.[23] For these two pairs, then, there is no need to map one abstract binyan onto another, as I did for Biblical Hebrew and as I still need to do for *qal*. Rather, we may specify the default realization of Passive as consisting of the *u a* melody, which will drive out the melody of the active binyan.

This is the realization of the passive in Hebrew. It also completes my analysis of the assignment and uses of the various binyanim, which we now see to be quite complex in relation to syntax, derivation, and inflection. Before going further, though, I should comment on the realization of the passive, for the passive morphology that I have just outlined is certainly quite far from a normal sort of morpheme, concatenative or otherwise. First, it involves a context-sensitive mapping, in that one must know the binyan of the active verb base in order to know which passive binyan to replace it with.[24] Second, it is abstract to the extent that the binyanim are themselves abstract, a point to which I will return in the next section. On this analysis, at least for Israeli Hebrew, the passive is also not morphophonologically uniform, consisting of a mapping between binyanim for *qal* verbs and a (replacive) vowel pattern for others. Finally, the mapping is an operation on the abstract morphological representation of the verb, triggered by the abstract morphosyntactic entity Passive or its analogue.

But within a lexeme-based framework in which morphology and syntax are autonomous, what Passive consists of syntactically is not directly relevant to its morphological realization. Syntactically, it may be a pronoun of some sort, as in Baker, Johnson, and Roberts 1989, or it may be something else. For my purposes, the question is just not interesting. Conversely, its morphology has no bearing on its syntax and should not be used as evidence for one syntactic analysis or another. This point emerges quite strongly from this analysis of Hebrew passives, for I see no sense in which either the Biblical or Israeli realizations of Passive can be construed as containing direct evidence for the place or nature of Passive in a syntactic representation.

5.3   The Abstract Nature of the Binyan

5.3.1   Prosody: Binyan and template
It should be clear by now that we must specify, for a given verb lexeme, both its root and its binyan, to be able to produce the paradigm of that verb.[25] The root alone will not do, as Schwarzwald (1973) has shown. Verbs that share the same root will either be listed as separate entries in the lexicon (if there is anything unpredictable about them, including possibly their binyan) or produced by lexeme-formation rules that assign membership in a binyan, among other things (Bolozky 1982). How is this information translated into actual forms? In particular, what information does a given binyan contribute to the forms that belong to that binyan? More concretely, what does a binyan sound like? Does it have its own phonological signifier at any level of analysis, however abstract? Readers familiar with McCarthy 1981 and the notion of an abstract prosodic template may assume that the signifier of a binyan is a purely prosodic template onto which the root is mapped, the prosodic template being abstract enough but still possessed of some semblance of sound form. As McCarthy points out, though, there are binyanim that consist not simply of a root prosodic template but additionally of another morph, usually a prefix.[26] Two Hebrew binyanim, *pi'el* and *hitpa'el*, demonstrate this point nicely: they share a root template (CVCCVC) and melody, but *hitpa'el* has a prefix as well. It is therefore impossible either to view each root template

as the realization of a distinct binyan or to think that binyanim are realized solely through root templates.

It is not even possible to associate each distinct binyan with a single root template, although the majority can be so associated. The problem cases in Hebrew are *qal* and *nif'al*. With each of these binyanim, there are two templates for every verb: one used for the past (perfect) tense and participle and one for the future (imperfect) tense and other forms.[27] I will refer to these as the unprefixed templates (for the past) and the prefixed templates (for the future). The unprefixed template of *qal* is of the form CVCVC, while the prefixed template is of the form CCVC. Neither one can be derived from the other by any plausible phonological means, even within a framework that tolerates quite abstract phonological analyses (Prince 1975).[28] The *qal* binyan, then, must be realized context-sensitively through two templates. I will discuss *qal* more fully below. The distribution of the stems in *nif'al* is similar, but they differ in more than the root template. The unprefixed stem is *niCCaC*, while the prefixed stem is *hinCâCeC*.[29] The *hin-* prefix never appears intact in actual surface prefixed forms, because the *n* is always assimilated to the following consonant, resulting in a geminate, while the *h* is similarly deleted after the consonant of the pronominal prefix. The *h* does surface in the infinitive and the imperative, however, to give forms like *hikkânes* 'enter!' If we disregard for the moment the prefix and vowel patterns and extract only the root templates, it is clear that there are two, CCVC and CVCVC, which are prosodically identical but distributed in an inverse fashion to the *qal* distribution.

I conclude that we cannot associate each binyan with a single root template. The presence of two root templates for *nif'al* is especially compelling. *Qal* verbs are all underived, and one might therefore expect them to be unusual. *Nif'al*, however, has been used productively both as a passive of *qal* and for derived intransitives throughout the history of the language, so that we cannot dismiss its significance so easily.

5.3.2 Prefixes
Each binyan has a fixed set of vowels that are intercalated with the root consonants in the stem prosody, and some also have prefixes. I will discuss these now, beginning with the prefixes. Two binyanim have prefixes that are constant throughout the paradigm. These are $h^o_u f'al$ and *hitpa'el*. If we assume that $h^o_u f'al$ is derived directly from *hif'il* by substitution of the passive vocalism, as suggested above, then we may exclude it from further discussion. I will assume that the *hitpa'el* prefix is *hit-*.[30] The

other binyanim with prefixes are *nif'al* and *hif'il*. *Nif'al*, as I noted above, has *ni* in the unprefixed stem and *hin* in the prefixed stem forms. I will follow Prince 1975 in my discussion of these. According to Prince, *i* in a #CiCCV sequence results from the sequential application of two rules. The first rule, cluster breakup, inserts a schwa in the environment #C_C. This schwa is then converted to *i* in the environment #C_CC. This analysis allows us to claim that the *ni-* prefix is actually *n-*. A form like *nixtav* 'it was written' thus enters the phonology as *nktab*, with the *i* resulting from the rules just mentioned. The *hin-* prefix of the prefixed stem contains the *n* and an additional *hi*. One might be tempted to derive the *i* by the same two rules used for the *i* of *ni*, which would make the *hi* sequence just *h*. However, this cannot be done for complex reasons, discussion of which would take me too far astray. I will therefore assume that the prefixed stem contains the additional prefix *hi-*. Remember that the *h* is deleted after the consonantal prefix. We thus have the phonological derivation in table 5.6 for a form like *yikkatev* 'it will be written', with the masculine prefix *y*.

The *hif'il* prefix shows two forms: *hi-* and *ha-*. The latter appears in the prefixed stem. The alternation between *i* and *a* is common in Hebrew. According to Prince, there is a rule of changing *a* to *i* in the same environment as the rule of changing schwa to *i* (#C_CC).[31] This rule is responsible for the *hi* form of the prefix. It does not apply in the prefixed forms, because the presence of the pronominal prefix blocks it. Sample derivations for unprefixed and prefixed forms are shown in tables 5.7 and 5.8. We may therefore claim that there is no variation in the basic form of the *hif'il* prefix, which leaves only *nif'al* with a different prefix pattern for the unprefixed and prefixed stems. This claim depends on an abstract analysis of *hif'il*. Readers with more concrete tastes may opt for two *hif'il* prefixes,

Table 5.6
Phonological derivation for *yikkatev*

Form	Description
y-hinkateb	underlying phonological representation
yinkateb	*h* deletion (h → $\emptyset$/C_V)
yikkateb	*n* assimilation
yikkatev[a]	spirantization

a. The *t* should also be spirantized, but I follow Israeli practice in not spirantizing *t*, *d*, and *g*.

Table 5.7
Sample derivation for unprefixed *hixtiv*

Form	Description
haktib	underlying phonological form
hiktib	*a* to *i*
hixtiv 'he dictated'	spirantization

Table 5.8
Sample derivation for prefixed *yaxtiv*

Form	Description
y-haktib	underlying phonological form
n.a. (blocked by $\#CC\_$)	*a* to *i*
yaktib	*h* deletion (h → $\emptyset$/C_V)
yaxtiv 'he will dictate'	spirantization

adoption of which would only strengthen my argument that the prefixed and unprefixed stems must be morphologically distinct.

5.3.3 Vocalism and stem templates

Three binyanim show a constant vocalism within the root template (except for indisputable surface phonological alternations) throughout the paradigm. They are *hitpa'el* and the two pure passives: $h_u^o f'al$, and *pu'al*. *Hif'il* is constant except for three forms (two of the four imperative forms and the feminine, plural, future), which show *e* instead of the expected *i*, as exemplified below:

(2) haqped 'be strict masc. sg.!'
    haqpidi 'be strict fem. sg.!'
    haqpidu 'be strict masc. pl.!'
    haqpedna 'be strict fem. pl.!'
    taqpedna 'you/they fem. will be strict'

If we follow Prince and others and analyze the imperative as being derived from the future by truncation, we can reduce the irregularity of the feminine plural imperative to that of its future counterpart. We also simultaneously account for the otherwise anomalous *a* of the prefix, which should be *i*, since the future prefix will block the rule of changing *a* to *i*, as it does in table 5.8.[32]

Pi'el shows different vowels in the unprefixed and the prefixed forms, but the difference is clearly due to the rule of changing *a* to *i*. The relevant forms are given below:

(3) qibbel 'he received'
    yqabbel 'he will receive'

The *i* of the unprefixed form results from the rule of changing *a* to *i*, which is prevented from applying by the prefix in the corresponding prefixed form.

We are thus left with *qal* and *nif'al* as the only binyanim that show truly distinct vocalisms in the unprefixed and prefixed stems under a fairly abstract analysis. Coincidentally, these are the two binyanim that show distinct root templates in the unprefixed and the prefixed stems, as I demonstrated above. This coincidence is resolved if we view the root template and its vocalism as a single unit consisting of a prosodic template with filled vowels. Each of these root templates also co-occurs with its own prefix, since the only binyan that shows variation in the form of its special binyan prefix is *nif'al*, which has two root templates, and the prefixes covary with the root templates and their vocalisms. I therefore suggest that we treat all the templates as *stem templates*, each consisting of a prosodic pattern for the root, a vocalism, and, in some cases, a prefix. The pronominal affixes are not part of this stem template but are affixed to it by separate realization rules.

In table 5.9, I list all the stem templates for active verbs except for *qal*, which still remains to be analyzed fully. From this table, we may interpret a binyan as a function that maps a root onto a corresponding set of stem templates. The result of this mapping is a stem that undergoes inflectional morphology. For a given binyan, the stem set usually has only one member, but it may have two, with the distribution of the two being determined by the presence or absence of any sort of prefix in the inflectional realization (hence the terms *prefixed* and *unprefixed* for the two tenses). Notice that whether the stem template itself contains a prefix is irrelevant to its distribution. What determines whether we call a stem *prefixed* or not is whether a prefix is attached to the stem: both of the *nif'al* templates have their own prefixes, but only one of these prefixed stem templates occurs after a pronominal or other inflectional prefix. Some interesting evidence that the simple presence of an inflectional prefix, and not some higher-level notion like tense or aspect, governs the distribution of the *nif'al* stems comes from participles. Table 5.10 contains a list of non-*qal* participial forms for the verb root *qtl*. Except for *nif'al*,

Table 5.9
Stem templates for non-*qal* Hebrew active binyanim

Binyan	Stem template
pi'el	CaCCeC
hif'il	haCCiC
nif'al	hinCâCeC (after a prefix)
	nCCaC (elsewhere)
hitpa'el	hitCaCCeC

Note: These templates should be interpreted as standing for prosodic templates in the style of McCarthy 1986 and McCarthy and Prince, to appear. McCarthy (1984) has shown that roots of more than three consonants necessitate a prosodic characterization of Hebrew, which I have ignored throughout my exposition, purely for the sake of brevity.

Table 5.10
Non-*qal* participles

Binyan	Participle
pi'el	mqattel
pu'al	mquttâl
hif'il	maqtil
h^o_uf'al	muqtâl
nif'al	niqtâl
hitpa'el	mitqattel

the prefix *m*- occurs on the participles of all non-*qal* binyanim. The *nif'al* participle has no *m*- prefix. The stem of this participle is therefore that of the unprefixed conjugation, *n*CC*a*C, as predicted by the prefix condition.

The infinitive may also be taken as evidence for the purely morphological character of the distribution of the prefixed template.[33] The infinitive has the prefix *l*-, which is homophonous with and historically identical to the preposition meaning 'to'. This prefix is obviously not pronominal, but still it triggers the prefixed stem template in both *qal* and *nif'al*.

5.3.4 Purely prosodic templates

The templates in table 5.9 are quite different from McCarthy's (1981), which are purely prosodic, containing neither vocalism nor stem prefix.

The templates in table 5.9 are, in fact, close to the traditional templates, though not identical to them. I have already given an argument for traditional stem templates for Hebrew, but let me make the argument clearer here by comparing these templates with the purely prosodic sort. The purely prosodic templates separate the vocalisms and the stem prefixes from the prosody. Prosody, vocalism, and prefix should therefore be demonstrably independent of one another in their distribution. But in Hebrew, and in most Semitic languages, there is no such independence for the templates. Instead, if we inspect the stems of table 5.9 carefully, we find no case where vocalism inhabits more than one prosody and that no two stem templates have the same prefix. The only commonalities between pairs of stem templates are the *n* of the two *nif'al* prefixes and the shared complete root template of *pi'el* and *hitpa'el*. Otherwise, every stem template (not every binyan) has its own peculiar specification for each of the three: prosody, vocalism, and prefix. This simultaneous divergence among templates along all three dimensions is entirely accidental if we have prosody, vocalism, and prefix each resulting from distinct morphological rules. Also, if we separate out prosody, vocalism, and prefix, we are at least implicitly claiming that the stem templates are morphologically complex. But there is no reason to view the stem templates in table 5.9 as morphologically complex, as a theory that uses prosodic templates would. In fact, I know of no instance where these stem templates must be treated as morphologically complex, and there is at least one argument, from passive morphology, for treating the stem templates as all morphologically simple. The same is true of Aramaic, as I will show later on.

5.3.5   Passive morphology revisited

As noted above, passive morphology is context-sensitive. The passive form of a verb is a function of its active binyan. For *qal* verbs, the morphological effect of the passive is *nif'al* morphology on the verb. For the other two passivizable binyanim (*nif'al* is not passivizable), we can treat the morphology as a realization rule. This rule can now be seen as an operation on the stem template of each binyan that replaces its vowels with the sequence *u a*. This will give us the correct result both for *pi'el*, whose stem is unprefixed and, more interestingly, for *hif'il*, which has a prefix in its stem. For this binyan, the *u* of the passive replaces the vowel of the prefix. The passive morphology thus operates on stems, oblivious to the apparent difference in morphological complexity between *pi'el* and *hif'il*, and this adds support to the claim that the apparent distinction in complexity between the two binyanim is a false one.

The precise nature of Hebrew passive morphology is now also clearer and can be described as a simple series of choices. To know how to specify the shape of a passive verb, we must first ask whether the active verb is *qal*. If yes, then we assign the corresponding active verb to *nif'al*. *Nif'al* morphology will then realize the stem of the passive verb as either *n*CC*a*C or *hin*Câ*C*e*c*, depending on whether the verb form in question is prefixed. If the active verb is not *qal*, then the passive morphology will ask for the binyan of the verb, create a stem according to the templates given in table 5.9, and substitute the stem vowels with *u a* to produce the passive stem. The passive stem then undergoes inflectional morphology (which does not distinguish active from passive verbs).

5.4 *Qal* Stem Templates

As with *nif'al*, so too the distribution of *qal* stems is determined by the presence or absence of a prefix. The CCVC stem occurs after a prefix, and the CVCVC stem elsewhere. But there is an added complication in the stem vowels. Most *qal*-verb lexemes have *o* in the prefixed stem and *â a* in the unprefixed stem. However, a relatively small number of verbs have *e* as the second vowel of the unprefixed stem and *a* in the prefixed stem. And a very small number of verbs have *o* as the second vowel of the unprefixed stem. The members of this last class are also odd in other respects, both morphological and syntactic, which suggests that the class is inherently unstable. These three distributions of stem vowels in the two templates can be historically traced to three syntacticosemantic classes of verbs, which Waltke and O'Connor (1990) call *fientive, temporary stative*, and *permanent stative*. These classes are very old. However, the syntacticosemantic principles are no longer operative in Hebrew, and the three sets of vowel patterns have also been augmented by three more.[34] The full set of six pattern classes is shown in table 5.11, adapted from Waltke and O'Connor 1990. For a good survey of these pattern classes, the reader should consult Waltke and O'Connor 1990, sec. 22.3. More detailed discussion can be found in Blake's masterful (1903) treatment of the actual forms in the Biblical text. As Waltke and O'Connor note (1990, 371), two of the three new classes (4 and 6) are apparently mixed derivatives of the two major original classes (1 and 2). Of these two new classes, 4 is much the larger, but many of its members are verbs whose middle or last root consonant is a guttural and in which the final vowel *a* is phonologically motivated.[35] Class 5 is somewhat mysterious, with its innovative stem vowel *e* in the prefixed stem, but it is very small, consisting of a number of

Table 5.11
Hebrew *qal* verb classes, by stem-vowel alternations

Class	Unprefixed stem	Prefixed stem	Pattern	Gloss
1	kâtav	ktov	a/o	'write'
2	kâved	kbad	e/a	'be heavy'
3	qâton	qtan	o/a	'be small'
4	lâmad	lmad	a/a	'learn'
5	nâtan	tten	a/e	'give'
6	ħâfec	ħpoc	e/o	'desire'

verbs with initial root consonant *y* (not all of them) and the frequent verb root *ntn* 'give'. Waltke and O'Connor (1990, 371) conclude that the old syntacticosemantic system is breaking down (this is undeniable; the system seems to have largely broken down already before Biblical Hebrew and is not very robust in Aramaic either, as I will show in section 5.7.4) and also conclude that pattern 1 is becoming dominant.

How do we represent the system of stem patterns shown in table 5.11? Chomsky and Halle (1968) treat the first three classes as ablaut classes (following the tradition of Gesenius and Kautzsch 1910 and Kuryłowicz 1961) and provide a polarity rule that derives the final vowel of the prefix *d* stem from that of the unprefixed stem. I repeat their rule in (4) below.

$$(4) \quad \begin{bmatrix} +\text{voc} \\ -\text{cons} \\ \alpha \text{ low} \end{bmatrix} \rightarrow \begin{bmatrix} -\text{low} \\ \alpha \text{ round} \\ +\text{back} \end{bmatrix} \underline{\quad\quad} C + \text{Imperfect}$$

There are several problems with this rule. First, it accounts not for the language in its present state but rather for a hypothetical earlier stage of the language at which only the three original classes presumably existed. The remaining classes must be marked in various ways. Classes 5 and 6 would presumably undergo a minor rule something like (5), for which class members would have to be marked:

$$(5) \quad \begin{bmatrix} +\text{voc} \\ -\text{cons} \\ \alpha \text{ low} \end{bmatrix} \rightarrow \begin{bmatrix} -\text{high} \\ -\text{low} \\ -\alpha \text{ back} \\ -\alpha \text{ round} \end{bmatrix} \underline{\quad\quad} C + \text{Imperfect}$$

Members of class 4 would be marked as exempt from all Imperfect ablaut rules.

If we fix up the rules so that they account for all the classes, the next problem is that the rules are directional and based on the unprefixed stem.[36] What is the motivation for this? For Chomsky and Halle, the use of the unprefixed stem as basic is dictated by the neutralization facts: both *e* and *o* in the input of the rule, as it is written, map onto *a* in the output. Writing the rule in the other direction using only phonological features would be impossible, since we could not distinguish the two classes of verbs with *a* in the prefixed stem. But if we try to account for all six classes, the answer to the directionality question becomes much less clear, and the question itself becomes more important. The two rules that I have proposed for all six classes handle the problem by Paninian rule ordering and outright exemption. With these devices, one could just as well go the other way, from prefixed to unprefixed, though I will not go through the exercise here. The point is that there is no rule-external justification, synchronic or diachronic, for choosing one stem type, prefixed or unprefixed, as basic. Semantically, we can't find a uniform semantics for each stem type (see the extensive survey in Waltke and O'Connor 1990, 455–674), so there is no reason to choose one as basic. Neither frequency nor syntax is decisive either. Instead, as with *nif'al*, it seems that we should simply acknowledge that we have two stem types, one each for prefixed and unprefixed verb forms, with neither one derived from the other.

Since there is no reason to assume that one stem type is more basic than the other, the ablaut relations expressed by Chomsky and Halle's rule (4) and my rule (5) become spurious generalizations. We are still left, though, with the problem of accounting for all the vowels. Remember that class 1 is much larger than all the rest put together. On the basis of this fact, I posit that *qal* is characterized basically by two stem melodies: $C\hat{a}CaC$ (unprefixed) and $CCoC$ (prefixed), which are the melodies of class 1.[37] I will account for the remaining classes by specifying for certain individual roots the final vowel of one or another *qal* stem. In other words, I will say of a root in class 5, for example, that the final vowel of its prefixed *qal* stem is *e*. That is all I will say for class 5 roots. In fact, the independent notion of class is not motivated within this treatment. All the other classes will be dealt with in a similar manner, by prespecifying certain stem vowels. I give a full set of specifications in table 5.12.

According to table 5.12, a verb may be irregular in *qal* in the final vowel of either its prefixed stem or its unprefixed stem. For each stem type, there are two possible irregular vowel specifications: *a* or *e* for the prefixed stem, *e* or *o* for the unprefixed stem. The possible irregularities of the two stems are independent of one another: a given root may have one or the other

Table 5.12
Vowel specifications for *qal* verb classes

Class	Vowel specification
2	The final vowel of the unprefixed *qal* stem is *e*.
	The final vowel of the prefixed *qal* stem is *a*.
3	The final vowel of the unprefixed *qal* stem is *o*.
	The final vowel of the prefixed *qal* stem is *a*.
4	The final vowel of the prefixed *qal* stem is *a*.
5	The final vowel of the prefixed *qal* stem is *e*.
6	The final vowel of the unprefixed *qal* stem is *e*.

or both of its stems prespecified as to its last stem vowel. Having isolated these four specifications, we see that they indeed have independent properties. Of the two possible irregular specifications for the prefixed stem, *a* is overwhelmingly more common than *e*. In fact, the specification of *a* in the prefixed stem is the most common of the four irregularities: verbs with *o* in their unprefixed stems are very few and have decreased in number over time, while the class of those with *e* in unprefixed stems is small and fixed. We see, then, that looking at the verb classes in this nonstandard way (severing the connection between the vowels of the two stem types) allows us not only to sort out the regular from the irregular but also to make some useful distinctions among the irregular verbs that cannot be formulated in a treatment that uses ablaut rules, even when an ablaut treatment is made to fit the data.[38]

5.4.1 Biconsonantal roots in *qal*

Further evidence for regarding the templates with stem vowels *a* and *o* as basic and for separating out the irregular vowel pairs comes from roots with two consonants. Although most Semitic verb roots are triconsonantal, there are a fair number with only two consonants. As McCarthy (1981, 396) has noted, forms built on these roots sometimes show repetition of the second consonant (doubled forms), which he has insightfully analyzed in terms of autosegmental spreading. McCarthy's analysis allows us to assimilate to normal patterns the forms of biconsonantal roots that show doubling. However, repetition of the second consonant in Hebrew is not nearly so widespread as one might hope, with the result that biconsonantal roots do sometimes show special forms.[39] These forms are quite complex and I cannot cover them in any depth here (see Prince

1975 for discussion), but they have one prevalent characteristic relevant to the issue at hand. To quote Gesenius and Kautzsch, "The biliteral stem always . . . takes the vowel which would have been required between the *second* and *third* radical of the ordinary strong form" (1910, sec. 67b). Furthermore, in the unprefixed *qal* stem, this vowel is always *a*, never *e* or *o*, even when the verb is stative (which is where *e* and *o* are common). In fact, as Gesenius and Kantzsch note (1910, sec. 67bb), while doubled forms like *sâvav* 'he turned' are common in the third-person, perfect *qal* forms of biconsonantal roots, it is precisely in third-person, perfect forms of *stative intransitive* verbs that we generally find instead undoubled forms like *mar* 'it was bitter'. In other words, in these marked circumstances (biconsonantal roots), the marked stative vowels do not appear in the unprefixed stem, and only the *a* vowel of unprefixed stems is tolerated. I take this neutralization in biconsonantal roots as evidence for the default nature of the *a* vowel in unprefixed *qal* stems.

Of the irregular vowels of the *qal* prefixed stem, the only one that appears with biconsonantal roots is *a*, which I singled out above as the most robust of all the irregular vowels. Furthermore, it shows up with stative intransitives like *yemar* 'it is bitter' (Gesenius and Kautzsch 1910, sec. 67p). Remember that this vowel is characteristic of prefixed stems of statives. Its presence with biconsonantal roots contrasts with the absence of *e* and *o* in unprefixed stems just noted. This difference can be traced to the greater robustness of the *a* in prefixed stems, which, as I pointed out above, is by far the most common of all the irregular vowels of *qal*. However, within an ablaut framework, which is rooted in the idea of alternation, we would not expect, and probably should not even permit, this sort of separation of the characteristic vowels of stative verbs. The presence of *a* in the prefixed stem should result from ablaut of the mid vowel of the unprefixed stem; more centrally, even if we treat ablaut as a relation between equals, the vowel specifications of the two stems should not be separable in the way that they clearly are in the case of two-consonant roots. But this has been my entire argument: the irregular specification of the prefixed vowel and the unprefixed vowel are entirely separate and, as we now see, separable phenomena.

5.4.2 Simplicity

The treatment of *qal* vowels that I am advocating assimilates *qal* stem templates to the stem templates of other binyanim: the stem templates each consist of a prosodic template whose vowels are fully specified. The *qal* stem templates differ from the others (compare table 5.9) in being simpler in form: they are unprefixed and are not "strengthened" by the addition of the extra medial consonant position that we find in the only other unprefixed stem template, that of *pi'el*. These templates thus accord with the traditional view of *qal* as being morphologically simple and the other binyanim as being morphologically more complex.

The treatment of *qal* stems that I have given is Gricean: I have accounted for the different stems and vowels of *qal* verbs by saying all that must be said and no more than that. I have also argued that this description is correct. One might propose a more radical solution: list each irregular *qal* stem in its entirety. Note that this solution mentions more than one must. As a consequence, it fails. If we list every irregular *qal* stem, we are saying that we permit these stems to vary in many ways. But they do not vary in many ways: all triliteral *qal* stems, irregular or not, have two basic prosodic shapes: CâCVC if they are unprefixed and CCVC if they are prefixed. My Gricean description is based on this fact, which is accidental in a solution that fully lists irregular stems. I conclude that the proper description of *qal* consists of a prefixed and an unprefixed stem template and the further specification of the final stem vowel of one or the other stem for certain roots.

5.4.3   *Qal* as default

Qal is the most common binyan in all stages of Hebrew, both in the number of roots that appear in each binyan and in total frequency of forms in the language. We may say that it is the default binyan, meaning that any verb root not assigned to another binyan by whatever means will occur in *qal*. Note that *qal* is not the most common binyan in terms of lexeme-formation rules. Quite the contrary: no lexeme-formation rule in any historically attested stage of the language has ever assigned a verb to *qal*. In this respect, it differs from the Latin *ā* conjugation and its Romance descendants, which are both the default and the most common inflectional class for the formation of new verbs. Nor is it semantically robust in the way that we expect of productive patterns. But this last fact is understandable from its nature as a default class: it doesn't have to be robust, for all it does is to sweep up what the more powerful classes have left in their wake. *Qal* is therefore derivationally marginal but inflectionally pervasive. Such a class would be difficult to account for without the notion of a default.

5.5 Varia

5.5.1 Stem suppletion

We must list separate stems where we find suppletion. In chapter 2, I used Latin verbs to show that suppletion takes place at the stem level. The same is true in Hebrew. Hebrew verb suppletion is much less common than in Latin and much less radical, usually involving differences of only a single root consonant, but where it does occur, it is not at the level of the individual form but rather at the stem level.

The most common type of suppletion involves roots with a variable initial glide: one stem contains the glide, another doesn't. Thus the root *ygr* 'to be afraid' has *y* in the *qal* unprefixed stem but is *gwr* in the prefixed stem. Conversely, *ṭb* 'to be good' is lacking the *y* in the unprefixed stem but has it in the prefixed stem and in *hif'il*. The most frequent suppletive verb is *hlk* 'to go', which has the root *ylk* only in *qal* prefixed forms and in *hif'il* but *hlk* everwhere else. Interestingly, *hlk* does show up in *qal* prefixed forms, but only in late or poetic passages (e.g., *yahalox* 'he will go', Psalms 58:9).

Some verbs are suppletive in a different way: not in the consonants of the roots for different stems but rather in using the stem of a different binyan for a missing *qal* stem. For example, the common verb *ngš* 'to approach' has a *qal* prefixed stem but a *nif'al* unprefixed stem. In contrast, *kšl* 'to stumble' has the reverse distribution. Again, though, we are dealing with stems in all the instances that I am aware of.

Gesenius and Kautzsch, from whom I have taken all my examples of suppletion, close their discussion of the subject with a very apt remark, which I quote here in full.

The early grammarians often speak of *mixed forms* (*formae mixtae*), i.e. forms which unite the supposed character and meaning of two different tenses, genders or conjugations. Most of the examples adduced are at once set aside by accurate grammatical analysis; some others appear to have arisen from misapprehension and inaccuracy, especially from erroneous views of unusual *plene* forms. Others, again, are either merely wrong readings or represent an intentional conflation of two different readings. (1910, 220)

5.5.2 Participles

All binyanim except for *qal* and *nif'al* show the prefix *m* in participles. *Qal* and *nif'al* participles have no prefix. The unprefixed stem is therefore found in the participles of these two binyanim, which are coincidentally the only ones to distinguish clearly between prefixed and unprefixed stems.

Nif'al participles also show the lengthening of the final *a* to *â*, which is found in all participles where the final stem vowel of the verb is *a*, except for *qal*.[40] With *qal*, if the unprefixed stem has the (characteristically stative) final vowel *e* or *o*, then we find the unprefixed stem appearing unchanged as the participle. However, if a verb takes the regular unprefixed *qal* vowel *a*, then the vowels of the participle are *o e*. Thus, in *qal* verbs that have *a* as the final vowel of the stem, this *a* is not lengthened, because it is changed to *e* "instead". In table 5.13, I have listed the stem from which the participle is formed for each binyan and the actual form of the participle. For the different *qal* types, I have used a subscript to indicate the last stem vowel. We see that four different steps are involved in forming the participle of any verb lexeme once we know its root and binyan. These steps are described informally below.

1. Form the verb stem set.
2. Prefix *m* to the verb stem if there is only one stem.[41]
3. Change the stem vowel melody *â a* to *o e*.
4. Lengthen the final stem vowel *a* to *â* in nominals.

These rules are in (intrinsic) feeding order, except for the last two, where Paninian principles give the order, (iii) being environmentally included in (iv). What is of special interest is that a given participle is formed by subjecting it to the *entire rule set*, with individual rule applications being completely determined by the stem set of the binyan. In table 5.14, I list the rules that apply for each binyan.

Participles are also important for another reason, which is that they provide the only hard evidence for my claim that the binyanim are conju-

Table 5.13
Hebrew participles

Binyan	Stem	Participle
pi'el	qattel	mqattel
pu'al	quttal	mquttâl
hif'il	haqtil	maqtil
hŭf'al	hoqtal	moqtâl
hitpa'el	hitqattel	mitqattel
nif'al	niqtal	niqtâl
qal$_a$	qâtal	qotel
qal$_e$	qâtel	qâtel
qal$_o$	qâtol	qâtol

Table 5.14
Hebrew participles according to the rules used in forming them

Binyan	Rules involved in forming the participle
pi‘el	1, 2
pu‘al	1, 2, 4
hif‘il	1, 2
h$_u^o$f‘al	1, 2, 4
hitpa‘el	1, 2
nif‘al	1, 4
qal$_a$	1, 3
qal$_e$	1
qal$_o$	1

gations: inflectional classes in the narrow sense of the term. With all other inflected forms of a verb, the binyan is irrelevant to everything except the stem: outside the participles, the prefixes and suffixes are the same for all binyanim. Thus if it weren't for participles, we should more properly call the binyanim stem categories and not conjugations, since, at least by a narrow etymological definition, the term *conjugation*, from the verb *conjugāre* 'to join together', should be confined to classes that differ in their affixes and not simply in their stems. In addition, some morphologists, e.g., Carstairs-McCarthy (1991), have argued that affixal and nonaffixal morphology are subject to different constraints. But the different binyanim do differ in whether their participles are prefixed, and hence they properly earn the name of *conjugation*, even on this narrow view. If we broaden the scope of the term to mean 'a class of verbs having the same inflectional forms', then the participles are not so crucial. In any case, though, it is clear that a Hebrew binyan is an inflectional class whose major morphological realization is in the shape of verb stems.

Let me close this section on stems with a remark about method: I have tried to show that a proper account of Hebrew binyanim must admit more than one stem for certain binyanim, *even* if we adopt an abstract analysis of many aspects of the morphology and phonology. In some instances, either the morphological or the phonological analysis may be too abstract for the taste of many readers, who would therefore posit more than one stem even for binyanim whose stems I have treated as unitary. Ravid (1991), for example, posits a unitary stem only for three binyanim. She posits two for *pi‘el, nif‘al,* and *hif‘il*. Such readers need no convincing, and so for them, many of my arguments are beside the point.

5.6   Aramaic Binyanim

Semitic is conventionally divided into four subfamilies, grouped according to the compass as Southwest (Arabic), Southeast (Old South Arabic
and Ethiopic), Northeast (Akkadian), and Northwest (the largest group,
in terms of early numbers of distinct languages). Among Northwest Semitic languages, which include all the languages of ancient Palestine and
Syria, one large group stands out quite clearly as forming a coherent
subfamily: Aramaic. Aramaic can be divided historically into four periods, as in table 5.15, constructed largely on the basis of Moscati, Spitaler,
Ullendorff, and von Soden 1964. Among these languages, many are of
great historical and cultural interest. Imperial Aramaic was the standard
language of the Babylonian and Persian empires; Palestinian was the language of Jesus; Syriac was the language of many of the early writings of
Christianity; and Babylonian is the language of the Talmud.

I will discuss the binyan systems of two Aramaic languages in this
section: Syriac, the late Aramaic language for which there exists the
largest literary record, and the modern Aramaic dialect of the Jews of
Amadia, a village in (Iraqi) Kurdistan, whose morphology has been described in detail by Hoberman (1989, 1991). The modern Northeastern
Aramaic dialects, of which modern Jewish Aramaic is one, are descended
historically from a language close to classical Syriac, but the two binyan
systems are quite distinct, as we will see. My main goal in discussing these
Aramaic binyanim is to show that they too are inflectional classes, albeit
quite different in many repects from those of Hebrew. By comparing these

Table 5.15
Aramaic languages

Period	Time frame	Languages
old Aramaic	< 700 B.C.E.	old Aramaic
classical Aramaic	700–200 B.C.E.	imperial Aramaic
late Aramaic	200 B.C.E.–800 C.E.	Nabatean ⎫ Palmyrene ⎬ West Palestinian ⎭
		Syriac ⎫ Babylonian ⎬ East Mandean ⎭
modern Aramaic	800 C.E.–now	various descendants of East and West

historically related systems, it will also be possible to trace the development from one type of inflectional class to another.

5.7   Syriac

There are six binyanim in Syriac. No Aramaic language has a binyan with a prefixed *n-*, corresponding to Hebrew *nif'al*. Similarly, there are no ablaut passives corresponding to *pu'al* and *h°ᵤf'al*. Instead, the cognate of the reflexive prefix of Hebrew *hitpa'el* is used to form passives. We thus find three active binyanim, corresponding historically to Hebrew *qal*, *pi'el*, and *hif'il*, and the passive of each, formed with the prefix *'et-*.[42] Table 5.16 gives the third-person, masculine, singular, past forms for each of the six binyanim with the root *qtl*. The final stem vowel of *pe'al* is variable in much the same way as in Hebrew *qal*, a matter that I will return to shortly. For the moment, I will consider only the most common *pe'al* stem type.

5.7.1   Passives
The most obvious feature of the table is that the passives are all transparently derived. They differ from their corresponding actives in two features: the prefix and the quality of the stem-final vowel. Since they pattern much like the Hebrew passives in their distribution, I will assume that they are all syntactically and morphologically derived. The syntax does not concern me. The morphology will consist of two parts, the prefix and an ablaut rule for the stem-final vowel, which is of the switching variety: if the final vowel of the active binyan is a back vowel, then the final vowel of the corresponding passive is *e*, and if the final vowel of the active binyan is *e*, then the final vowel of the corresponding passive is *a*. The prefix is simple. Interestingly, the prefix parallels the Hebrew default passive *u a* vowel pattern in that it must operate on a verb stem and not on a

Table 5.16
Sample forms of Syriac binyanim

Binyan	Masc. 3sg. past	Masc. 3sg. future
pe'al (qal)	qṭal	neqṭul
'etpe'el	'etqṭel	netqṭel
pa'el	qaṭṭel	nqaṭṭel
'etpa'al	'etqaṭṭal	netqaṭṭal
'aph'el	'aqṭel	naqṭel
'ettaph'al	'ettaqṭal	nettaqṭal

root. The reasoning here is similar: the prefix attaches to the already prefixed *'aph'el* stem to give us *'ettaph'al*, just as the Hebrew *u a* passive operates on the prefixed *hif'il* stem to give *huf'al*.[43]

It is clear that the Syriac passive is similar to the Hebrew in its general outline: passive binyanim are derived morphologically from the stems of their corresponding actives. The exact morphological means by which this is done is quite different in detail, but not in spirit. I conclude for the moment that Syriac has three basic binyanim: *pe'al*, *pa'el*, and *'aph'el*. The same is true of Babylonian (Levias 1900), although I do not have the space to demonstrate the point here.

5.7.2 *Pa'el* and *'aph'el* as one

The two "derived" binyanim, *pa'el* and *'aph'el*, are quite similar to one another morphologically. For one, they share the melody *a e*. For another, their prosodies are identical: CVCCVC. We may say that they share the abstract prosodic stem shape $CaCCeC$, but that one is mapped onto this stem by doubling of the second root consonant, while the other achieves the same by means of the prefix *'a-*. Further shared characteristics are the nominal prefix *m-*, which is not found with *pe'al* participles, and the shared vocalism of the passive participle, *a a*, which differs from the *pe'al* participle vocalism *i*: *mqaṭṭal* and *maqṭal* (underlyingly *m'aqṭal*), as opposed to *qṭil*.[44] Phonologically, the only difference between the two is the deletion of the glottal stop of *'aph'el* after a consonantal prefix, a phenomenon that is quite general. It is therefore reasonable to treat them as instances of a single binyan that is not assigned to lexemes directly but rather by way of the two morphological operations of doubling the second root consonant and prefixing a glottal stop to the root, both of which may be either lexical properties or assigned by a lexeme-formation rule. Each of these realizations will result in a four-consonant radical.[45] The binyan itself will then consist of the prosodic stem template $CaCCeC$. Nominal *m-*, which shows up on *pa'el* and *'aph'el* participles, may be assigned to $CaCCeC$ participles by default, with the *pe'al* participial melodies being assigned by their binyan. This same *m-* also appears on the participles of the derived passive binyanim (e.g., *metqṭel*, participle of *'etqṭel*) and on all infinitives. The result of making the *m-* prefix the default realization for participles is that the *pa'el*/*'aph'el* binyan is now reduced to the stem template $CaCCeC$. If we further assume that this template is assigned to all pluriconsonantal radicals, then there will be no need for lexical assignment of the binyan.[46] We will see below that treating of Syriac *pa'el* and *'aph'el* as a single phonologically driven binyan in terms of their forms also makes sense in terms of their subsequent history.

5.7.3   Distribution of active binyanim

The semantic distribution of the active binyanim is similar to that of their Hebrew counterparts: *pe'al* is the most common; many but not all *pa'el* and *'aph'el* verbs are transparently derived; and few verb roots occur in all three binyanim.[47] Semantically, *pa'el* has a distribution similar to the Hebrew *pi'el*. It is often intensive but also has other uses (including causative) and is the binyan that usually occurs with denominal and pluriliteral verbs. The binyan *'aph'el* is often causative but is also inchoative or detransitive. Just as in Hebrew, the binyan system is obligatory in that every root must occur in at least one binyan. The Syriac active binyanim would thus seem to constitute inflectional classes onto which lexemeformation rules are mapped, just as in Hebrew. Given the analysis just proposed of the two derived active binyanim as forming a single pluriconsonantal binyan, we may assume that this binyan is assigned phonologically to all pluriconsonantal radicals and that *pe'al* is the default, and hence the most common binyan, even though it is not associated with any lexeme-formation rule, like its Hebrew *qal* counterpart.

5.7.4   *Pe'al* stems

Just like the Hebrew *qal*, the Syriac *pe'al* has a prefixed and an unprefixed stem (i.e., different stems occurring in prefixed and unprefixed verb forms). Although the unprefixed stem is generally held to be of the form CCVC, it is easy to show from forms like *qaṭlan* 'he killed us' with object suffixes (Aronoff 1971) that there is a vowel *a* between the first two vowels. There is no such vowel in the prefixed stem, which must therefore be of the form CCVC. Just as in Hebrew, the final vowel of each stem is variable. In the unprefixed stem, it may be *a* or *e*, and one verb (*kpud* 'roll oneself up') has *u*. In the prefixed stem, it may be *u* or *a*, and a very small number of verbs show *e*. Just as in Hebrew, the prefixed and unprefixed stem vowels may be paired in various ways. Table 5.17 shows the distribution of these pairs. The class numbers are identical to those for the corresponding Hebrew classes in table 5.11.

If we compare the two languages, we find that class 2 (stative intransitive) is larger in Syriac. Class 3, moribund in Hebrew, has only one survivor in Syriac. Syriac class 4 is similar to its Hebrew counterpart, although it is interesting to note that certain verbs that belong to this class in Hebrew have moved out of it in Syriac.[48] Syriac class 5 has only two

Table 5.17
Syriac *pe'al* verb stems, by stem vowel alternations

Class	Unprefixed stem vowel	Prefixed stem vowel
1, default	a	u
2, stative intrans	e	a
3, *kpud*	u	a
3, mixed$_1$	a	a
5, prefixed *e*	a	e
6, mixed$_2$	e	u

members, according to Costaz (1964), and is not used with *y*-initial roots, as it is in Hebrew. Instead, *y*-initial roots fall into class 2. Class 6 is larger in Syriac than in Hebrew, which makes sense, since class 2, the other class that shows *e* in the unprefixed stem, is also larger. If we separate the vowel specifications of the prefixed and unprefixed stems, as in Hebrew, the greater size of these two classes is the result of a single phenomenon: the greater robustness of *e* in unprefixed stems. Overall, the Syriac situation with respect to the stem vowels of the *pe'al* binyan is similar enough to the Hebrew *qal* situation for us to adopt the same solution: the basic stems are C*a*C*a*c (unprefixed) and CC*u*C (prefixed), with some overrides of individual stem vowels analogous to those in table 5.12.

A general comparison of Hebrew and Syriac binyanim reveals that the two systems differ in most details but have essentially the same architecture. Syriac thus tells us very little that is new, and it would not be of great interest were it not for the morphological changes that have taken place in the last two millennia. For as I will now show, modern Aramaic dialects, while still retaining the basic characteristic of the binyan as an inflectional class and arguably retaining the same binyanim, have restructured the factors that determine the distribution of the binyanim so that they have become phonologically driven along the lines of Arapesh gender. The significance of Syriac, for my purposes at least, thus lies in what followed it.

5.8 Modern Aramaic

My discussion of modern Aramaic binyanim is based almost entirely on the work of Hoberman (1989, 1991). Most of Hoberman's work deals with a single dialect, the Jewish Aramaic dialect of Amadia, a town in northwestern Iraqi Kurdistan, which he abbreviates as JA.[49] Hoberman also discusses briefly certain features of a dialect of Persian Azerbaijan, the data for which come from the classic work Garbell 1965. This dialect belongs to a different subgroup of Northeastern Neo-Aramaic from the subgroup to which JA belongs. As we will see, its binyan system represents yet a further development away from the Syriac model but along the same general lines as that of JA.

The structure of the verb paradigm in JA is radically different from that of the classical languages. All the original tensed perfect and imperfect forms have disappeared entirely, and the new forms are built for the most part on old participles and nominals. Only the imperative is anything like a direct descendant of the cognate category in the classical languages. Although radically restructured, the paradigm is nevertheless very rich both in the number of forms and in their morphological and semantic complexities, more so in fact than the classical languages. As in the classical languages, the affixation pattern of the verb paradigm does not vary by binyan, and so we do not need to look at it here. Interested readers should consult Hoberman 1989 for detailed discussions of all aspects of the verbal paradigm. Despite the radical restructuring, though, the binyanim remain in their old function of stem categories: to know the form of the stem of a verb lexeme, one must know its binyan.

There are two binyanim in JA, one (called binyan i by Hoberman) descended from Aramaic *pe'al* and the other (binyan ii) descended from the combined *pa'el*/*'aph'el* binyan. Their historical origins are clear from the stem melody of the imperative, which is *o* in binyan i and *a i* in binyan ii, exactly analogous to the basic prefixed stem vowel *o* of *pe'al* and the *a e* melody of the *pa'el*/*'aph'el* binyan.[50] Note that the victory of *o* over other possible prefixed stem vowels supports my analysis of CC*u*C (historically CC*o*C) as the basic *pe'al* prefixed stem in Syriac. Also, the coalescence of *pa'el*/*'aph'el* into a single binyan is expected from the account that I gave of Syriac, according to which they were already a single binyan at the earlier stage. Further evidence for the origin of binyan ii in the *pa'el*/*'aph'el* binyan is the presence of the prefix *m-* throughout binyan ii: all binyan ii stems begin with *m-*. This *m-* is quite transparently descended from the *m-* prefix that appears on participles and other nominal forms of the *pa'el*/*'aph'el* binyan.

Morphosyntactically, the two JA binyanim are very similar in their general characteristics to the binyanim of Hebrew and Syriac: there exist lexical verbs in both binyanim; both include transitive and intransitive verbs; there is a productive lexeme-formation rule forming causatives of binyan i verbs in binyan ii. The binyan system is obligatory: all verb lexemes must belong to one or the other binyan. In other words, the JA binyan system is a system of inflectional classes, partially driven by derivation, just as in Hebrew and Syriac.

Each binyan has four stems, according to the system given in Hoberman 1991. These are the continuous, preterite, imperative, and jussive. Table 5.18 contains a list of stem vowels for the stems of each binyan. The distribution of the stems among the actual forms of the verb is not crucial to my discussion, although it is a complex and fascinating matter. I refer the curious reader to Hoberman 1989. Among the stem melodies, only those of the jussive are shared by both binyanim. Hoberman argues that this stem results from an independent morphological rule for forming jussives that operates across binyanim. I will therefore factor out the jussive, which leaves us with three stems. I will follow Hoberman 1991 in citing forms in the continuous stem. This stem is nounlike and hence is always followed by a nominal suffix, which is -a for binyan i and -e for binyan ii.[51]

5.8.1   Distribution of JA binyanim

The three stems remaining when we factor out the jussive all have one vowel in binyan i and two vowels in binyan ii. This forms the basis of Hoberman's analysis, which is that monosyllabic verbs are assigned to binyan i and disyllabic verbs to binyan ii. Each verb lexeme, on this analysis, contains a radical and a prosody that is independent of the number of consonants in the radical and that specifies the number of syllables in the stem as well as whether the first consonant of the stem is extrametrical. The prosody of a given verb lexeme is fixed throughout the entire paradigm of that lexeme. For binyan i (monosyllabic) verbs, we can predict the entire prosody from the number of consonants in the radical: all three-consonant binyan i verbs have the prosody Cσ in all stems, since this is the only monosyllabic prosody that can accommodate three consonants; all two-consonant binyan i verbs have the prosody σ for the same reason.[52]

Table 5.18
Jewish Aramaic stem melodies

Stem	Binyan i	Binyan ii
Continuous	a	ao
Preterite	i	oi
Imperative	o	ai
Jussive	ai	ai

In other words, for lexemes whose prosody is specified as monosyllabic, we need make no further stipulations concerning extrametricality. For verb lexemes with two-syllable prosodies, though, we sometimes have a choice among phonologically possible two-syllable prosodies, and so we must specify for a given lexeme whether the first consonant is extrametrical.

Compare the verb lexemes listed in table 5.19 (adapted from Hoberman 1989). Remember that the continuous stem has a vowel suffix, *a* or *e*, depending on the binyan. In table 5.19 each verb lexeme is listed by its radical and prosody. All disyllabic lexemes have two syllables in their prosody, by definition. The second syllable is always open for phonological reasons, but lexemes differ as to whether the first consonant of the stem is extrametrical (the first consonant of the stem will always be *m*, since all disyllabic, binyan ii, verbs have this prefix added to their radical consonants). We see that the prosody of disyllabic lexemes is partly independent of the number of consonants in the radical: disyllabic lexemes with three radical consonants may have either of two possible different prosodies;[53] disyllabic lexemes with two radical consonants may similarly have either one of two different prosodies; only lexemes with four consonants are restricted to a single prosody (which is perforce disyllabic), because no other prosody but the maximal one will accommodate four consonants plus the prefix *m-*. In other words, the table shows first that the stem of a verb lexeme may have one of a number of prosodies and second that it is sometimes phonologically possible for the consonants of a verb radical to map onto different prosodies; in that case, the "choice" is a property of individual lexemes. Once the prosody of a lexeme is "chosen", the binyan follows automatically: binyan i if the prosody is monosyllabic and binyan ii if the prosody is disyllabic.

Table 5.19
Possible prosodies for Jewish Aramaic verbs

Lexical representation	Continuous stem
⟨/šql/, σ⟩	šqal(a)
⟨/xl/, σ⟩	ixal(a)
⟨/lp/, σσ⟩	malop(e)
⟨/xθ/, Cσσ⟩	mxaθθoθ(e)
⟨/rpy/, Cσσ⟩	mrapoy(e)
⟨/rpy/, σσ⟩	marpoy(e)
⟨/hrhr/, Cσσ⟩	mharhor(e)

The following parameters for verb-stem prosodies cover all the possibilities if we assume the recoverability principle that all the root consonants of a lexeme must be mapped onto its stems.

1. A verb lexeme may have from two to four consonants in its radical in its lexical representation.
2. A verb lexeme may be specified as having a monosyllabic or disyllabic stem.
3. The first consonant of a stem may be specified as extrametrical.

The first parameter allows for three different types of verb lexemes. Of these three, the four-consonant lexemes are exempted from parameters 2 and 3 by the simple fact that all consonants of a lexeme must surface: a lexeme with four consonants must be disyllabic if all consonants are to surface, and the presence of the *m*- prefix on disyllables means that all four-consonant lexemes will have five consonants in their stems. There is therefore only one possible type of four-consonant stem. Parameter 2 says that two- and three-consonant verb lexemes may each be of two types. Parameter 3 would seem to double these. However, for phonological reasons, a monosyllabic stem can have only two shapes: CVC or CCVC. The recoverability principle thus dictates that a three-consonant lexeme have the shape CCVC in monosyllables. Similarly, the phonological fact that there are no initial geminates in the language means that two-consonant lexemes must have the shape CVC in monosyllables. So there is no choice on parameter 3 for monosyllabic stems. This parameter therefore governs only disyllabic stems. We are thus left with seven possible verb prosodies, arising from the interaction of the three parameters with a universal principle and the general phonological properties of the language.[54]

This remarkable and beautiful system is highly robust. Hoberman, who discovered it, notes (1989) that there is only one significant exception in the language: the verb /nbl/ 'take', which is binyan ii but does not show the *m*- prefix, so that its continuous stem is *nabole*, preterite *nobil*, and imperative *nabil*. It must be marked as an exception to the *m*-prefixing rule for disyllabic stems, but otherwise all verb forms are perfectly regular with respect to the binyan system.

5.8.2 The workings of the binyan system

The binyan of a JA verb is never a lexical property: it is governed by the number of syllables in its stem (which may or may not be lexical). But once we know that number, the binyan system operates independently of phonology or anything else. Thus binyan i takes the nominal suffix- *a* in the continuous stem, and binyan ii takes the nominal suffix *-e*. There is no good phonological or other reason for this difference (as Hoberman stresses); the choice of suffix vowel is simply a property of the abstract binyanim, which, like all abstract inflectional classes, characteristically determine choices like this (compare Latin verb-stem vowels). Similarly, the choice of vowel melodies for each stem type is determined entirely by the binyan of a verb; there is no phonological or other synchronic reason for these vowels to be what they are. Furthermore, nothing but the binyan ever determines the quality of a stem vowel. Hoberman shows that the binyanim differ in one other morphological respect, which is that binyan i verbs take the prefix *b-* in the continuous, exactly the sort of difference that is characteristic of abstract morphological classes.

In all these instances, the JA binyanim pattern like inflectional classes: they organize those properties of the forms of the lexeme not governed by other factors. One might wonder why languages should permit words to have such properties, but the fact is that they do and that they almost invariably organize themselves into inflectional classes, a long-ignored but fundamental fact that Carstairs (1987) has emphasized. In the case at hand, we have dramatic evidence of how a system of verb classes in Aramaic has persisted over two millenia unchanged in its essence, against all obvious reasons, reorganized itself along totally new lines, with no syntactic or conceptual roots, and emerged much stronger and more regular in its present state than ever in the recorded history of the Semitic languages.

5.8.3 A remark on the Jewish Neo-Aramaic dialect of Persian Azerbaijan

I have already noted that the binyan system of JA has no exceptions of the ordinary Arapesh sort: items that should normally be assigned to one inflectional class by their phonology but instead belong to another default class by virtue of being exceptions to the rules assigning inflectional class. In JA the rule assigning inflectional class assigns monosyllabic stems to binyan i and disyllabic stems to binyan ii, and that is that. In the Jewish Neo-Aramaic dialect of Persian Azerbaijan, described by Garbell (1965), we do find just the sort of exception that we found in Arapesh, as Hoberman (1991) notes. Here only the continuous stem has different forms in the two binyanim, which are identical to those of JA: melody *a* and suffix *-a* in binyan i and melody *a o* and suffix *-e* in binyan ii. Whether a verb falls into one binyan or the other is determined phonologically, but directly from the segmental makeup of the verb root rather than from some intermediate prosody. To quote Hoberman, "If there are three seg-

ments in the radical, and the first two segments are not both consonantal"
(1991, 60), then the verb belongs to binyan i. Otherwise, the verb belongs
to binyan ii, which is therefore the default. However, there are five verbs
that should belong to binyan i by the above rule but that instead are
conjugated according to binyan ii. This dialect is clearly further along in
its progress from Syriac than is JA: the two binyanim show distinctions
only in one stem-type, not three, and the more restricted binyan shows
exceptions. We may conjecture that it will eventually lose the more
restricted binyan, which will result in a language with only one inflectional
class. I will now turn to such a language.

5.9   Michal: A Semitic Language without Binyanim

Kaufman and Aronoff (1990, 1991) describe the language of Michal, a
native Israeli-Hebrew-speaking child who moved to an English-speaking
environment at the age of $2\frac{1}{2}$. Over a period of about two years, Michal
simultaneously acquired English and lost Hebrew. Our publications have
dealt with various aspects of this simultaneous loss and acquisition, including the effects of each language on the other. For present purposes, I
am concerned solely with the morphology of the later stages in Michal's
loss of Hebrew. At these stages, Michal's language still bore a resem-
blance to Hebrew, but it was different enough to warrant giving it another
name. The name I have chosen is *Michal*.

5.9.1   Michal noun morphology

Morphologically, Michal shows a strong distinction between nouns and
verbs. Just as in Hebrew, the forms of nouns are quite unrestricted. There
is also a great deal of code mixing and direct borrowing of nouns intact
from English. We also find the default English plural marker, used alone
or in combination with a Hebrew plural marker, on both English and
Hebrew nouns. Table 5.20 lists Hebrew nouns with Michal plurals and
standard Hebrew plurals (of a sort that Michal had already mastered
when the process of attrition began). In general, the Hebrew -ot (feminine)
plural marker is lost in Michal, except in words that have a final *t* in
the singular. The default -*im* plural marker is retained, along with English
/z/, one or both of which may appear. When both appear, either order
of them is possible. In other words, Michal nominal morphology is a
mix of English and Hebrew, both of which are largely suffixal and not
templatic.

Table 5.20
Hebrew versus Michal noun plural forms

Singular	Gloss	Hebrew plural	Michal plural
pérax	'flower'	praxím	péraxim
			péraxs
séfer	'book'	sfarím	séferim
			séfers
magévet	'towel'	magavít	magavóts
—	'tights'	garboním	garbonímzız
cimúk	'raisin'	cimukím	cimukímzız
agalá	'stroller'	agalót	agalazim

5.9.2 Michal verb morphology

Kaufman and Aronoff (1991), which I summarize here, is devoted almost entirely to Michal verb morphology. Michal had already mastered Hebrew verb inflection at the very earliest period for which we have data. Beginning quite early in her exposure to English, she began to mix English verbs into her Hebrew. This mixing was morphologically of two types. First, she would mix an intact English verb stem with a Hebrew prefix. This yields forms like *aklin*, consisting of the Hebrew first-person, singular, future prefix *a-* followed by the English verb stem *clean*. The most common such prefix was the infinitive *lV-*, where the vowel was either *a*, *e*, or *i*, as in Hebrew, but not distributed in accord with Hebrew patterns.[55] Examples are *laflush* and *lestep*. The other, admittedly rarer but much more dramatic, form of mixing occurred with suffixed verbs and involved apparent extraction of the root consonants of the borrowed verb and mapping onto a Hebrew template. For example, the verb form *balati* 'I blew' contains the English verb *blow*, whose consonants *bl* have been extracted and mapped onto a two-consonant past-tense *qal* template CaCa, followed by the appropriate first-person, singular, past-tense suffix *-ti*. It is unclear why one morphological type, which we may call *stem borrowing*, was used for prefixed forms and the other, which we may call *root borrowing*, for unprefixed forms. Nor do we have enough data to decide whether the difference is real.

We see signs of the disintegration of the Hebrew system even in these early forms. For example, a two-consonant verb in Israeli Hebrew has the form CaCa in the past tense when it has no suffix: *šata* 'he drank'. Although a three-consonant stem retains the *a* when suffixed (*katavti* 'I wrote'), a two-consonant verb does not: *šatiti*, **šatati*. But Michal's form is *šatati*, and she is quite consistent, as is shown by her borrowed form *balati*, *baliti.

Later on Michal's verb morphology begins to collapse in the usual manner, which is to say that we first find morphologically correct forms used in the wrong context. These include use of the wrong person marker, the wrong tense, the wrong binyan, and occasional mixing of Hebrew and English morphology of a sort that is much more prevalent with nouns. At this point (age 3 years, 6 months), Michal's use of English has become dominant, and she begins to mix Hebrew verbs into her English. An example of such speech is given in (6) below:

(6) I'm *me-nagev-ing* myself. I want to *i-nagev* myself. Can you *it-labeš* me.
   I'm drying myself. I want to dry myself. Can you dress me.'

In these English sentences we find three Michal verb forms. The first is an instance of mixed English and Hebrew morphology in *me-nagev-ing*. Here the expected Hebrew form, if the sentence were in Hebrew, would be *me-nagev-et*, where -*et* is a gender-agreement suffix, so the correspondence is quite close. The second is an instance of a form that I will describe in detail in the next section, 5.9.3. The third is a well-formed masculine singular third-person reflexive, clearly out of context here (the addressee is the child's mother).

5.9.3 The idiosyncratic template

The variety of verb forms used soon gives way to a single idiosyncratic template that is similar to an actual colloquial Israeli Hebrew form but generalized to all occurrences of Hebrew verbs. This template is of the form $iCaCeC$.[56] The template first emerged in Michal's bilingual transition period, but it persisted into the period when Michal was speaking English almost exclusively, so most but not all of the attested forms are from mixed utterances. I will give one example from an actual utterance where we find a switch precisely at the form in question. Note also the well-formed infinitive in this example, which comes from Michal's bilingual period, when the idiosyncratic form first appeared.

(7) Hey, can you *i-kapel et ze? at   yexol-a   le-kapel et ze?*
         fold   obj this you.fem.sg can-fem.sg to-fold obj this
   'Hey, can you fold this, can you fold this?'

Other examples of idiosyncratic verb forms, but without context, can be found in table 5.21, which is taken from Kaufman and Aronoff 1991.

Table 5.21
Michal's idiosyncratic verb template, with date of first occurrence

Age (yrs., mos.)	Form	Gloss	Age (yrs., mos.)	Form	Gloss
3, 1	ikapel	'fold'	3, 9	ikašet	'decorate'
3, 5	isaref	'burn'		inake	'clean'
	ikarer	'cool'		ixabes	'wash'
	isader	'arrange'		icalcel	'ring'
	inagev	'dry, wipe'		išatef	'rinse'
3, 6	igared	'itch'		ixaded	'sharpen'
	isarek	'comb'		igalgel	'roll'
	inagen	'play (music)'	3, 11	itate	'sweep'
3, 7	ikalef	'peel'		isaxek	'play'
	ixabet	'turn off'		itafer	'sew'
	isaben	'soap'		idapes	'type'
	išaber	'break'	4, 1	ikalkel	'spoil'
	igamer	'end'		ivarex	'bless'
	ixamem	'warm'	4, 5	icalem	'take photos'
3, 7	ixaten	'marry'	4, 6	ibalbel	'be confused'
	ixatex	'cut'			
	ixasot	'cover'			

Where does this template come from? The root template CaCeC is easily recognizable. In Israeli Hebrew, it is the *pi'el* and *hitpa'el* template and also the prefixed *nif'al* template: the characteristically geminate middle consonant of the Biblical Hebrew *pi'el* has been neutralized, because there are no morpheme-internal phonetic geminates in Israeli Hebrew. Given the productivity of *pi'el* and *hitpa'el* in both general colloquial Israeli Hebrew and the language of children (Berman 1980, 1982), the use of this root template is not surprising. The prefix *i-* is also frequent in children's Israeli Hebrew: *ye-*, *yi-*, and *hi-* are all neutralized to *i-* (as they are in adult colloquial speech), and in addition, the first-person singular prefix, which is *-a* or *e-* in adult colloquial speech, is realized as *i-* in most binyanim in children's speech. In other words, *i-* is the most frequent verb prefix in Israeli children's Hebrew. This frequency does not explain the simple presence of a prefix in the template, since many verb forms have no prefix at all, but it does explain why this particular prefix is chosen if we must have one.

To return to the analysis of Hebrew binyan templates in section 3, we see that this prefixed idiosyncratic template is in fact not so odd from a Hebrew-internal perspective: most Hebrew stems consist of a prefix and a root template with a fully specified vowel melody. Thus, $iCaCeC$ is a well-formed template of the normal type. If i- is the most frequent prefix in children's Hebrew (which seems likely) and $CaCeC$ is the most frequent root template and an archetypical template is of this general form, then $iCaCeC$ is in fact expected.

The larger question of why use a template of any sort is at once simpler and more difficult. Put simply, what choice does Michal have? If she wants to mix a Hebrew verb into her English, that verb must have some form, and we have seen that this is the most likely form for any verb to have. But the more difficult question is why she does not produce a variety of forms, more or less unsystematically, rather than a single form, no matter how reasonable that form may be. Here we must rely on our belief in the power of grammar: she has a language, which, being a language, must be systematic; it is this systematicity that drives her to select a consistent form.

All verbs must fall into a single form, determined to the point of rigidity. The binyan system ends at this point. We have followed a steady erosion, from Hebrew through Syriac through the Modern Aramaic dialects, from five down to two binyanim and now with only one remaining. Yet through its very persistence it becomes transformed: for if we did not know its history, we would not hesitate to call it what it must be in this language, the marker of the lexical category Verb. By virtue of its survival, an inflectional-class marker, the essentially unmotivated morph, becomes a motivated grammatical sign. This is surely the exact reverse of the expected course of history, whereby motivated signs become grammaticized (Haspelmath 1992), but it is just as real.

Chapter 6
Conclusion

Morphology is not necessary. There are languages that do without it, and languages with morphology vary quite remarkably in their morphological structure and complexity. Because morphology is not essential to all languages, general theorists of language have often tried to do without it, positing theories in which there is no specifically morphological component. From a reductionist point of view, this move makes excellent sense: general linguistic theory is meant to account for just those properties shared by all languages, and if some languages have no morphology, then our general theory too should have no morphology. By this reductionist logic, morphology is an excrescence, and when we find a language with morphology, we must either account for it in terms of some more universally available piece of the language machine, say syntax or phonology, or we may choose to ignore it as simply an accident of history that has nothing to do with the real object of our study, the Universal Grammar that governs the shared properties of all human language.

The reductionist view of morphology has flourished in American linguistics for decades. On this view in its various incarnations, the difference between morphology and syntax is basically junctural; whether a language expresses something syntactically or morphologically may be accounted for on language-particular historical grounds, but this kind of historical account has no place in synchronic linguistics, which is concerned centrally with what permits a child to acquire a natural language.

Many morphologists, by contrast, are impressed less by the fact that morphology is so variable across languages than by the mysterious complexity of the morphological systems within individual languages. To these observers, the remarkable fact is not how little morphology a language can get along with but rather how much morphology a language can accommodate. To those who are struck by this efflorescence in languages like Navajo or Mohawk or classical Greek, where each verb may have hundreds of different forms, reactive reductionism holds no charm. Instead, they wish to understand such systems in all their complexity. This can be a daunting task. Navajo verb morphology has probably been the most intensely studied single aspect of any of the indigenous languages of North America, yet its true nature remains largely a mystery. Similarly for other Athabaskan languages: Rice's prize-winning comprehensive grammar of Slave (1989) is not quite 1,400 pages long, and more than 500 of these pages are devoted to a purely descriptive treatment of its verb morphology. Algonquian verb morphology too, though it has occupied some of the best minds in the field over most of the century, is still little understood.

For me, the most comfortable scientific strategy to adopt in the study of these complex and daunting morphological systems is not the confrontational stance of reductionism but rather one of accommodation: to try to understand each system on its own terms. To many, this may smack of Boasian relativism or, even worse, of descriptivism, but remember that it is a strategy and not a theoretical claim. In the theoretical end, all morphological systems must be learnable and hence must conform to universal principles of grammar. But if we do not understand how the systems themselves work, how can we find out whether their workings conform to our putative general claims? This approach lies behind the title of this work and its purpose: to understand morphology by itself on its own terms and not on terms imposed on it from outside; to understand nature, not to subdue it. To a philosopher, this goal may seem naive, but I am not claiming any privileged insight, I am only stating the purpose of the enterprise.

From this perspective, the strategy of rooting out morphological phenomena grounded in some other aspect of language and brandishing such phenomena as vindication of the reductionist method makes little sense. There may be a myriad of these reductions, but it is precisely the opposite that attracts me: the morphological fact that is not easily reducible to another aspect of language and hence that is morphological in more than name. So I have set out over the last few years to uncover morphological generalizations that are not plausibly analyzed as something else, and I have presented a number of these in this book within a general framework that allows a great degree of autonomy to morphology. Theoretically, one such true generalization would suffice to show the reality of morphology and the value of the general framework, but despite the appeal of the well-worn phrase, we cannot know whether the generalizations we capture are real or imagined. So I seek safety in numbers.

I have focused on a particular type of phenomenon, the irreducible abstract morphological categories that partially determine the form of a word, because these categories seem to me to be the clearest examples of the purely morphological. Let me review these briefly. In chapter 2, I showed that Latin verb morphology is organized in terms of three verb stem. For each inflected form of a Latin verb paradigm and for certain derived stems, the choice among these three stems is systematically determined: each form is built on a particular one of these three stems. I have concentrated my analysis on what I have called the third stem, which has been very little studied in the long history of Latin grammar. My main point has been to show that this stem can be defined in neither phonological nor semantic nor syntactic terms, but only in terms of which forms are built on it, which is to say in terms of its place in the morphological system of the language, a place that is quite rigid. In other words, the stem system of Latin verb morphology is autonomous.

In chapter 3, I reviewed some of the now fairly large literature showing that gender and nominal inflectional classes are independent of one another in many languages. This independence is evidence for another type of, usually unmotivated, abstract morphological category, the inflectional class, which determines not the stems but rather the inflections of lexemes. I would like to emphasize again that what I have said about gender and inflectional class is truly ancient. It was not for nothing that the Latin grammarians only gave numbers to inflectional classes for both nominals and verbs. The numbers are arbitrary, which shows the arbitrary basis of the inflectional classes. That linguists, in their quest for motivation, still ignore this important finding despite its frequent repetition may tell us something about ideology, but it should not gainsay the truth of the original observation: that Latin inflectional classes are demonstrably divorced from gender and singularly unmotivated.

In this same chapter, I addressed a question that arises as soon as one divorces gender from inflectional class, which is how the two are related. I followed a fairly conservative tack here: adopting the common idea that gender and inflectional classes are related by implicational rules, often called redundancy rules. Separate from these redundancy rules are the rules for spelling out actual inflected forms. I stated these in terms of what I called realization pairs: pairings between morphosyntactic-feature arrays and morphophonological realization rules. Each inflectional class is a set of such pairs, defined simply by means of its members. This treatment of morphological realization is not meant to be of great theoretical or formal significance but is to my mind primarily a way to present morphological realization clearly, especially as it relates to inflectional class.

Once we divorce inflectional class from gender but permit the two to be related implicationally, other possibilities arise. In particular, the separation allows the relation between gender or inflectional classes and phonological form to be more complex than we usually think. Inflectional classes rooted in phonological form are not uncommon. For example, it has been known for centuries that inflectional classes may be determined phonologically: traditional classical Greek grammar treats the nominal inflectional classes in terms of the final segment of the nominal stem (*a*, *o*, or default). But there has been very little discussion in the general morphological literature about the possible relation between gender and phonological form. As it happens, Latin has a fair number of examples of just this phenomenon in its third declension (what I call inflectional class 3), and I end chapter 3 with these.

Chapter 4 moves on to two languages of Papua New Guinea in which the phonological forms of nouns quite reliably determine their inflectional class and gender. I discussed Arapesh morphology in some detail to show precisely how conceptual categories, genders, inflectional classes, and phonological form can be related in a fairly complex fashion within a single language and yet remain independent from one another. My discussion of Yimas is meant to reinforce this point and to extend the discussion to a language in which conceptual categories play a larger role in the morphology than in Arapesh.

In chapter 5, I brought together the two strands of the three previous chapters, stems and inflectional classes, in an analysis of Semitic verb classes (binyanim). I argued for a treatment of binyanim as inflectional classes. However, unlike typical inflectional classes, which determine the forms of inflectional endings, binyanim determine the forms of verb stems: if a verb lexeme belongs to a particular binyan, the stem of each inflected form of that lexeme will have a form determined by the binyan. Some binyanim have only one stem, but others have two, with the distribution of the two stems being determined by the verb morphology of the language. The existence of two phonologically unrelated stems for some binyanim is important, for it shows that a binyan, which combines the two notions of stem and inflectional class, is also an abstract morphological category. I treated several Northwest Semitic languages in this chapter, arranged in terms of the number of binyanim they contain and also, for Aramaic, in terms of their historical development. For Aramaic, although the basis of the binyanim has changed over the millennia, they have retained their essential nature as stem-determining inflectional classes. I closed the chapter and the book with a description of the interlanguage of a young child in which the Semitic binyan system has collapsed into a single stem that characterizes all verbs, a motivated sign.

Much more remains to be done. Thus, although I made a clear distinction between productive morphology and the lexicon of listed words, I have avoided any detailed discussion of the two in languages with unmotivated stems and inflectional classes. Classical Greek springs readily to mind as such a language, with several verb stems for each verb and a great deal of irregularity in the forms of these stems. Another topic I have not touched on is that of affixal position class, which has been discussed within an autonomous framework by Stump (1991). In Athabaskan languages, we find both a great deal of irregularity in the forms of stems and a wonderfully rich system of affixal position classes. For a morphological reductionist, languages like these are mere sports, deviating beyond the normal limits of variation. If I have laid the groundwork properly, you will see instead that they may hold the key to knowledge. My charge to you: find it.

Notes

Introduction

1. In Aronoff 1976, I claimed that *-ive* adjectives were normally derived from *-ion* nouns, with accompanying truncation of the noun suffix. *Formative* is an example of this sort of derivation: its meaning shows that it is derived from *formation* and not directly from the verb or noun *form*.

2. The formative letters of Hebrew are so called because they are restricted to a set of seven letters, called in traditional grammar by the acronym *h'mntyv*, pronounced [he'emantiv]. The English translation is *hemantic*, which may be etymologically related to *semantic*, a much later coinage.

3. Bopp writes, "The only thing which we will leave untouched is the secret of the roots, that is, the basis for the naming of the original concepts" (1833, vol. 1, iii, cited in Stam 1976).

4. I do not have space here to explore the adjective *formal*, which, in modern technical usage, is often almost synonymous with *formalized*, another word worth studying. In this sense, we can and do speak of formal syntax. See Chomsky (1975, 83) for a discussion of the two terms. It is also true that linguists who have worked with syntactic tree notation for many years tend to think in terms of syntactic structures much more tangible than a nineteenth-century grammarian could conceive of. For modern syntacticians, sentences do have form, but we should remember that this form is immaterial, unlike the sound shape of morphology.

Chapter 1

1. In the first chapter of this work, Selkirk introduces an informal morphosyntactic definition of stems and roots, in which "*Stem* is simply a convenient term for the [recursive] type X^{-1} that is one down in the X-bar hierarchy from Word ($=X^0$) .... A case can also be made for a yet lower (recursive) category level X^{root} (or X^{-2}) contained within Stem" (1982, 7). This definition is intuitively close to the traditional one. It is the attempt to assimilate it to the theory of junctural types of affixes that results in the later oddity in the definition of the term *root*.

2. One possible account of the phenomenon may lie in the inherent prescriptivism of definitions. Linguists, perhaps because they have been so indoctrinated against

prescriptivism in language, seem to find the bonds of normative terminology especially chafing. By using a term in their own way, they are, like Humpty Dumpty, declaring their right as individuals to use the language however they please. Unfortunately, even the informal language of science is not ordinary language but is closer, at least in purpose, to mathematics. Just as we try in mathematics to avoid nonstandard and especially idiosyncratic notations and definitions, so too must we in our informal scientific discourse. That is one of the rules of the game.

3. It is important to note, though, that the actual arguments given in *WFGG* for truncation are independent of this problem. To the extent that truncation is systematic and morphologically restricted, it is still a theoretically useful device, regardless of whether one allows a stem to be something other than a free form.

4. Baudouin de Courtenay, in the introduction to his monograph on phonetic alternations, says the following about the early days of modern linguistic terminology:

Both works of Kruszewski ... belong to a time [1879–1881] when the Kazan' linguists became infatuated with nomenclature, developing a mania for inventing new and unusual technical terms; Kruszewski was wise enough to use some restraint in this respect in his works. This disease reached monstrous proportions in my own [work], the reading of which could only be hampered by such technical terms as *coherents, homogenes, heterogenes, monogenes, polygene, amorphism* and *secondary heterogeneity of morphemes, amorphous correlatives, divergence* and *anthropophonic coherence, mobile correlation* and *morphological coincidence, coincident correlatives, coexistent correlatives,* etc.

However, despite this frightful number of newly coined technical terms, there is a sound kernel of useful observations in this work.... Of a certain methodological value are also: first, distinction of the concepts *sound* and *phoneme*; second, the unification of the concepts of root, affix, prefix, ending, and the like under the common term, *morpheme*. (1972 [1895], 150)

Thus from the great number of terms coined by Baudouin de Courtenay and Kruszewski for their newly discovered concepts, we are left with the phoneme and the morpheme. Not bad. Incidentally, Baudouin states clearly that Kruszewski coined the term *phoneme*, but *morpheme* is apparently his own.

5. Matthews (1991, chap. 10) emphasizes that the ancient Latin and Greek grammarians had no notion of morphemes. One can view the work of Matthews and his followers as an attempt to do morphology without morphemes, in the ancient manner.

6. I assume without argument that adverbs are adjectives and that adposition is not a lexical category. I also assume that all languages have the three categories of noun, adjective, and verb as syntactic categories, although morphology does not usually reliably distinguish all three.

7. DeSaussure puts it well: "The sound-image is sensory, and if I happen to call it 'material,' it is only in that sense, and by way of opposing it to the other term of the association, the concept, which is generally more abstract" (1959, 66).

8. The temptation of form extends to the morpheme too. There is a tendency in American linguistics to think of a morpheme as being essentially a form or a set of forms.

9. I assume that whether a given lexeme is actual or not is a question about the mental lexicon. Stemberger and MacWhinney (1988) have shown that a word can be used without having to be stored in the mental lexicon. For other recent discussion of morphology in the mental lexicon, see Henderson, Coltheart, Cutler, and Vincent 1988.

10. I am not claiming here that every lexeme must be representable by a single decontextualized *form* (usually called the *lexical representation*), from which all contextual forms are generated. This claim, which may be sustained in the vast majority of cases (Carstairs 1987), in some instances runs up against the conflicting demands of the (permanent) lexicon: there are many lexemes for which some contextualized forms must be listed in the lexicon because of morphophonological irregularities of varying degrees. Some linguists assume that each lexeme is a set of fully inflected forms. De Saussure says, "Latin *dominus, dominī, dominō*, etc. is obviously an associative group formed around a common element, the noun theme *domin-*" (1959, 126). Bybee (1985, 1988) and others have proposed network models that dispense with lexical representation in all cases. I mention all of this only to underscore that for the moment it is irrelevant to me exactly what the internal organization of a lexeme is. I care only that each lexeme be given some independent status.

11. Only the term *lexeme formation* is less than common. I have borrowed it from Matthews 1991.

12. I use the terms *morphosyntactic property* and *morphosyntactic category* in the sense of Matthews 1991 to refer to the syntactic properties of a word that have a role in morphology (understood narrowly) and to the categories of these properties. Latin gender, for example, will be a morphosyntactic category, and individual genders will be morphosyntactic properties. I use the term *morphosyntactic property array* in instances where more than one property is realized by a single morph, as frequently occurs in inflectional languages. I use the term *property* instead of *feature*, because on some views, some morphosyntactic properties are not features but independent elements. I also assume for the moment that the morphology is ignorant of the syntactic side of these properties—an assumption that I will explore further in chapters 3 and 4.

13. Some reader's might feel that I am begging a central question here: whether the spelling out of lexeme and higher-level categories is done by a single mechanism or not. There are arguments on both sides (Lieber 1992; Beard, to appear), but since the issue is not yet decided, it seems more prudent to preserve the distinction for now.

14. The exact nature of this distinction is never made totally clear in Chomsky's work. At one point, Chomsky says, 'Formatives are of two types: grammatical and lexical (among the grammatical we count, as subtypes, class markers and junctural elements introduced by syntactic rules, e.g. word boundary). Each grammatical formative is represented by a single symbol. Each lexical formative is represented in a systematic [phonological] orthography as a string of symbols" (1964, 85). Chomsky's discussion in *Aspects* is even more enigmatic: "The ques-

tion of substantive representation in the case of the grammatical formatives and the category symbols is, in effect, the traditional question of universal grammar" (1965, 66). That Chomsky does make a distinction, though, is quite clear.

15. Some people use the term *morphosyntax* to mean sublexical syntax. The problem here is that the term is usually used to mean any aspect of syntax that has morphological realization, inflectional or derivational, and is therefore too broad.

16. Note that Bloomfield's morphological definition of the word quite clearly treats compounds and phrasal lexemes as containing more than one word.

17. If we go by spelling (which we shouldn't), these would include the English articles, demonstratives, prepositions (unless we include prepositions as a separate major lexical category), conjunctions of various sorts, auxiliary verbs, and pronouns. Phonology reveals that many orthographically separate members of non-lexical categories are clitics, but polymoraic prepositions like *under*, *beside*, and *through* are still separate phonological words in English, as are their counterparts in many other languages. Similarly for certain modals.

18. Even the terms *lexical category* and *lexical formative* are unfortunate, since they conjure up another false connection, that between minimal projections and the lexicon. I discuss this problem below.

19. Some might object to *lexeme formation* as a term, because it intimates a constructive treatment of the workings of this domain. I would counter that such an intimation is in fact correct. I have argued at length elsewhere (WFGG, Aronoff 1983) that the core of lexeme formation involves the creation of new lexemes and that the analysis of existing lexemes, if it has any theoretical validity at all, is derivative. I see no reason to change this view and I therefore prefer *lexeme formation* to a term like *lexicology*, which is more neutral.

20. Chomsky suggests that we "characterize a zero element of the level **L** as a prime of **L** that happens to correspond to the unit [identity] element of some lower level. For example, consider the two levels **Pm** and **M**, the phonemic and morphemic levels. We can 'spell' a certain utterance in terms of phonemes or in terms of morphemes; i.e., we can associate with this utterance a certain string in **Pm** and a certain string in **M**. But these strings are related. The 'morphophonemic rules' tell us which string of phonemes corresponds to a given string of morphemes. If a certain morpheme corresponds, under these rules, to the [identity] unit U of the phonemic level, i.e. if it disappears on this lower level, then we call this morpheme a 'zero morpheme' and we write it with the symbol 0 (perhaps with subscripts). We might say, then, that the element 0 has real morphemic content, but no phonemic content" (1975, 106).

21. This dichotomy may have to be relaxed or rethought in the light of Drijkoningen 1989, 1992, where it is argued that category-changing affixes occur above the level of minimal projections and that their adjunction is a case of derivation in syntax. Whatever the final outcome, it is clear that if there is a genuine difference between derivation and inflection, that difference lies in their syntax and not in their morphology.

22. This is not to deny that one or both members of a compound may show a special form. The first members of Greek compounds have a "compounding-stem," as discussed by Bloomfield (1933, 229). But as I point out in chapter 3, bound stems, which are contextually determined forms of lexemes, must be distinguished from the bound realizations of morphosyntactic properties. What makes compounds different is that they lack the latter.

23. Some authors, e.g., Selkirk (1982), posit a very broad account of English compounding according to which even the categories are variable. Selkirk's system would include all English compounding under a single rubric:

(i) $[[\ ]_X [\ ]_Y]_Z$

(where X, Y, and Z range over the lexical categories.) Such an account, if valid, does not gainsay my observation.

24. Baudouin de Courtenay defines a morpheme as "that part of a word which is endowed with psychological autonomy and is for the very same reasons not further divisible" (1972 [1895], 153). My thanks to Przemyslav Pawelec for pointing out this definition.

25. Later in the book Bloomfield goes on to "extend the term *lexical* to cover all forms that can be stated in terms of phonemes, including even such forms as already contain some grammatical features (e.g. *poor John* or *duchess* or *ran*)" (1933, 264). This is certainly nonstandard, and it shows the extent to which, for Bloomfield, *lexical* had lost its connection with words. On the other hand, this use of the term may be defended as a return to its etymological origin. It has also recently been revived by syntacticians, who distinguish lexical pronouns, which have phonological substance, from null pronouns, which have none.

26. Bloomfield's use of *formative* is more restricted than that of Chomsky, who extended it to all morphemes, thus obliterating a useful distinction.

27. In a footnote, Chomsky discusses, without conclusion, the question of whether *modal* should be considered as a lexical category. In later work (e.g., 1972, 210), the lexical categories are characterized as just N, V, and A.

28. In restricting the sense of the term *morphological realization* to bound realization as opposed to the realization of free forms, I am attempting to preserve Chomsky's distinction.

29. The following story has circulated for years, though one of the main protagonists tells me that it has little basis in reality. Noam Chomsky is being interviewed by Joshua Whatmough, as a candidate for a junior fellowship at Harvard in the early 1950s. Whatmough asks Chomsky what he thinks of the term *morpheme*. Chomsky launches into a learned disquisition concerning Harris's distributional definition of the morpheme. Whatmough patiently lets him finish and says that he had something else in mind. To which Chomsky responds with another long disquisition, this time about the morphemic level versus the phonemic level. Again Whatmough waits and then replies that his question was about the term *morpheme* and not the concept. The term *phoneme*, says Whatmough, is etymologically justified by the Greek term φώνημα 'a sound'. The Greek word for 'a form' is μόρφωμα, with a different stem vowel, so the modern technical term should therefore be *morphome* and not *morpheme*. Chomsky agreed and got his fellowship.

30. Andrew Carstairs-McCarthy tells me that he has never encountered such an ideal regular agglutinative language. Neither have I.

31. Inflectional homonymy, or syncretism, as discussed at length by Carstairs (1987), might look like an example of many-to-one mapping. However, if we treat each realization rule as a separate function, then the mapping within each function is one-to-one, although the total paradigm is not.

32. The underlying form of the suffix *D* is usually taken to be /d/, but this is not a settled issue (Bloomfield 1933, Zwicky 1975).

33. Some of these realizations are shared with irregular past-tense formation, but the *-n* suffix is limited to the perfect participle in standard English (*I seen him* is nonstandard), whence Chomsky's use of the name *-en* for the perfect participle, regardless of its realization, even though *-n* is in the minority, even for irregular verbs.

34. These realization rules themselves are clearly quite free of any signification, but discussing of this observation would take me too far afield.

35. Some readers may feel that a complex morphological identity of this sort is impossible without corresponding syntactic identity. While I agree that complex morphological identity is a good heuristic for syntactic identity, nonetheless, to elevate this heuristic to a theoretical claim is both to beg an important question and to downplay the prevalence of homophony in natural language. Note also that I am using the assumed homophony of the English passive and perfect participles simply as a familiar example. It might very well turn out in the end that the two constructions are synchronically related in their syntax in such a way that the identity of the participles is explained. In that eventuality, the reader should substitute the Hebrew example that I give below.

36. Note, by way of contrast, that the English adjectival passive is sometimes distinct in its form from the verbal passive for individual verbs (e.g., *rotten* versus *rotted*), which would seem to indicate that in the case of the two passives we are not dealing with constructions that are morphologically identical constructions in the way that the two participles are identical. In general, if the adjectival and verbal passive differ in form, the verbal passive is the innovative form. A synchronic analysis that always morphologically derives one of the two passives from the other must be mistaken.

37. Positing this level allows for more complexity than the conventional morpheme-based ideal, which envisions morphology as consisting of a direct mapping between syntax and phonology. Since positing this level is a priori undesirable, it is important that it be justified empirically.

38. The present tense differs from other finite tenses in modern Hebrew in not allowing subject prodrop, presumably because it lacks person agreement.

39. I will not take up here the question of participles in Biblical Hebrew participial relative clauses, which sometimes pattern like adjectives and sometimes like verbs with respect to the diagnostics under discussion. See Waltke and O'Connor 1990, chap. 37, for a discussion of the facts.

Chapter 2

1. Monteil, for example, defines the theme as "le mot complet amputé de sa désinence" (the whole word with its desinence cut off).

2. For the moment I will be using terms like *root* and *stem* in a pretheoretical sense. Later I will clarify more precisely what I mean by these terms.

3. In the system of the classical Latin grammarians, e.g. Donatus (fourth century) or Priscian (sixth century), and in subsequent traditional Western school grammars based on the Latin model, one member of an inflectional paradigm was formed from another, rather than both being formed from a third more abstract form, as in the Sanskrit and modern formal traditions. Hence the name *Priscianic* for such a formation when it is called for in modern treatments.

4. The future participle, because it is an adjective, always carries an agreement suffix after the *-ūr*-suffix. However, in this chapter, future participle will designate the "abstract" form that ends in *-ūr-*, without any agreement suffix.

5. In addition to the standard abbreviations, I will use the following in the Latin glosses: Th, theme vowel; T, third stem marker (the notion of the third stem will be explicated in section 2.2.3); FP, future (active) participle.

6. In the tables, I note only the morphs that are relevant to the discussion. Irrelevant morph boundaries are not indicated.

7. In this chapter, the term *perfect participle* and its abbreviation *PP* will designate the perfect participle minus any agreement suffix, i.e., the form that ends with the *-t-* (or *-s-*) suffix. This form never actually occurs alone "on the surface," since an agreement suffix is obligatory.

8. Whether the perfect-participle suffix is *s* is not always predictable on phonological grounds.

9. The best-known exception is the verb *mor-i-* 'die', whose perfect participle is *mortu-* but whose future participle is *moritūr-*. Most of the other exceptions are first-conjugation verbs with a theme-vowelless perfect participle but a thematic future participle. An example is *sec-ā* 'cut', with the perfect participle *sect* but the future participle *sec-ā-t*. There are perhaps a half dozen of these.

10. With the verbs *posse* and *velle* in table 2.2, the absence of both the perfect and future participles can be attributed to the absence of the former. With *esse*, one might wish to claim that the perfect participle is not used for semantic or syntactic reasons, although it "exists" in some potential sense and surfaces in the Romance languages.

11. There is one fairly widespread circumstance under which the perfect participle is not passive: with the so-called *deponent* verbs, which are passive in form throughout the paradigm but active in meaning. These will be discussed in section 2.6.

12. The distinction that Bloomfield makes may be important, yet I will not discuss it in this work.

13. The contemporary theoretician who has discussed the importance of stems most cogently is Arnold Zwicky (e.g., 1990).

14. One might invoke solutions involving existing but nonoccurring forms, but these are too dangerous for my blood.

15. The Latin word literally means 'lying on the back' and is intended to convey that the verb here is inert, neither active nor passive in force. It is derived from the Greek grammatical term *hyption*, originally a wrestling term. The etymology of *supinum* is discussed in Benveniste 1932.

16. The supine appears to be defective, having only two of the expected five case forms. However, this may be due to its syntax rather than to its morphology.

17. Unlike nouns, whose declension is fixed, first- and second-declension adjectives have their declension (first or second) determined by the gender (not declension) of their head noun. Feminine nouns trigger the first declension, while masculine and neuter nouns trigger the second declension. Third-declension adjectives do not vary in this way.

18. Historically, the past participle has an -*o* stem, while the supine has a -*u* stem. However, a sound change in old Latin changed *o* to *u* under certain circumstances, resulting in the homophony of the accusative singular case forms. It is also worth noting here that there is another type of nominal, identical to the supine in form, found in such words as *fructus* 'enjoyment, profit', *sensus* 'perception', and *actus* 'movement'. This nominal is related historically to the supine in the same way that English -*ing* developed a nominal as well as a gerund use (Wasow and Roeper 1972). For an illuminating discussion of the relation between the two, see Panagl 1987. The classic discussion of Latin -*t* nominals of all sorts is Benveniste 1948.

19. One might counter on the side of the supine that its neutrality with respect to voice makes it a better candidate semantically for the base of the future participle than the usually passive past participle. But this argument is not much more forceful than the last.

20. The suffix is underlyingly -*ōr*, but the vowel shortens by a regular rule in the nominative citation form. In general, a -*trix* feminine can be found corresponding to a -*tor* masculine form, but for -*sor* masculines, -*rix* feminines are systematically lacking, except for *expultrix* 'she who drives away' (compare *expulsor*) and *tonstrix* 'hair-dresser' (compare *tonsor*). *Expultrix* is irregular, the expected form being *expulstrix, and in both cases we see that the -*t* has been reanalyzed as part of the suffix rather than as part of the stem.

21. With verbs whose theme vowel is *ā*, the iterative form is regularly built on the bare stem, rather than on the third stem. So we find forms like *rōgitō*, from *rogō*, *rogāre* 'ask', rather than the expected *rōgātitō. This is probably due to some sort of haplology (Menn and MacWhinney 1984), although it might have to be formulated as a truncation rule.

22. These form types are systematically built on the third stem. Other types are sometimes built on this stem, but I will not consider them here.

23. A similar solution is proposed by Kuhner and Holzweissig (1912).

24. Remember again that this definition of *stem* is very different from Bloomfield's. For Bloomfield, a stem is a bound form, and he has no term that expresses the notion that I am getting at. Mel'čuk (1982) seems to have in mind a concept

similar to mine, but he says, "The notion of stem is quite important for morphological description, but at present I am not able to suggest a rigorous definition for it (1982, 131).

25. As Robert Hoberman has reminded me, in the Semitic tradition, the citation form is not the address, for which the root is normally used, dictionaries being alphabetized according to roots.

26. This is essentially equivalent to Halle's (1973) list of morphemes, though one might quibble about the confusion of terminal elements (which are purely syntactic) and morphemes.

27. Robert Beard points out to me that the term morpholexical rule was coined by Bloomfield (1939) to distinguish lexically governed morphological alternations from more general morphophonemics.

28. Lieber does not broach the question of the semantic relation between the terminal elements related by her morpholexical rules. The question is not trivial, since these terminal elements, being listed in the permanent lexicon, must have semantic representations, unless we distinguish the morphological lexicon from another lexicon, the syntactic one.

29. For suffixed verbs, the theme vowel is usually determined by the suffix.

30. Incidentally, for productively derived lexemes (what I call *potential lexemes*) whose stems are predictable, as in this case, it is impossible to say that these nonexistent stems of nonexistent lexemes are listed in a permanent lexicon. Thus even if we were to allow the more than 96 percent of actual first conjugation verbs whose stems are all predictable from the theme vowel to have all their stems listed (following, say, Bybee), we would still not be able to claim that the rules for regularly derived stems are not productive.

31. There is no special connection between a theory's being lexeme-based and its permitting a complex mapping between form and meaning. For instance, Marantz (1984), while not having an explicitly lexeme-based theory, certainly argues for nonisomorphism.

32. In general, when a morph occurs with a particular possible meaning only in a morphologically restricted environment, it is difficult to decide whether that morph has significance or whether its presence simply as a form is conditioned by the environment or construction, which as a whole bears the significance in question. Thus one might wish to claim for Greek compounds that the stem vowel signals that the stem preceding it is a bound member of a compound or that it links the members of a compound, but since the stem vowel only occurs by itself between members of compounds, the traditional analysis, that the stem vowel is semantically empty, is equally reasonable and more parsimonious, especially since some compounds show no stem vowel and would have to contain $\emptyset$ if the stem vowel were semantically significant. Troubetskoy (1949) calls such junctural phonological phenomena as word-final devoicing *boundary signals*, even though they are automatically conditioned phonological alternations. At a superficial level, they do serve to mark the juncture even though they are, strictly speaking, predictable from it. My claim is that we are dealing here with a similar phenomenon.

33. Note that the theme vowel -*ā* appears "after" the null suffix for intensives. If we do not allow zero morphs and if we insist that morphs (forms) rather than lexemes condition the quality and quantity of the theme vowel, then we must say that the -*ā* theme vowel is the default. This conclusion is based on frequency and further historical development (it is the default theme vowel in all Romance languages).

34. There is, as I have already mentioned, a small number of very-high-frequency irregular verbs that lack a theme vowel. These verbs, to the extent that they are regular, take the same inflections as *e*-theme verbs.

35. Of the five, three occur independently as verbs. One, -*lē*, occurs only in the verb *dēlē*, which quite transparently contains the privative prefix *dē*-. The other (-*plē*) occurs with a number of prefixes (e.g. *ex*-, *con*-) and has the general meaning 'fill'.

36. I assume that the *i* of *viē* is a glide.

37. The fact that a stem and not a lexeme has a theme vowel is consonant with my claim above that morphs determine the quality of theme vowels. Most interesting in this regard are the third-conjugation verbs that show mixed conjugation. This class includes all verbs with the intensive suffix -*ess*, which have the theme vowel -*e* in the present stem but -*ī* in the perfect and third stems. The suffix thus determines the form of the resulting verb in a complex manner, selecting different theme vowels for different stems. Sometimes included with -*ess* are verbs with the inceptive suffix -*sce*, whose perfects lack the suffix (e.g., *quiēscō*, *quiēvī* 'become quiet'). Here, however, the derived verb is lacking the perfect stem altogether, and the perfect stem of the base is used instead.

38. Where the nasal is retained throughout, we know from etymology that the root has no nasal. For example, *iunge* is transparently derived from the root *iug* 'yoke'. In this case, a less frequent verb, *iugā* 'tie together', is also formed from the same root without a nasal infix.

39. Traditional grammars say that the nonpresent stems of these verbs are formed on the root. For morphologically simple verbs, the lexical representation will indeed be the root.

40. Note that this type of idiosyncratic stem selection would be much more difficult to state in a simple morpheme-based treatment, since we may do severe damage to the notion of allomorph if we always treat as allomorphs the different forms of a single lexeme that may be selected as stems. That is because some stems are morphologically complex, while others are not, for the same realization rule. Semantically, the two stem types must be treated identically, which leads to difficulties in grouping forms into traditional morphemes.

41. I have not included any verb without a theme vowel, since they are all idiosyncratic, but you should note that these verbs by and large take the same endings as *e* verbs and that they are perfectly regular in the nonpresent forms.

42. For example, the *ī* and *i* conjugations are identical in all but a few cases, and in just those cases where they differ, the *i* and *e* conjugations are identical.

43. This analysis of the function of theme vowels can be traced to the Latin grammarians. Monteil (1970) restates it within a "Benvenistean" framework.

44. The term *stem type* is used to refer to general notions on the level of present stem, perfect stem, third stem, etc., as opposed to individual stem tokens like *portāt-* or *portā-*.

45. This generalization holds only for inflection. In derivational word formation we do find exceptions, so that a given suffix that usually selects a given stem type may exceptionally be formed on another stem type in a particular instance. Derivational suffixes also vary in regularity in this respect. But such variation is the hallmark of derivation.

46. All deponents have the following active forms: present and future participles, future infinitive, gerund, and supine.

47. There are a few verbs (all of them very frequent) that occur only in one or two individual verb forms. Two common ones are *aiō* 'affirm', which occurs only in the present and imperfect indicative, and *inquam* 'say', which occurs in a few scattered forms.

48. Note also that I am looking at stem types, not morphs. It should be very clear by now that each stem type is a phonologically abstract morphomic entity realized in a great variety of ways, rather than a phonologically specified (albeit abstract) entity on the level of, say, English /z/, the marker for the plural noun, the third person present verb, and the genitive.

49. I assume that this suffix is followed by a theme vowel, *-ā* in the imperfect and *-e* in the future. This will ensure that the person and number suffixes have the proper forms.

50. The first-person singular suffix *-am* deletes the preceding vowel in all instances. Similarly, the third-person singular suffix- *t* shortens the preceding vowel in all instances.

51. We also see from this particular example that the former type can sometimes be constructed on the latter, the *b* stem being built on the present stem.

Chapter 3

1. Whorf would call gender a covert category because membership in a given gender is not marked on the category member itself but rather by what Whorf (1945) calls *reactance*.

2. Unless otherwise indicated, translations are mine.

3. I will not address in this work the general question of why grammars should tolerate unmotivated morphophonological, or for that matter morphosyntactic classes. It is sometimes said that "Classification systems allow a language to impose order within this set of nouns." (Foley 1986, 78). But this explanation usually is predicated on the observation that the classification system is externally motivated by inherent features of the nouns' referents. When such external motivation cannot be found, as it cannot in the case that Foley has in mind, we may instead appeal to an inherent human desire for order, however ungrounded the particular order may be. See the psychological literature on memory for further elaboration (Cohen 1989, Zachmeister and Nyberg 1982).

4. "Each independently provides information concerning regularities in selected aspects of human behavior. The general methods of scientific technique are the same in both .... But the results in each ... are different" (Z. Harris 1960, 22).

5. The editorial marginalia in Joos 1966 directed against grammatical prerequisites to phonemic analysis provide the best example of this school of thought.

6. Strictly speaking, a language whose major lexical categories each have only one inflectional class will still have inflectional classes. In practice, however, interest in inflectional classes only arises when a language has more than one such class for a given major lexical category. The reason for this is simple: the major question about inflectional classes is what determines membership in one or another of these classes for a given lexeme. This question is already answered for languages with only one inflectional class for a particular major lexical category, which makes the study of inflectional classes less interesting for such languages.

7. The one exception is the combination neuter, plural, and nominative or accusative, which is always realized as -a. I discuss this exception in some detail below.

8. We almost never find free variation among realizations for a given noun or adjective. In other words, the mapping is a function, as noted for other similar cases in chapter 2.

9. I exclude vocative and locative, which are restricted in their distribution.

10. I will not explore the basis of this principle or its relation to language acquisition.

11. When we find pairs of nouns like Spanish *tio* 'uncle' and *tia* 'aunt', we assume that these are distinct lexemes (Matthews 1991).

12. Only one common feminine noun, *mano* 'hand', belongs to the *o* class. This noun is irregular in Latin, being one of the few feminine nouns (*manus*) belonging to the predominately masculine fourth declension. Similarly, *tribu* 'tribe', which is irregular in ending in *u*, is a feminine, fourth-declension noun in Latin.

13. Spanish is peculiar in that the inflectional class triggers only one rule rather than an entire set of realizations. Spanish is also peculiar in that it is not clear what property beyond the inflectional class is being realized. In the next section I will deal with Russian, which is a more typical language.

14. I state the realizations in terms of rules because I believe that there are circumstances under which process morphs are called for (Hoeksema and Janda 1988). Advocates of pure item and arrangement morphology may substitute other methods of realization here without harm.

15. A larger question about disjunction lurks here. Imagine two classes, one of which triggers one suffix and the other of which triggers both. Nothing that I have said rules this out, nor does the elsewhere condition (see n. 30), since there is no subset principle to appeal to here. The interested reader should consult Anderson 1992 and Stump 1991 for further discussion of the problem of disjunction and position class in morphological realization.

16. Feminine nouns might be specified lexically for membership in class 2, but because this class is assigned to feminine nouns by rule, we can't tell for any given

feminine noun whether it receives this class membership by rule or bears it idio-syncratically. The same holds for masculine nouns ending in *o* and class 1. There is in fact experimental evidence that lexemes that are both very frequent and regular may be specified lexically for features that are otherwise assigned by rule (Stemberger and MacWhinney 1988).

17. I have no ready explanation for the fact that class 1 is almost never specified idiosyncratically for feminine nouns. We might say that this is the default class and that the default class is not usually specified lexically, but I am not sure of the general validity of this assertion, especially since default inflectional classes may be context-sensitive in other cases, as I show in my discussion of Hebrew participles in section 3.

18. *Heroe* is odd in having a final *e* that is not inserted phonologically. It repre-sents a fairly substantial class.

19. There are no adjectives idiosyncratically specified as belonging to class 1. This is not surprising, as the number of nouns so specified is vanishingly small and the total number of idiosyncratically specified adjectives is much smaller than the corresponding number of nouns.

20. My account of Spanish gender and its morphology differs somewhat from Harris's. Harris argues that there is no masculine gender in Spanish, only feminine.

21. Animacy is distinct from gender but also plays a role in Russian declension. I omit here any discussion of animacy or of the neuter gender but I will return to the subject below, in the section on neuter gender in Latin nouns, since the two systems are similar in certain respects.

22. Corbett (1991) gives a much more detailed account of Russian nouns classes and their relation to gender, and it differs somewhat from mine.

23. Robert Beard points out to me that most of the masculine members of class 2 are there for systematic reasons. First, all hypocoristics, regardless of gender, go into class 2 (*Saša*, for example, is the nickname for *Aleksandr* as well as for *Aleksandra*. Second, pejorative agentives like *p'janica* 'drunkard' and *plakša* 'cry-baby' are always class 2 (syntactically, they may be either masculine or feminine, depending on pragmatic context).

24. The most productive of these is the suffix *-ost'* '-ness', which is responsible for a large proportion of class 3 nouns.

25. This is the default rule. It is written without any gender specification, so that any noun that is not feminine and is not inherently specified for a noun class will be assigned by default to this class.

26. It is usual to distinguish the stage of Hebrew that one is talking about: Biblical, Masoretic, Mishnaic, rabbinic, or modern. But when it comes to gender and number in nouns and adjectives, which is what I am concerned with here, there is no systematic difference among the various stages. I use Berman's (1978) orthography, which is designed for modern Hebrew, throughout this section.

27. In Hebrew, nouns, adjectives, and participial forms of the verb are considered to be *nominal* in their morphology, as opposed to morphological verbs, which have person markers (nominal forms of the verb do not) and differ morphologically from nominals in various other ways. The morphologically nominal verb participles were discussed briefly in chapter 1. Henceforth in my discussion of Hebrew, you should understand the term *nominal* in this narrow Hebrew sense in which a verb participle may be morphologically nominal, even when it is syntactically a full-fledged verb.

28. There is a very small set of Biblical titles like *qohelet* 'teacher' that are masculine but show the feminine suffix -*t*. Interestingly, this set has disappeared in later stages of the language. Note that I exclude cases like *moledet* 'offspring', which is an abstract feminine noun but sometimes shows masculine agreement, according to the sense.

29. In the account of Spanish given above, the most marked class (class 3, which is never assigned by rule) is realized by the identity rule. In terms of markedness, this is an instance of reversal (Battistella 1990), since all other classes carry a formal marker.

30. The ordering principle commonly known as the elsewhere condition (Koutsoudas, Sanders, and Noll 1974), according to which a specific rule will always precede a more general one that properly includes its domain, will guarantee the proper order of application here, since the stipulated nouns form a subset of the set of all nouns.

31. One might even wish to combine (11) and (12) into a single pairing, as in (i):

(i) $\langle$[N, Feminine or stipulated, Plural], $(X \rightarrow Xot)\rangle$

This rule would state that the plurals of either feminine nouns or those nouns that are stipulated for it are paired with the realization "suffix -*ot*." This entails allowing disjunctions in morphosyntactic property arrays, a possibility that I do not wish to explore here.

32. The -*a* suffix shows up as *at* before suffixes and in the construct form, where the noun is closely joined to the following word. Otherwise, the *t* is absent word-finally, and the *a* lengthened (with the length distinction being lost in later stages of the language). The occurrence of *t* in this form might tempt one to try to reduce all the feminine suffixes to -*at*. Additional support for such a reduction comes from the fact that the suffix -*et* is always unstressed, the vowel being inserted by the well-attested "segholate" rule. This suffix is therefore synchronically -*t*. Historically, the two suffixes -*a*(*t*) and -*t* do arise from the former, with the *a* being deleted after a vowel-final stem, which results in -*t*. Synchronically, though, -*a*(*t*) and -(*e*)*t* must be seen as two distinct suffixes throughout the recorded history of the language. This is because the -*t* suffix is found attached to consonant-final stems from the earliest records, especially in participles and infinitives, so that the two forms are not in complementary distribution. We find variation between -*a*(*t*) and -(*e*)*t* participles in Biblical Hebrew, although the -(*e*)*t* form wins out with most feminine participles at later stages and is completely standard in the modern language for all but one template (*hif'il*, in which only -*a* appears). Thus Gesenius and Kautzsch (1910) list both *qotelet* and *qotla* as paradigm feminine forms of the

simple *qal* active participle, noting that the first is more common. The distribution of the two affixes among nominal forms and the changes in this distribution over time are a complex and fascinating object of study but would take me too far afield. For my purposes, it is sufficient to conclude that the forms of the participle prove that these two feminine nominal suffixes are not phonologically predictable allomorphs but rather two separate suffixes. The other two *t* suffixes, *-ut* and *-it*, are similarly unreducible to *-at*, for a variety of reasons.

33. This point is made most clearly in James Harris's work on Spanish (1991a, 1991b).

34. As in Russian and many other Indo-European languages, neuters are restricted to the inflectional classes that also have masculine members. I could represent this fact by calling both of these genders [−Feminine], following Jakobson (1984, chap. 9), but note that this would call for the use of a binary feature, which I have tried to avoid.

35. The symbol *N* in these rules stands for *nominal*, including adjectives, nouns, and participles, so that the rules also apply to nouns and participles unspecified for gender. The default class for feminine nouns is thus class 1, and for masculine and neuter nouns it is class 2. This prediction accords with the statistical distribution of nouns in Latin and with the subsequent history of the Romance languages, where classes 1 and 2 predominate and the associations between gender and class statistically follow these rules.

36. Class 3 words ending in a sonorant, like *consul*, with no visible nominative suffix, are normally treated as having the suffix *-s*, which is deleted by the phonology.

37. Almost the same solution is given in Carstairs 1987.

38. Both of these facts can be traced back to Indo-European. According to Meillet (1964 [1937]), the Indo-European neuter had its own case forms only for the nominative-vocative-accusative, for which there was a single form for each of the singular, dual, and plural numbers. The plural form was *-ā*. Frank Anshen points out that it is natural to expect the neuter not to have either distinct nominative or vocative forms. The vocative, after all, is largely reserved for animates, and neuter nouns are seldom, if ever, animate. Similarly, subjects are archetypically animate, making neuter nominatives uncommon. We might therefore assume that neuters originally had no nominative or vocative form because they did not occur with these cases and that the accusative was extended to the nominative, which made it at least historically prior.

39. One might wish to claim that the case suffix here is *-ibus*, as in classes 3 and 4, and that the *ē* is the class suffix. A phonological rule would delete the *i*, which results in *-ēbus*. This is reasonable, but orthogonal to the question at hand.

40. The identity of neuter nominative and accusative case forms also extends to the pronoun, but the nominative and accusative plural form is not always *a* (compare *haec* 'this', *quae* 'which').

41. In the singular, the dative and ablative forms are identical in class 2 and certain class 3 forms, but in class 1 and class 5, the dative and genitive forms are identical.

42. The fact that there are exceptions to this observation (e.g., *acer* 'maple tree' neut.) shows that we are dealing here with the gender of the plant name and not simply with deletion of a feminine head noun, as we are with names of cities, which are all feminine, presumably because the noun *urbs* 'city' is feminine and is understood when we use the bare name of the individual city.

43. On the surface, we find alternations between *us* and *er* in word like *foedus* (nom.) *foederis* (gen.) 'treaty' and between *us* and *or* in words like *corpus, corporis* 'body'. I am assuming that the *u* is phonologically basic in the former class and that the *o*, changing to *u* by a well-known rule, is basic in the latter.

44. On the surface, there is an epenthetic *e* between the consonant (usually a stop) and the word-final *r*, as the cited forms show. This *e* disappears when *r* is followed by a vowel.

45. Ernout and others note the influence here of those class 2 masculine adjective stems ending in C*r* that also end in C*er* (rather than C*erus*) in the nominative singular, e.g., *tener* 'tender' as opposed to *properus* 'hasty'. Ernout also notes that the lack of the nominative singular suffix -*is* was variable and that some adjectives (e.g., *mediocris* 'ordinary') always show the suffix. In other words, the facts are complex, but they do not contradict my central point. A related but even more anomalous fact is that class 3 names of plants ending in C*er* are neuter, rather than feminine, as most plant names are. Examples are *papāver* 'poppy' and *sūber* 'corktree'. According to what we have seen so far, we can understand why these are not feminine (there is only one feminine noun ending in -*er* in Latin, *linter* 'tub') but they should be masculine and not neuter.

Chapter 4

1. Pashto is another language in which gender appears to be based on phonology (Shafeev 1964).

2. R. F. Fortune is Reo Fortune, a well-respected British-trained social anthropologist who may be best known as Margaret Mead's second husband. He was the one whose canoe Mead abandoned literally in midstream for Gregory Bateson's, according to legend. His work on Arapesh was done in the mid 1930s, when he was at the peak of his career, on one of the two major field trips that he and Mead took together. Mead describes this trip in her autobiography (1972). It is notable that the major theme of Mead's early work was the social construction of sex roles and how it differs across societies. This interest of hers may have heightened Fortune's interest in gender in Arapesh. In any case, a great deal of Fortune's grammar of the language is devoted to gender.

3. I use the term *proword* here, rather than the more usual *pronoun*, because the language does not distinguish pronouns from determiners like *which*. On the simplest analysis, all demonstratives and interrogatives in the language can be treated as determiners, but I will not take up this issue here.

4. All subject prefixes have the vowel *a*. This may be a separate morph from the subject-agreement marker.

5. This peculiar condition on relative sonority covers cases like *røb*, whose corresponding free pronoun is *abarøb*, rather than the expected *ararøb, which would arise from reduplicating the first consonant of the base. But when *r* is the only consonant, it does reduplicate, and when there is no consonant in the class marker, the vowel reduplicates as a glide: *u* reduplicates as *awau*. We may therefore say that we reduplicate the least sonorous segment of the base. I know of no other reduplications that can be described quite like this.

6. Obviously, this state of affairs is not universal, since there are many languages that show gender agreement on non-third-person verbs as well as gender-distinct forms of at least second-person pronouns. Semitic languages provide examples of both. Exactly how to distinguish a Semitic type of language from the Arapesh type is beyond the scope of this work.

7. It is possible that these "affixes" are clitics. The grammar does not provide enough information to permit us to choose between the two analyses.

8. The verb classes may be syntactically motivated, but Fortune's grammar does not provide enough information to allow us to say so with ease.

9. Certain nouns belong to Gender viii legitimately, rather than by default. This state of affairs is typical with default genders.

10. It is worth quoting Fortune in full here: "Of the demonstrative pronouns meaning this near me, that near you, and that yonder near him, the forms for class VIII (terminals of nouns in *ñ* and *š*) are used where the class of the noun specified is not specially singled out, or in the plural to refer to a compound subject of nouns of various disparate noun classes. This usage agrees with the general use of the forms in *ñ* and *š* for exceptional or non-specific purposes" (1942, 49).

11. In the texts that accompany the grammar, Fortune always glosses this form as 'what things'.

12. I am treating this sentence as an example of default agreement of the verb, rather than agreement of the proword: *ña* is found only as a subject prefix on verbs, and the corresponding nominal form, if one exists, should end in *ñ*, with no final *a*. However, Fortune gives the form *amwiña*, as if *ña* were a suffix on the noun rather than a prefix on the verb. I would therefore not hang a theory on this example.

13. Further evidence for the outlying status of the first person is the fact that only the first person has a distinct dual form. The numeral for 'two', used only in the third person, shows plural agreement.

14. It is entirely possible, as I noted above, that there exist languages in which gender and inflectional class cannot be empirically distinguished, i.e., in which the mapping between them is perfect. Within my framework, this is accidental, though nothing in the framework prevents such perfect mappings from occurring. In this regard, it is less restrictive than a framework that permits only perfect mappings, which is why I must empirically demonstrate that gender and inflectional class are nonisomorphic.

15. Fortune also includes all nouns ending in a voiced vowel in the set of nouns whose terminals do not fit any inflectional class. However, these are numerous enough that one might claim instead that they are assigned to the *ehas* class by rule.

16. In addition to defaults, gender viii is regularly assigned to members of the inflectional class of nouns whose singular form ends in *ñ* and whose plural is *š*. For this inflectional class, gender viii is assigned by normal means rather than by default.

17. The problem is that they do seem to belong to an inflectional class (to judge from their plurals), albeit the wrong one, so that if gender is dependent simply on inflectional class, we would expect them to belong to gender i, which they do not. There are various solutions to this problem but too few examples to warrant exploration of it.

18. The only items that I cannot account for remain those five nouns with anomalous class 1 plurals but default gender. They are also the only clear examples of positive exceptions in the entire morphological system of the language. Gender iv, the only one that is morphologically diverse but phonologically unified, presents a different problem, which I will return to shortly.

19. Remembering that these rules are feature-filling and implicational, one might be tempted to turn (5b) into a biconditional, but the many-to-one mapping of some inflectional classes onto genders makes this move unwarranted as a general solution.

20. I assume that the *u* of the singular is inserted by regular phonology, though nothing here hinges on that assumption.

21. The conditions are not sufficient under the conservative treatment, since we must ensure that those "stems" that end in the appropriate segment(s) for a given class and result from segmenting off a singular suffix are not put in that class. For example, the "stem" *war-* should be eligible for membership in class 10 (with final *r*) and have the plural form **waguh*, but it doesn't, because is a member of class 5. Under such an analysis, though, since stems like *war-* are all lexically marked for membership in their inflectional class, they will be exempted from the regular class-assignment rules by the elsewhere condition.

22. This same *mi* also appears on a few male kinship terms.

23. Fortune lists nouns that denote objects used in male initiation ceremonies but that do not belong to gender vii, e.g., *wagitur* 'tree-trunk seats for initiated boys'. Specifically male or female body parts or articles of clothing also fall outside the two genders in question. It is thus clear that the scope of these classes is restricted to persons, both actual and mythical.

24. In English, we find them only in compounds, and then only when the first component of a compound is suppletive in its plural and of very high frequency. A search of *Webster's Third* gives the list below:

man-child	men-children
manfish	menfish
man Friday	men Fridays
manfriend	menfriends
manservant	menservants
man-woman	men-women
woman-suffragist	women-suffragists

All the examples but one involve the word *man*, which is the most frequent noun in the language (Francis and Kučera 1982). Semantically, all but one (*man Friday*) are of what Marchand (1969) calls the *girlfriend* type, in which there is no discernible semantic head or modifier (a girlfriend is both a girl and a friend, a girl who is a friend and a friend who is a girl). Note that it is impossible to have a form like **girlsfriends* or **boysfriends*. Note also that these are not dvandvas.

25. Foley (1986) reconstructs such a system for Proto–Lower Sepik. No similar reconstruction has been done for Torricelli, and there is no simple way to determine in which family the system originated, but the answer to that question is somewhat orthogonal to my purposes.

26. Foley says that this is also the gender for human beings whose sex is not highlighted, and hence is the unmarked human gender.

27. This class "includes higher animals, those important to humans, such as pets, domesticated livestock, other sources of food, ceremonial accoutrements or mythological figures. There is not a sharp boundary between the animals of this class and those included in class V or the other inanimate classes" (Foley 1991. p. 129).

28. Foley notes that only two words in the language end in *c*, which otherwise is prohibited from occurring word-finally. These may be recent loans. As expected if it is indeed the default gender, these anomalous nouns end up in gender v.

29. Alternatively, we could list the exceptions to these two genders, which would then fall into the default gender automatically. I see no empirical grounds for choosing between these two solutions, although the latter is more elegant.

30. How do we characterize this default relation without using rule ordering? The problem is as follows: given a noun with a conceptual property P_c and a phonological property P_p, why should the first take precedence? The answer is that nouns with both properties are a subset of those with only P_p, and so the conceptual definition takes precedence.

31. Gender ii, the female gender, has affixes for adjective and possessive agreement that are distinct from those of any other gender. Otherwise, its agreement affixes are identical to those of gender i. Its nominal inflections are also distinct.

32. This gender constitutes a problem for Carstairs's (1987) notion of paradigm economy, since it has no affix of its own. Carstairs-McCarthy (1991) discusses similar examples from other languages.

Chapter 5

1. Waltke and O'Connor point out that "in the earliest grammars presented with Hebrew and Latin *en face* the Latin term *conjugatio* appears opposite Hebrew

binyan" (1990, 351). Gesenius and Kautzsch, by contrast, note in a footnote that "the term *conjugation* thus has an entirely different meaning in Hebrew and Greek or Latin grammar" (1910, 115).

2. A dozen or so other binyanim are rarely found in Biblical Hebrew. Altogether, verbs in these rare binyanim comprise less than 1 percent of the total number of verb forms in the Biblical text. Most of these have disappeared completely in later stages. In Israeli Hebrew, as R. A. Berman points out (1978, 85), *nitpa'el* is found, and *šif'el* is fairly productive in the sense of the English verbal prefix *re-*. The former consists morphologically of the *nif'al* prefix *n* added to the *hitpa'el* template; Berman analyzes the latter as derived by prefixation of *š* to the root of a *pi'el* verb, which thus turns it into a quadriliteral. Alternatively, since quadriliterals are automatically *pi'el*, we may simply say that *š* is prefixed to the root of its base lexeme and that the resulting quadriliteral root is automatically *pi'el*. Also found in Israeli Hebrew is *hitpu'al*, with the meaning 'to act involuntarily', as in *hitputar* 'be forced to resign', from *hitpater* 'resign'. Morphologically, this is the passive of *hitpa'el*. All three of these less common Israeli Hebrew forms may therefore be analyzed as consisting of a combination of an already existing binyan and another morphological operation. Berman uses the term *subconjugation* in discussing these forms.

3. In this chapter I use a version of Schramm's (1964) phonological transcription, modified in the direction of R. A. Berman's (1978). Schwa is not indicated; long kamats is transcribed as *â*, rather than as open *o*. Double consonants are indicated as such, rather than with a daghesh. For the vowels written with matres lectionis, I do not include the mater in the transcription, again following Schramm. I use the smooth breathing mark for aleph and the rough breathing mark for ain.

4. In the Hebrew grammatical tradition, these are called *past* and *future* tenses. In Israeli Hebrew, they are unequivocally past and future tenses. Their exact meanings in Biblical Hebrew, which are clearly more aspectual and may be only minimally temporal, have been a matter of great debate for centuries. See Waltke and O'Connor 1990 for a comprehensive analysis. Waltke and O'Connor call the tenses *conjugations* because they differ in affixation patterns. I would prefer to reserve this term for inflectional classes and therefore persist in the traditional term *tense*.

5. In Israeli Hebrew, one infinitive as well as the optative and jussive are gone.

6. In Biblical Hebrew, object pronouns are suffixes, which greatly expands the size of the paradigm. In Israeli Hebrew, object pronouns are common only in very formal and poetic registers. The suffixed forms are not germane to my discussion.

7. Most irregularities in the forms belonging to the paradigm of a given verb can be characterized in terms of the phonological peculiarities of certain root consonants. Roots are classified into strong roots, which have none of these consonants, and weak roots, which are further classified according to the position and nature of the offending consonant. The weak roots include those in which one consonant is a glide and those in which the first consonant is *n*, as well as those in which the second and third consonants are identical (i.e., two-consonant roots). Once the nature and position of the weak consonant is given, the properties of the verb

paradigm follow automatically. In this sense, Biblical Hebrew has very few irregular verbs, verbs whose forms are arbitrarily irregular with no phonological basis, as there are in English: most "irregular" verbs in Biblical Hebrew owe their irregularity to their root consonants. This predictability holds only for Biblical Hebrew. The irregular root classes became morphologized in later stages, due to various phonological changes. At these later stages, one might treat the root classes analogously to the binyan system, so that there are two morphological class systems for verbs, each comprising one dimension of a matrix. For any given verb, the intersection of its binyan and its root class will give its paradigm. But here I am stepping ahead of my argument. There are also suppletive verbs, which I discuss briefly in section 5.5.1.

8. Remember that normal nouns with no inherent inflectional class will be assigned a class by implicational rules of various sorts. The set of nouns under discussion is different, since we must make sure that none of the implicational rules operate on these nouns. In other words, we must somehow assure that these nouns remain outside the inflectional system of the language. A central issue here is lexical borrowing, especially the relation between borrowing and code mixing.

9. I do not know of any instance of an indeclinable nonauxiliary verb. This is most likely due to the fact that verbs are rarely borrowed. See, however, the discussion in Aquilina 1965 on the conjugation of verbs borrowed from Italian into Maltese. Thanks to Bob Hoberman for drawing my attention to the Maltese case.

10. Lieber 1981 is an extended argument for the morphological unity of derivation and inflection within a very different general framework. As far as I can see, Lieber's arguments carry over to the framework adopted here.

11. None of what I am saying here depends on there being a genuine distinction between lexeme formation and syntax, although I do believe that such a distinction is valuable (see chapter 1). Those who wish may therefore treat the syntacticosemantic dimensions of what I am calling lexeme formation as (sublexical) syntax.

12. This is not to say that the morphological effects of derivation will always be linearly external to inflectional morphology, a point that I have discussed in Aronoff 1988.

13. I am not claiming that inflectional morphology is never abstract in this way. For example, for those Indo-European languages that have separate passive-verb paradigms, one may argue that the morphological reflex of syntactic passive (and whatever the passive is syntactically varies quite dramatically from one theory to another) is the abstract marker of the passive paradigm. In languages like Sanskrit or Greek, where the passive paradigm is not unified but coincides to some extent with the middle form of the verb, the abstract nature of the notion of passive morphology is even clearer.

14. Diminutive suffixes are a well-known exception. They often inherit the gender of their base. Again, Latin provides good examples: the diminutive suffixes, *-l* and *-cul* are always first or second declension, regardless of the declension of their base, but they almost always inherit the gender of their base. This is another

demonstration of the distinction between syntax and morphology: gender, being syntactic, can be passed on by percolation, or feature passing. Inflectional class cannot, as discussed in detail in chapter 4.

15. This suffix is historically distinct from the -*or* agentive suffix, which is also masculine. The agentive attaches to the third stem, as discussed in chapter 2, while the abstract suffix attaches to the root or present stem, which gives us contrasts like *amātor* 'lover' versus *amor* 'love'; also, the abstract suffix was originally -*os* and not -*or*, later alternating with intervocalic -*or* because of rhotacism, the well-known phonological rule of Latin whereby [s] becomes [r] between vowels. The change of final [s] to [r] is usually viewed as a result of analogy or paradigmatic leveling. Not all nouns ending in *os* underwent the analogical leveling, and it is interesting to note that nouns are less likely to undergo the change where the *os* was not strippable (because it would leave a vowelless stem): *flos* 'flower', *mos* 'custom', *ros* 'dew'. This may be taken as evidence that the suffix itself was undergoing the leveling, perhaps under the influence of the agentive suffix. The subsequent history of the two suffixes is complex: they fall together in the Romance languages (as with Italian -*ore* for both), but the borrowing of Latin terms led to such contrasts as French *amour* versus *amateur*. In English the two suffixes became differentiated in spelling: -*or* (*cantor*) versus -*our* (*valour*). See Aronoff 1978a for a discussion of the English facts and later developments.

16. To cite one example among many, Waltke and O'Connor (1990) devote 9 pages to noun *mishkalim* and 109 pages to binyanim.

17. Although they are not obligatory, *mishkalim* do play an important role in Hebrew morphology. See Ravid 1991 for an enlightening discussion of their importance in Israeli Hebrew lexeme formation.

18. Classical Arabic differs from Hebrew and Aramaic in having overt case endings on nouns. It also has two distinct inflectional classes of nouns: one in which the nominative, accusative, and genitive are all distinct and one in which the latter two fall together. Some Arabic *mishkalim* also assign inflectional class to their members, as expected. However, as Bob Hoberman points out to me, Arabic diminutives normally inherit the inflectional class of their base nouns, contrary to general expectation (Wright 1896, 1: 242). This matter warrants further investigation.

19. There are exceptions, though not many. For example, as Bob Hoberman points out to me, the Israeli Hebrew verb *qibel* 'receive' has as its passive *hitqabel* or *nitqabel* but not **qubal*. Such cases can be handled by listing the passive binyan for this lexeme and consequent preemption of the passive rule.

20. See Waltke and O'Connor 1990, sec. 22.6 for discussion of and further references to this fascinating textual problem.

21. Gesenius and Kautzsch put it this way: "In consequence of a looseness of thought at an early period of the language, *Niph'al* comes finally in many cases to represent the passive of *Qal*" (1910, secs. 51 f.).

22. The first stem vowel of the binyan that I have designated as $h_u^o f'al$ varies in the Masoretic text between a symbol for *u* and one that is usually interpreted as

standing for an open o. The conditions under which each symbol appears are not completely understood. In Israeli Hebrew, u wins out over o in all forms, a point to which I will return below.

23. This same melody is also used for internal passives in Arabic, as Shmuel Bolozky points out to me.

24. Remember also that the binyan of a given active verb will sometimes be an arbitrary part of its lexical entry, and sometimes not, as with any inflectional-class marker.

25. Rosén (1977) distinguishes between the root and what he calls the three-position radical, which may include derivational material in addition to root consonants and which is "extracted" from a base by stripping off external affixes and internal vowel patterns. Rosén's observations have been taken up and elaborated on in a modern theoretical framework by Bat-El (1986, 1988, 1989). Although my sympathies are with the radicalists, I will continue to use the term *root* and its associated notions, because they are familiar.

26. In Arabic, these affixes may also be infixes or, in one case, a suffix. Most other Semitic languages tolerate only prefixes in forming binyanim. I should mention here that McCarthy's templates span the entire inflected verb form. In my use, which is closer to traditional practice, I exclude from the template all pronominal prefixes and suffixes. I also distinguish the root template as being filled by only the root consonants.

27. The two tenses have analogues in other Semitic languages. They also differ in their patterns of agreement affixation: the past tense has only suffixes, while the future has prefixes in all forms and some suffixes. For this reason, the two are called the suffix and the prefix conjugations or stems, or the prefixed and unprefixed stems. The two stem types date at least to Proto-Semitic and possibly to Afro-Asiatic. The question of their meanings in Biblical Hebrew is one of the great enigmas of Biblical scholarship. By the time of Mishnaic Hebrew, a simple tense distinction had begun to emerge (Segal 1927), and it has continued through to its logical end in Modern Hebrew. In later Hebrew, there has also developed a distinct present tense, which is participial in form.

28. Prince explores this issue at length, concluding that "for the purposes of phonology, there never is a vowel between C_1 and C_2 in the imperative/imperfect stem $C_1C_2VC_3$.... The internal workings of morphology remain as inscrutable as activity inside the En-Soph" (1975, 116).

29. This discussion ignores the first-person, singular form that is usually given in paradigms, which is 'εppâ'el. This form has the vowel ε instead of i in the prefix. However, as Gesenius and Kautzsch note (1910, sec. 51) the expected i vowel is as frequent as ε in the actual Biblical text. I will therefore assume that the paradigm contains the i form.

30. There is no evidence to decide whether this prefix is morphologically complex or not. The *hi* shows up in the future of *nif'al* in the *hin-* prefix, but I see no reason to claim that the *hi* sequence of *hit-* is the same as this one or even that the *hi* of *hin-* is a separate prefix. The *hi-* of the *hif'iyl* binyan is often analyzed as *ha-*,

as I will show shortly. In any case, in the analysis of binyanim that I develop below, there is little sense to the question, since the prefix, prosody and vocalism are treated as a single unit.

31. Blake (1950) surveys this alternation in detail and concludes that it is lexically and morphologically conditioned. As Bob Hoberman points out, we can fruitfully regard the alternation as part of the morphology of the *hif'il*.

32. We cannot account completely for the masculine singular imperative, since its future counterpart shows the expected *i* between the second and third root consonants (*yaqpid*). It may be relevant that all other masculine singular imperatives except for *qal* have this same *e* vowel, but I have no real explanation for this vocalic anomaly.

33. There are two types of infinitives in Biblical Hebrew: the infinitive absolute and the infinitive. Because the former is quite complex and only the latter occurs in Israeli Hebrew, I will not discuss the infinitive absolute, which is not germane to my point in any case.

34. The idea that the first three patterns are old and the other three innovations is traditional in Semitic grammar (see Waltke and O'Connor 1990, 367). However, not all scholars agree with this scheme. Lambdin (n.d.) reconstructs five patterns for West Semitic: *a, u; i, a; a, a; a, i;* and *u, u*. The reflexes of the last two do not occur in Hebrew.

35. I do not say *determined*, because stem vowels other than *a* may appear before guttural consonants. When they do, an epenthetic *a* is inserted between the vowel and certain gutturals. So, for example, with the root *šm'* 'hear', the *qal* prefixed stem is *šma'*, but the participle is *šomea'*, with the characteristic *e* of the participle followed by *a*. Similarly, the infinitive is *šmoa'*, with the stem-vowel *o*. In other words, the prefixed stem could be *šmo'* or even *šme'*, and it would still be pronounceable by means of the epenthetic *a*.

36. If we were to start with the prefixed stem, we would have to write an entirely different set of rules. I should also note that a corresponding rule for classical Arabic would have to go from the prefixed stem to the unprefixed stem.

37. I should also note that the template of the qal infinitive stem is usually CC*o*C, even with verbs whose prefixed template is CC*a*C. This may be further evidence in support of the basicness of CC*o*C.

38. There is a downside to this treatment: three of the nine theoretically possible verb classes are not found. Two of these would have *e* in the prefixed stem, which is rare, so that their absence is easily understood, but one would have *o*, which is common. However, this class (*o/o*) would also have the stem vowel *o* in the unprefixed stem, which is the least common. That may be a factor in why this does not exist. Also, we expect class 6, with default prefixed *o* and unprefixed *e*, to be common, but it is in fact very rare. One might respond to this by observing that prespecification of the vowel of the unprefixed stem normally implies that the vowel of the prefixed stem will be *a*. In any case, we are dealing here with details that may in fact be accidental.

39. McCarthy (1986, 237) treats these biconsonantal forms as the result of a rule of geminate verb deletion, which, he points out, precedes all known rules of the phonology. I would prefer to assume that there is no spreading in these verbs to begin with, and hence no need for geminate verb deletion, whose only purpose is to undo the effect of spreading.

40. This lengthening is due to the nominal nature of participles: stressed stem-final *a* is normally lengthened to *â* in nominals but not in verbs. Note also that the distinction between *a* and *â* is lost in Israeli Hebrew.

41. If a verb has more than one stem, the rule stated in this way will not apply. If the rule does not apply, then there is no prefix and the unprefixed stem will be used, which is just what we want.

42. The Syriac transcription is my own and uses Jacobite, or Syrian Orthodox, pronunciation, in which *o* and *u* have fallen together. For the most part, I do not mark spirantization. I do mark gemination. Otherwise, the consonant transcription is the same as for Hebrew. I transcribe the "Greek vowels" by means of the corresponding Latin vowel letters.

43. It is said that *'ettaph'al* is rare, with the other passives being substituted for it in many cases. It may be that some users of the language restricted the application of the prefix to unprefixed stems, which would account for the observed rarity. This is merely a conjecture, though, and not based on any analysis of textual materials. In any case, *'ettaph'al* future forms are the only ones in the language to have three prefixes.

44. The passive participles of the active binyanim are distinct from the participles of the passive binyanim, which are not relevant here.

45. I follow Hoberman (1991), who follows Rosén's (1977) treatment of Hebrew in distinguishing a root from a radical in Aramaic. Hoberman defines the radical as "what is left when the prosody and vocalic melody are extracted from a stem" (1991, n. 2).

46. Note that the two cognate binyanim in Hebrew (*pi'el* and *hif'il*) cannot be similarly reduced to one, since they differ in their final stem vowel: *e* versus *i*. This difference is an anomaly historically, but it is undeniable.

47. Levias has studied the occurrence of all the verb roots by binyan in the Babylonian Talmud. Of 1,013 triconsonantal roots, 287 occur only in *pe'al*, 116 only in *pa'el*, and 56 only in *'aphel*. Only 43 roots occur in all three. Of course, the Talmud is a text (albeit large), and these numbers cannot be extrapolated directly to the language as a whole, but they are indicative of the overall distribution pattern, which seeems to be generally similar to that of Hebrew.

48. Although the *a/a* class with nonguttural roots is small in Hebrew and Syriac and nonexistent in Arabic, Lambdin reconstructs it for Proto–West Semitic.

49. This dialect is one of a group known as Northeastern Neo-Aramaic, which is the largest group of modern Aramaic dialects, in numbers both of speakers and of dialects. Although these dialects are sometimes called modern Syriac, they are probably not direct descendants of Syriac but rather of some closely related dialect that was more similar to Babylonian. For my purposes, the exact nature of the

historic relation between Northeastern Neo-Aramaic and Syriac is not crucial. The binyan system of Babylonian is almost identical to that of Syriac, and so whatever dialect was the ancestor of the modern dialects under discussion must have had more or less the same system as Syriac and Babylonian.

50. The *u* of Jacobite Syriac is *o* in other forms of Syriac and is descended from *o*. This is the *o* that appears in modern Aramaic.

51. Most nouns show *a*, but some show *e*.

52. The continuous stem of two-consonant verbs is preceded by *i*. See Hoberman 1991 for discussion.

53. Only two are possible, because the addition of the binyan prefix *m*- to the three-consonant root gives us four consonants, and therefore either the first consonant of the stem must be extrametrical or the first syllable heavy. Otherwise, the stem could not accommodate four consonants.

54. The careful reader will note that the system underdetermines one case: given a two-consonant lexeme like /xθ/ mapped onto a disyllabic prosody with the first consonant extrametrical, from a purely phonological point of view, the stem could be either *mxaθθoθe*, which is what we find, or **mxaθoθe*, without the middle consonant doubled, which we never find for any two-consonant root. The morphological system doesn't tell us which to use. We must therefore add a codicil to the effect that the form with the doubled middle consonant is the only one used in this case.

55. The actual distribution seems to follow a sort of vowel harmony.

56. The root template is in fact prosodic, consisting of two syllables with vowels specified as *a* and *e* and all else unspecified. The use of C is therefore a somewhat misleading convenience. See McCarthy 1984 for a more complete discussion of this template.

References

Allen, J. H., and H. B. Greenough. 1894. *New Latin Grammar*. Ginn and Co., Boston.

Allen, M. 1978. "Morphological Investigations." Dissertation, University of Connecticut.

Anderson, S. R. 1982. "Where's Morphology." *Linguistic Inquiry* 13, no. 4: 571–612.

Anderson, S. R. 1988. "Inflection." In M. Hammond and M. Noonan, eds., *Theoretical Morphology: Approaches in Modern Linguistics*, 23–43. Academic Press, San Diego.

Anderson, S. R. 1992. *A-morphous Morphology*. Cambridge University Press, Cambridge.

Anshen, F., and M. Aronoff. 1988. "Producing Morphologically Complex Words." *Linguistics* 26:641–655.

Aquilina, J. 1965. *Maltese*, Teach Yourself Books. English University Press, London.

Aronoff, M. 1971. "The Syriac Regular Verb." Unpublished paper, MIT.

Aronoff, M. 1976. *Word Formation in Generative Grammar*. Linguistic Inquiry Monograph, no. 1. MIT Press, Cambridge.

Aronoff, M. 1978a. "An English Spelling Convention." *Linguistic Inquiry* 9, no. 2: 299–303.

Aronoff, M. 1978b. "Lexical Representations." In D. Farkas, W. M. Jacobsen, and K. W. Todrys, eds., *Papers from the Parasession on the Lexicon*, 12–25. Chicago Linguistic Society, Chicago.

Aronoff, M. 1983. "Actual Words, Potential Words, Frequency, and Productivity." *Proceedings of the Thirteenth International Congress of Linguists*, Tokyo, 163–171.

Aronoff, M. 1988. "Two Senses of 'Lexical'." *Proceedings of the Annual Meeting of the Eastern States Conference on Linguistics* (*ESCOL*), 1–11.

Aronoff, M. To appear. "Generative Grammar." In G. Booij, C. Lehmann, and J. Mugdan, eds., *Morphology: A Handbook on Inflection and Word Formation.* Handbooks of Linguistics and Communications Science. Walter de Gruyter, Berlin.

Aronoff, M., and S. N. Sridhar. 1988. "Prefixation in Kannada." In M. Hammond and M. Noonan, eds., *Theoretical Morphology*, 179–191. Academic Press, San Diego.

Baker, M., K. Johnson, and I. Roberts. 1989. "Passive Arguments Raised." *Linguistic Inquiry* 20, no. 2: 219– 251.

Bat-El, O. 1986. *"Extraction in Modern Hebrew Morphology."* M.A. thesis, UCLA.

Bat-El, O. 1988. "Remarks on Tier Conflation." *Linguistic Inquiry* 19, no. 3: 477–485.

Bat-El, O. 1989. "Phonology and Word Structure in Modern Hebrew." Dissertation, UCLA.

Battistella, E. 1990. *Markedness: The Evaluative Superstructure of Language.* SUNY Press, Albany.

Baudouin de Courtenay, J. 1972. "An Attempt at a Theory of Phonetic Alternations." Trans. Edward Stankiewicz in Edward Stankiewicz, ed., *A Baudouin de Courtenay Anthology*, 144–212. Indiana University Studies in the History and Theory of Linguistics. Indiana University Press, Bloomington. First published in 1895.

Bazell, C. E. 1949. "On the Problem of the Morpheme." *Archivum Linguisticum* 1:1–15. Reprinted in Eric Hamp, Fred Householder, and Robert Austerlitz, eds., *Readings in Linguistics, II.* University of Chicago Press, Chicago, 1966.

Bazell, C. E. 1952. "The Correspondence Fallacy in Structural Linguistics." *Studies by Members of the English Department, Istanbul University* 3:1–41.

Beard, R. 1981. *The Indo-European Lexicon: A Full Synchronic Theory.* North-Holland Linguistics Series, no. 44. North-Holland, Amsterdam.

Beard, R. 1987. "Morpheme Order in a Lexeme/Morpheme Based Morphology." *Lingua* 72:73–116.

Beard, R. 1990. "The Nature and Origin of Derivational Polysemy." *Lingua* 81: 101–140.

Beard, R. To appear. "Lexeme-Morpheme Based Morphology." Manuscript. Bucknell University.

Benveniste, E. 1932. "Supinum." *Revue de Philologie* 38:136–137.

Benveniste, E. 1948. *Noms d'agent et noms d'action en Indo-Européen.* Adrien-Maisonneuve, Paris.

Benveniste, E. 1966. "«Être» et «avoir» dans leurs fonctions linguistiques." In his *Problèmes de linguistique générale*, 187–207. Gallimard, Paris.

Berman, R. 1978. *Modern Hebrew Structure*. University Publishing Projects, Tel Aviv.

Berman, R. 1980. "Child Language as Evidence for Grammatical Description: Preschoolers' Construal of Transitivity in the Verb System of Hebrew." *Linguistics* 18:677–701.

Berman, R. 1982. "Verb Pattern Alternation: The Interface of Morphology, Syntax, and Semantics in Hebrew Child Language." *Journal of Child Language* 9, no. 1: 169–191.

Blake, F. R. 1903. "The So-Called Intransitive Verbal Forms in Hebrew." *Journal of the American Oriental Society* 24:145–204.

Blake, F. R. 1950. "The Apparent Interchange between *a* and *i* in Hebrew." *Journal of Near Eastern Studies* 9:76–83.

Bloomfield, L. 1933. *Language*. Henry Holt, New York.

Bloomfield, L. 1939. "Menomini Morphophonemics." In *Études phonologiques dédiés à la mémoire de M. le Prince Trubetzkoy*, 105–115. Travaux du Cercle Linguistique de Prague, no. 8. Jednota Českých Matematiků A Fysiků, Prague.

Bloomfield, L. 1970. "A Set of Postulates for the Science of Language." In Charles F. Hockett, ed., *A Leonard Bloomfield Anthology*. Indiana University Press, Bloomington. First published in *Language* 2 (1926): 153–164.

Bolozky, S. 1978. "Word Formation Strategies in the Hebrew Verb System: Denominative Verbs." *Afro-Asiatic Linguistics* 5, no. 3: 111–136.

Bolozky, S. 1982. "Strategies of Modern Hebrew Verb Formation." *Hebrew Annual Review* 6:69–79.

Bolozky, S. 1986. "Semantic Productivity and Word Frequency in Modern Hebrew Verb Formation." *Hebrew Studies* 27:38–46.

Bopp, F. 1833. *Vergleichende Grammatik des Sanskrit, Zend, Grieschischen, Lateinischen, Littauischen, Gottischen und Deutschen*. Berlin.

Botha, R. 1968. *The Function of the Lexicon in Transformational Generative Grammar*. Mouton, The Hague.

Bresnan, J. W. 1978. "A Realistic Transformational Grammar." In M. Halle, J. Bresnan, and G. Miller, eds., *Linguistic Theory and Psychological Reality*, 1–59. MIT Press, Cambridge.

Bybee, J. 1985. *Morphology*. John Benjamins, Amsterdam.

Bybee, J. 1988. "Morphology as Lexical Organization." In M. Hammond and M. Noonan, eds., *Theoretical Morphology*, 119–141. Academic Press, San Diego.

Carstairs, A. 1987. *Allomorphy in Inflexion*. Croom Helm, London. Also see Carstairs-McCarthy.

Carstairs-McCarthy, A. 1991. "Inflection Classes: Two Questions with One An-swer." In F. Plank, ed., *Paradigms: The Economy of Inflection*, 213–253. Mouton de Gruyter, Berlin.

Carstairs-McCarthy, A. 1992. *Current Morphology*. Routledge, London.

Chomsky, N. 1957. *Syntactic Structures*. Mouton, The Hague.

Chomsky, N. 1962. "A Transformational Approach to Syntax." In A. Hill, ed., *Proceedings of the Third Texas Conference on Problems of Linguistic Analysis in English*, 124–158. University of Texas, Austin. Reprinted in Jerry A. Fodor and Jerrold J. Katz, eds., *The Structure of Language*. Prentice-Hall, Englewood Cliffs, 1964.

Chomsky, N. 1964. *Current Issues in Linguistic Theory*. Mouton, The Hague.

Chomsky, N. 1965. *Aspects of the Theory of Syntax*. MIT Press, Cambridge.

Chomsky, N. 1970. "Remarks on Nominalization." In R. A. Jacobs and P. S. Rosenbaum, eds., *Readings in English Transformational Grammar*, 184–221. Ginn and Co., Waltham, Mass.

Chomsky, N. 1972. *Language and Mind*. Enlarged ed. Harcourt, Brace, Jovanovich, New York.

Chomsky, N. 1975. *The Logical Structure of Linguistic Theory*. Plenum, New York.

Chomsky, N., and M. Halle. 1968. *The Sound Pattern of English*. Harper and Row, New York.

Cohen, G. 1989. *Memory in the Real World*. Lawrence Erlbaum, Hillsdale, N.J.

Corbett, G. 1991. *Gender*. Cambridge University Press, Cambridge.

Costaz, L. 1964. *Grammaire Syriaque*. 2nd ed. Imprimerie Catholique, Beirut.

De Saussure, F. 1959. *Course in General Linguistics*. Trans. Wade Baskin. McGraw-Hill, New York.

DiSciullo, A. M., and E. Williams. 1987. *On the Definition of Word*. Linguistic Inquiry Monograph, no. 14. MIT Press, Cambridge.

Dixon, R. M. W. 1982. *Where Have All the Adjectives Gone?* Mouton, The Hague.

Drijkoningen, F. 1989. *The Syntax of Verbal Affixation*. Linguistische Arbeiten, no. 231. Max Niemeyer, Tübingen.

Drijkoningen, F. 1992. "Derivation in Syntax." In M. Aronoff, ed., *Morphology Now*, 48–68. SUNY Press, Albany.

Ernout, A. 1974. *Morphologie Historique du Latin*. 3rd ed. Klincksieck, Paris. First published in 1914.

Farkas, D. 1990. "Two Cases of Underspecification in Morphology." *Linguistic Inquiry* 21:539–550.

Foley, J. A. 1965. "Spanish Verb Morphology." Dissertation, MIT.

Foley, W. A. 1986. *The Papuan Languages of New Guinea.* Cambridge University Press, Cambridge.

Foley, W. A. 1991. *The Yimas Language of New Guinea.* Stanford University Press, Stanford.

Fortune, R. F. 1942. *Arapesh.* Publications of the American Ethnological Society, no. 19. J. Augustin, New York.

Francis, N., and H. Kučera. 1982. *Frequency Analysis of English Usage.* Houghton Mifflin, New York.

Garbell, I. 1965. *The Jewish Neo-Aramaic Dialect of Persian Azerbaijan: Linguistic Analysis and Folkloric Texts.* Janua Linguarum, Series Practica, no. 3. Mouton, The Hague.

Gesenius, W., and E. Kautzsch. 1910. *Gesenius' Hebrew Grammar.* 2nd English edition. Trans. A. E. Cowley. Oxford University Press, Oxford.

Goldsmith, J. 1990. *Autosegmental and Metrical Phonology.* Blackwell, Oxford.

Halle, M. 1973. "Prolegomena to a Theory of Morphology." *Linguistic Inquiry* 4:3–16.

Halle, M. 1990. "An Approach to Morphology." *NELS* (North Eastern Linguistics Society) 20:150–184.

Harris, J. W. 1991a. "The Exponence of Gender in Spanish." *Linguistic Inquiry* 22, no. 1: 27–62.

Harris, J. W. 1991b. "The Form Classes of Spanish." *Yearbook of Morphology* 4:65–88.

Harris, Z. 1960. *Structural Linguistics.* University of Chicago Press, Chicago. Originally published as *Methods in Structural Linguistics,* 1951.

Haspelmath, M. 1992. "Grammaticization Theory and Heads in Morphology." In M. Aronoff, ed., *Morphology Now,* 69–82. SUNY Press, Albany.

Hayes, B. 1986. "Inalterability in CV Phonology." *Language* 62:321–351.

Henderson, L., M. Coltheart, A. Cutler, and N. Vincent. 1988. *Linguistic and Psychological Approaches to Morphology.* Special issue of *Linguistics* 26, no. 4.

Hoberman, R. D. 1989. *The Syntax and Semantics of Verb Morphology in Modern Aramaic: A Jewish Dialect of Iraqi Kurdistan.* American Oriental Series. American Oriental Society, New Haven, Connecticut.

Hoberman, R. D. 1991. "Formal Properties of the Conjugations in Modern Aramaic." *Yearbook of Morphology* 4:49–64.

Hockett, C. F. 1947. "Problems of Morphemic Analysis." *Language* 23:321–343.

Hoeksema, J. 1985. *Categorial Morphology.* Garland, New York.

Hoeksema, J., and R. Janda. 1988. "Implications of Process Morphology for Categorial Grammar." In R. T. Oehrle, E. Bach, and D. Wheeler, eds., *Categorial Grammars and Natural Language Structures*, 199–247. Reidel, Dordrecht, Neth.

Jaeggli, O. 1986. "Passive." *Linguistic Inquiry* 17:587–622.

Jakobson, R. 1971. *Selected Writings*. Vol. 2, *Word and Language*. Mouton, The Hague.

Jakobson, R. 1984. *Russian and Slavic Grammar: Studies, 1931–1981*. Ed. Linda R. Waugh and M. Halle. Janua Linguarum. Mouton, Berlin.

Jensen, J. T., and M. Stong-Jensen. 1984. "Morphology Is in the Lexicon!" *Linguistic Inquiry* 15:474–498.

Joos, M. 1966. *Readings in Linguistics, I*, 4th ed. University of Chicago Press, Chicago.

Joseph, B. 1983. *The Synchrony and Diachrony of the Balkan Infinitive: A Study in Areal, General, and Historical Linguistics*. Cambridge University Press, Cambridge.

Kaufman, D., and M. Aronoff. 1990. "Morphological Interaction between L1 and L2 in Language Attrition." In S. Gass, C. Madden, D. Preston, and L. Selinker, eds., *Variation in Second Language Acquisition*, 202–215. Multilingual Matters, Clevedon, Avon, England.

Kaufman, D., and M. Aronoff. 1991. "Morphological Disintegration and Reconstruction in First Language Attrition." In H. W. Seliger and R. M. Vago, eds., *First Language Attrition*, 175–188. Cambridge University Press, Cambridge.

Kiparsky, P. 1982. "From Cyclic Phonology to Lexical Phonology." In H. van der Hulst and N. Smith, eds., *The Structure of Phonological Representations, Part 1*, 131–175. Foris, Dordrecht, Neth.

Klein, W. 1992. "The Present Perfect Puzzle." *Language* 68, no. 3: 525–552.

Koutsoudas, A., G. Sanders, and C. Noll. 1974. "The Application of Phonological Rules." *Language* 50:1–28.

Kuhner, R., and F. Holzweissig. 1912. *Lateinische Grammatik*. 2nd ed. Hahnsche Buchhandlung, Hannover. Reprinted 1974.

Kuryłowicz, J. 1961. *L'Apophonie en Sémitique*. Polska Akademia Nauk, Warszawa.

Lambdin, T. O. N.d. Notes on Comparative Semitic, Harvard Divinity School, Cambridge.

Lane, G. M. 1970. *A Latin Grammar for Schools and Colleges*. Rev. ed. Ed. Morris H. Morgan. AMS Press, New York. First published in 1903.

Levias, C. 1900. *A Grammar of the Aramaic Idiom Contained in the Babylonian Talmud, with Constant Reference to Gaonic Literature*. Bloch, Cincinatti.

Lieber, R. 1981. *On the Organization of the Lexicon*. Indiana University Linguistics Club, Bloomington.

Lieber, R. 1992. *Deconstructing Morphology*. University of Chicago Press, Chicago.

Lyons, J. 1977. *Semantics*. Cambridge University Press, Cambridge.

McCarthy, J. J. 1981. "A Prosodic Theory of Nonconcatenative Morphology." *Linguistic Inquiry* 12, no. 3: 373–418.

McCarthy, J. J. 1984. "Prosodic Organization in Morphology." In M. Aronoff and R. T. Oehrle, eds., *Language Sound Structure*, 299–317. MIT Press, Cambridge.

McCarthy, J. J. 1986. "OCP Effects: Gemination and Antigemination." *Linguistic Inquiry* 17, no. 2: 207–263.

McCarthy, J. J., and A. Prince. 1990. "Foot and Word in Prosodic Morphology: The Arabic Broken Plural." *Natural Language and Linguistic Theory* 8, no. 2: 209–283.

McCarthy, J. J., and A. Prince. To appear. *Prosodic Morphology*. MIT Press, Cambridge.

Marantz, A. 1984. *On the Nature of Grammatical Relations*, MIT Press, Cambridge

Marchand, H. 1969. *The Categories and Types of Present-Day English Word-Formation*, 2nd ed. Beck, Munich.

Masica, C. 1976. *Defining a Linguistic Area: South Asia*. University of Chicago Press, Chicago.

Matthews, P. H. 1972. *Inflectional Morphology: A Theoretical Study Based on Aspects of Latin Verb Conjugation*. Cambridge University Press, Cambridge.

Matthews, P. H. 1974. *Morphology*. Cambridge University Press, Cambridge.

Matthews, P. H. 1991. *Morphology*. 2nd ed. Cambridge University Press, Cambridge.

Mead, M. 1972. *Blackberry Winter: My Earlier Years*. Morrow, New York.

Meillet, A. 1964. *Introduction à l'étude comparative des langues Indo-Européennes*. 8th ed. University of Alabama Press, University, Alabama. First published in 1937.

Mel'čuk, I. 1982. *Towards a Language of Linguistics*. Wilhelm Fink, Munich.

Mel'čuk, I. 1991. "Subtraction in Natural Language." In M. Grochowski and D. Weiss, eds., *Festschrift for Andrzej Bogusławski*, 279–293. Otto Sagner, Munich.

Menn, L., and B. MacWhinney. 1984. "The Repeated Morph Constraint." *Language* 60: 519–540.

Monteil, P. 1970. *Éléments de phonétique et de morphologie du Latin*. Fernand Nathan, Paris.

Morin, Yves-Charles. 1987. "Remarques sur l'organization de la flexion des verbes français." *ILT Review of Applied Linguistics* 77/78:13–91.

Morin, Yves-Charles. 1990. "Parasitic Formation in Inflectional Morphology." In W. U. Dressler, H. C. Luschützky, O. E. Pfeiffer, and J. R. Rennison, eds., *Contemporary Morphology*, 197–202. Mouton de Gruyter, Berlin.

Moscati, S., A. Spitaler, E. Ullendorff, and W. von Soden. 1964. *An Introduction to the Comparative Grammar of the Semitic Languages*. Ed. S. Moscati. Porta Linguarum Orientalium. Otto Harrasowitz, Wiesbaden.

Nespor, M., and I. Vogel. 1986. *Prosodic Phonology*. Foris, Dordrecht, Neth.

Ornan, U. 1971. "Binyanim ubasisim, niot ugzarot." *Ha-universita* 16:15–22.

Panagl, O. 1987. "Productivity and Diachronic Change in Morphology." In W. U. Dressler, W. Mayerthaler, O. Panagl, and W. U. Wurzel, eds., *Leitmotifs in Natural Morphology*, 127–151. John Benjamins, Amsterdam.

Perlmutter, D. 1988. "The Split Morphology Hypothesis." In M. Hammond and M. Noonan, eds., *Theoretical Morphology*, 79–100. Academic Press, San Diego.

Pinker, S. 1991. "Rules of Language." *Science* 253 (2 August): 530–535.

Prince, A. 1975. "The Phonology and Morphology of Tiberian Hebrew." Dissertation, MIT.

Quirk, R., S. Greenbaum, G. Leech, and J. Svartvik. 1985. *A Comprehensive Grammar of the English Language*. Longman, London.

Raffelsiefen, R. 1992. "A Nonconfigurational Approach to Morphology." In M. Aronoff, ed., *Morphology Now*, 133–162. SUNY Press, Albany.

Ravid, D. 1991. "Internal Structure Constraints on New-Word Formation Devices in Modern Hebrew." *Folia Linguistica* 24:289–347.

Rice, K. 1989. *A Grammar of Slave*. Mouton de Gruyter, Berlin.

Roberts, I. 1987. *The Representation of Implicit and Dethematized Subjects*. Foris, Dordrecht, Neth.

Robins, R. H. 1979. *A Short History of Linguistics*. 2nd ed. Longman, London.

Robinson, T. H. 1962. *Paradigms and Exercises in Syriac Grammar*. Revised by L. H. Brockington, Oxford University Press, Oxford.

Rosén, H. 1977. *Contemporary Hebrew*. Trends in Linguistics, State-of-the-Art Reports. Mouton, The Hague.

Sadock, J. M. 1988. "The Autolexical Classification of Lexemes." In M. Hammond and M. Noonan, eds., *Theoretical Morphology*, 271–290. Academic Press, San Diego.

Salmon, V. 1988. *The Study of Language in Seventeenth-Century England*. 2nd ed. Amsterdam Studies in the Theory and History of linguistic Science, series 3, no. 17. John Benjamins, Amsterdam.

Sapir, E. 1921. *Language*. Harcourt Brace, New York.

Schane, S. A. 1968. *French Phonology and Morphology*. Research monograph no. 45. MIT Press, Cambridge.

Schramm, G. M. 1964. *The Graphemes of Tiberian Hebrew*, University of California Publications in Near Eastern Studies. University of California Press, Berkeley and Los Angeles.

Schwarzwald, O. 1973. "Roots and Patterns in the Modern Hebrew Lexicon." *Hebrew Abstracts* 14:95–96.

Schwarzwald, O. 1981. "Frequency Factors as Determinants in the *Binyanim* Meanings." *Hebrew Studies* 22:131–137.

Segal, M. 1927. *Mishnaic Hebrew Grammar*. Oxford University Press, Oxford.

Selkirk, E. O. 1982. *The Syntax of Words*. Linguistic Inquiry Monograph, no. 7. MIT Press, Cambridge.

Shafeev, D. A. 1964. *A Short Grammatical Outline of Pashto*. Ed. Herbert Paper. Trans. Herbert Paper. Indiana University Press, Bloomington.

Smith, H. W. 1956. *Greek Grammar*. Revised by Gordon M. Messing. Harvard University Press, Cambridge.

Spencer, A. 1988. "Bracketing Paradoxes and the English Lexicon." *Language* 64, no. 4: 663–682.

Spencer, A. 1991. *Morphological Theory*. Basil Blackwell, Oxford.

Stam, J. H. 1976. *Inquiries into the Origin of Language*. Harper and Row, New York.

Stemberger, J. P., and B. MacWhinney. 1988. "Are Inflected Forms Stored in the Lexicon?" In M. Hammond and M. Noonan, eds., *Theoretical Morphology*, 101–116. Academic Press, San Diego.

Stump, G. 1991. "On the Theoretical Status of Position Class Restrictions on Inflectional Affixes." *Yearbook of Morphology* 4:211–241.

Troubetzkoy, N. S. 1949. *Principes de phonologie*. Trans. J. Cantineau. Klincksieck, Paris.

Ungebaun, B. 1967. *Russian Grammar*. Oxford University Press, Oxford. Reprinted with corrected sheets of the 1957 edition.

Walker, J. 1936. *The Rhyming Dictionary of the English Language*. Dutton and Co., New York. Revised and enlarged by Lawrence H. Dawson.

Waltke, B. K., and Michael P. O'Connor. 1990. *Biblical Hebrew Syntax*. Eisenbrauns, Winona Lake, Ind.

Wasow, T., and T. Roeper. 1972. "On the Subject of Gerunds." *Foundations of Language* 8:44–61.

Wheelock, F. 1960. *Latin*. 2nd ed. Barnes and Noble, New York.

Whorf, B. L. 1945. "Grammatical Categories." *Language* 21:1–11. Reprinted in John B. Carroll, ed., *Language, Thought, and Reality*. MIT Press, 1956.

Williams, E. S. 1981. "On the Notions 'Lexically Related' and 'Head of a Word'." *Linguistic Inquiry* 12:245–274.

Wright, W. 1896. *A Grammar of the Arabic Language*. Cambridge University Press, Cambridge.

Wurzel, W. U. 1989. *Inflectional Morphology and Naturalness*. Reidel, Dordrecht, Neth.

Wurzel, W. U. 1990. "The Mechanism of Inflection: Lexicon Representations, Rules, and Irregularities." In W. U. Dressler, H. C. Luschützky, O. E. Pfeiffer, and J. R. Rennison, eds., *Contemporary Morphology*, 203–216. Mouton de Gruyter, Berlin.

Zachmeister, E., and S. Nyberg. 1982. *Human Memory*. Brooks/Cole, Monterey, Calif.

Zwicky, A. 1975. "Settling on an Underlying Form: The English Inflectional Endings." In D. Cohen and J. Worth, eds., *Testing Linguistic Hypotheses*, 120–185. Hemisphere Publishing Co., New York.

Zwicky, A. 1986. "The General Case: Basic Form versus Default Form." *Berkeley Linguistics Society* 12:305–314.

Zwicky, A. 1989. "Quicker, More Quickly, *Quicklier." *Yearbook of Morphology* 2:139–173.

Zwicky, A. 1990. "Inflectional Morphology as a (Sub)component of Grammar." In W. U. Dressler, H. C. Luschützky, O. E. Pfeiffer, and J. R. Rennison, eds., *Contemporary Morphology,* 217–236. Mouton de Gruyter, Berlin.

Zwicky, A., and G. Pullum. 1989. "Misconceiving Morphology." Manuscript. Stanford University.

Index